C000076982

Select poetical works of the late William Dunkin, D.D. In two volumes. ... Volume 1 of 2

William Dunkin

ECCO

PRINT EDITIONS

Select poetical works of the late William Dunkin, D.D. In two volumes. ... Volume 1 of 2
Dunkin, William
ESTCID: N047958
Reproduction from British Library
The titlepage to vol. 2 bears the imprint: printed by S. Powell, 1770. Vol. 1 contains parallel Latin and English, and Greek and English texts.
Dublin : printed by W. G. Jones, 1769-70.
2v. ; 4°

Eighteenth Century
Collections Online
Print Editions

Gale ECCO Print Editions

Relive history with *Eighteenth Century Collections Online*, now available in print for the independent historian and collector. This series includes the most significant English-language and foreign-language works printed in Great Britain during the eighteenth century, and is organized in seven different subject areas including literature and language; medicine, science, and technology; and religion and philosophy. The collection also includes thousands of important works from the Americas.

The eighteenth century has been called "The Age of Enlightenment." It was a period of rapid advance in print culture and publishing, in world exploration, and in the rapid growth of science and technology – all of which had a profound impact on the political and cultural landscape. At the end of the century the American Revolution, French Revolution and Industrial Revolution, perhaps three of the most significant events in modern history, set in motion developments that eventually dominated world political, economic, and social life.

In a groundbreaking effort, Gale initiated a revolution of its own: digitization of epic proportions to preserve these invaluable works in the largest online archive of its kind. Contributions from major world libraries constitute over 175,000 original printed works. Scanned images of the actual pages, rather than transcriptions, recreate the works *as they first appeared.*

Now for the first time, these high-quality digital scans of original works are available via print-on-demand, making them readily accessible to libraries, students, independent scholars, and readers of all ages.

For our initial release we have created seven robust collections to form one the world's most comprehensive catalogs of 18th century works.

Initial Gale ECCO Print Editions collections include:

History and Geography
Rich in titles on English life and social history, this collection spans the world as it was known to eighteenth-century historians and explorers. Titles include a wealth of travel accounts and diaries, histories of nations from throughout the world, and maps and charts of a world that was still being discovered. Students of the War of American Independence will find fascinating accounts from the British side of conflict.

Social Science

Delve into what it was like to live during the eighteenth century by reading the first-hand accounts of everyday people, including city dwellers and farmers, businessmen and bankers, artisans and merchants, artists and their patrons, politicians and their constituents. Original texts make the American, French, and Industrial revolutions vividly contemporary.

Medicine, Science and Technology

Medical theory and practice of the 1700s developed rapidly, as is evidenced by the extensive collection, which includes descriptions of diseases, their conditions, and treatments. Books on science and technology, agriculture, military technology, natural philosophy, even cookbooks, are all contained here.

Literature and Language

Western literary study flows out of eighteenth-century works by Alexander Pope, Daniel Defoe, Henry Fielding, Frances Burney, Denis Diderot, Johann Gottfried Herder, Johann Wolfgang von Goethe, and others. Experience the birth of the modern novel, or compare the development of language using dictionaries and grammar discourses.

Religion and Philosophy

The Age of Enlightenment profoundly enriched religious and philosophical understanding and continues to influence present-day thinking. Works collected here include masterpieces by David Hume, Immanuel Kant, and Jean-Jacques Rousseau, as well as religious sermons and moral debates on the issues of the day, such as the slave trade. The Age of Reason saw conflict between Protestantism and Catholicism transformed into one between faith and logic -- a debate that continues in the twenty-first century.

Law and Reference

This collection reveals the history of English common law and Empire law in a vastly changing world of British expansion. Dominating the legal field is the *Commentaries of the Law of England* by Sir William Blackstone, which first appeared in 1765. Reference works such as almanacs and catalogues continue to educate us by revealing the day-to-day workings of society.

Fine Arts

The eighteenth-century fascination with Greek and Roman antiquity followed the systematic excavation of the ruins at Pompeii and Herculaneum in southern Italy; and after 1750 a neoclassical style dominated all artistic fields. The titles here trace developments in mostly English-language works on painting, sculpture, architecture, music, theater, and other disciplines. Instructional works on musical instruments, catalogs of art objects, comic operas, and more are also included.

The BiblioLife Network

This project was made possible in part by the BiblioLife Network (BLN), a project aimed at addressing some of the huge challenges facing book preservationists around the world. The BLN includes libraries, library networks, archives, subject matter experts, online communities and library service providers. We believe every book ever published should be available as a high-quality print reproduction; printed on-demand anywhere in the world. This insures the ongoing accessibility of the content and helps generate sustainable revenue for the libraries and organizations that work to preserve these important materials.

The following book is in the "public domain" and represents an authentic reproduction of the text as printed by the original publisher. While we have attempted to accurately maintain the integrity of the original work, there are sometimes problems with the original work or the micro-film from which the books were digitized. This can result in minor errors in reproduction. Possible imperfections include missing and blurred pages, poor pictures, markings and other reproduction issues beyond our control. Because this work is culturally important, we have made it available as part of our commitment to protecting, preserving, and promoting the world's literature.

GUIDE TO FOLD-OUTS MAPS and OVERSIZED IMAGES

The book you are reading was digitized from microfilm captured over the past thirty to forty years. Years after the creation of the original microfilm, the book was converted to digital files and made available in an online database.

In an online database, page images do not need to conform to the size restrictions found in a printed book. When converting these images back into a printed bound book, the page sizes are standardized in ways that maintain the detail of the original. For large images, such as fold-out maps, the original page image is split into two or more pages

Guidelines used to determine how to split the page image follows:

• Some images are split vertically; large images require vertical and horizontal splits.
• For horizontal splits, the content is split left to right.
• For vertical splits, the content is split from top to bottom.
• For both vertical and horizontal splits, the image is processed from top left to bottom right.

SELECT

POETICAL WORKS

OF THE LATE

WILLIAM DUNKIN, D.D.

IN TWO VOLUMES.

VOL. I.

DUBLIN:

PRINTED BY W. G. JONES, IN SUFFOLK-STREET.

MDCCLXIX.

RB23 b.130T

CONTENTS.

TECHNETHYRAMBEIA:

SIVE

MURPHÆIS.

In tenui labor: at tenuis non gloria, si quem
Numina læva sinunt, auditque vocalus Apollo.

Virg.

THE

ART

OF

GATE-PASSING:

OR,

THE MURPHÆID.

Nec fum animi dubius verbis ea vincere magnum
Quam fit, et angustis hunc addere rebus honorem.

VIRG.

VOL. I.   B

MURPHÆIDOS.

L I B. I.

EN! ego Mufarum blando perculfus amore,

Pieriis haud ante modis vulgata per orbem

Aggredior, non magna quidem, fed digna poeta,

Quem pauci accingunt anni, nec fata tulerunt

In medium, famæ cupidum, quem diva bilinguis

Ignoravit adhuc, luctantem in limine primo.

THE

MURPHÆID.

BOOK I.

I FEEL the Muſes, and confeſs their charms;
A gentle flame my panting boſom warms:
No common ſubject claims the tuneful ſtrings,
Such as each trifling Poetaſter ſings:
Slight is the theme; but yet a theme ſo rare
Is not unworthy of a Poet's care,
Who yet a novice to the double tongue
Of public Fame, with youthful ardour ſtung,
And unacquainted with the craggy way,
Explores Parnaſſus in his firſt eſſay.

THOMPSON,

Tu vero, pennis quem jam plaudentibus effert,

Dexter ades, Musæque vias oftende vaganti:

Egregios inter vates memorandus, et ipfe

Avia Pieridum peragras umbrofa piarum,

Caftas propter aquas Phœbi fecreta recludens:

Tu mihi nunc aures ne mites abnue, Thompson,

Veftra nec erubuit quondam feftiva Thalia

Stramineas ceciniffe cafas et fordida rura,

Mendicofque tori genialia vincla petentes,

Hanc oculis captam, labefactum cruribus illum:

Hos melior fortuna manet per lubrica rerum,

Quorum culta manu veftra fplendefcit egeftas,

Alternique vigent æternis verfibus ignes.

Tuque

THOMPSON, aufpicious Bard, whofe laurel'd name,
Mounts on the pinions of eftablifh'd fame,
O! fmile propitious on the lines I write,
Affift my genius, and direct my flight.
Though calmly wand'ring through fequefter'd fhades,
Of old frequented by the Thefpian Maids,
By chryftal fountains you fublimely hail
The God of Numbers, and his rites reveal;
Yet will you not difcourage, nor refufe
Indulgent audience to the modeft Mufe.
In doric drefs thy fportive Mufe, I ween,
With youthful vigour gambol'd on the green,
Nor whilom blufh'd to fing the fordid plains
And lowly cottages of rural fwains:
The begging pair, that languifh'd long to prove
The facred pleafures of connubial love,
The crippled Bride-groom and his eyelefs Bride,
In Hymen's bands indiffolubly ty'd,
Whofe poverty with matchlefs glory fhines,
Deck'd by the graces of thy lovely lines,
Above the frowns of fickle fortune reign,
And live, and love for ever in thy ftrain.

AND

Tuque adeo, cui rara fides, et pectoris ardor

Ingenui, facilifque decor; fed nefcia flecti

Mens patria pietate potens, mihi candidus adfis,

Adderley comes; tecum quippe impiger aufim

Ignotas tentare vias, tecum ire per atras

Serpentum latebras, ac triftia luftra ferarum.

Et jam tempus erat numeris expandere fcenam

Mirandam, partefque fenem monftrare per omnes.

Ecce, nova prodit cinctum formidine monftrum

Patricius, craffo Murphæi fanguine plenus,

Murphæi magnis Murphæis regibus orti!

Jamque fecunda tenens portarum munera multum

Fafcibus, at multo magis alta ftirpe tumefcit.

Quem fefe oie ferens! quam fronte et vellere nigro!

Monftrum quale fuit quondam Polyphemus in antro

Horrendum, tefta nec major claufus in arcta

Diogenes, licet ille fophos, fubjanitor hic fit.

Hic

AND thou, whofe bofom, which no changes knows,
With friendly faith and inbred honour glows,
Whofe grace is eafy, but whofe loyal heart
Is fixt for ever to the patriot part,
Come, honeft ADDERLEY, and bring along
Thy truth and candour, to protect my fong.
The willing Mufe, with ADDERLEY her guide,
Would boldly rove through devious paths untry'd,
With him explore, where Nature never fmil'd,
The dens of ferpents and the favage wild.

AND now to bring expanded on the ftage
A fcene furprifing, and difplay the Sage
In all his various attitudes, behold
A dreadful monfter of uncommon mould :
From great O MURPHY's thickeft blood he fprings,
Auguft defcendant of Hibernian kings,
Second in Porter's penfion, as in place,
Proud of his poft, but prouder of his race.
How ftern his vifage ! how uncouth his hairs !
How black ! how fhaggy, and how like a Bear's !
Mark well his figure, and imagine then,
You fee dread Polyphemus in his den :
High in his lodge he ftands, although a fub,
Nor grander look'd the Cynic in his tub.

FULL

Hɪc jam bis denos annos regnavit et unum
Luſtrum in veſtibulo, ſemper contentus eodem
Stare loco: proh grande nefas! ingrata priorum
Turba poetarum, Mater quibus annuit Alma
Sublimes habitare domos, et condere turres
Nubigenas, puraque poli depaſcier aura!
Uſque adeone virum potuiſtis cernere talem,
Tantorum immemores operum? ſtat limine Phœbi
Patricius, nulla redimitus tempora fronde,
Quamvis hic lauri naſcatur plurima paſſim
Sylva; nec alterno ceciniſtis carmine nomen,
Rauca nec Eblanæ triviæ præconia norunt;
Quæ memorare piget, verum et memorare neceſſe eſt.

Nᴏɴ illum gazæ, non illum ſplendida regum
Sceptra movent, cæcove trahit Fortuna tumultu,
Nec læto tollit, nec triſti deprimit ore:
Non illum Boreas, gelida torpente pruina,
Strinxit, nec veſtes maduerunt imbribus atris,

FULL five-and-twenty years the radiant Sun,
His annual journey through the figns hath run,
Since PADDY firft affum'd the gate-command,
Content for ever with his narrow ftand.
O crying fhame! O barren of rewards,
Ungrateful herd of Alma Mater's bards,
To whom fhe gave to dwell aloft, and rear
Caftles of clouds, and feed on polar air!
Could ye behold his obvious worth fo long,
And yet deny the tribute of a fong?
Juft at the threfhold of the tuneful Nine
He ftands, without one tributary line.
Phœbean laurels here unnumber'd grow,
But not a branch will any Bard beftow:
That all our Poets thus remain a-fleep,
Eblana fuffers, and the Hawkers weep.

THE fplendid pomp and pageantry of kings
To him are vain, imaginary things:
Fortune the blind divinity, that rules
The giddy crowd, and is ador'd by fools,
Exerts on him her idle charms in vain,
Her fmiles nor pleafure, nor her frowns give pain:
Boreas, which binds the rapid-rolling flood
In icy fetters, never numbs his blood:

Nec lateri increpuit lapidofæ grandinis ictus,

Quæ furit in tectum; placidis quin auribus haurit

Immitem cœli rabiem, potiturque procella :

Non calor æftivus, non Sirius attigit antrum.

Quicquid habet, fine fraude tenet : fine limite latos

Expofcant alii campos: huic mucida piftæ

Sint frufta, et coctæ Cereris modo fuccus in urna,

Nil ultra rogat ille Deos: vixiffe per annos,

Inque diem vixiffe, brevem victurus in horam,

Seu moriturus ovat fapiens, ridetque potentum

Militiam, rerumque vices, neque cafibus ullis

Flectitur, in fefe totus teres atque rotundus.

Qualis inacceffa longum nutritus in aula

Divitis, acer opum et rerum tutela, Moloffus

(Affuetum

His garments brave the cloud-collected pow'rs,
Nor ſpongy drink the diſſipated ſhow'rs:
He hears the tempeſt, and ſerenely ſmiles
At peals of hail, that rattle on the tiles :
As cool amid the hot extreme he lies,
When Summer ſcorches, and the Dog-ſtar fries:
Whate'er he has, he holds as fixt, as fate:
Let others languiſh for a vaſt eſtate :
Grant him, ye Gods, his body to regale,
A cruſt of bread, and but a pot of ale;
He ſeeks no more, who chearfully can ſay,
He liv'd for years, yet liv'd from day to day,
Well arms himſelf with philoſophic pow'r
To live, or periſh with the flying hour,
And mocks the conteſts of the guilty great,
Their ſhifting ſcenes, and all the farce of ſtate.
The ſhafts of chance againſt him, ſmooth and round,
Innoxious rage, and glancing but re-bound:
He ſnugly ſits immur'd, and warmly pent,
His life in one perpetual watching ſpent;
Thus in ſome griping miſer's bolted court,
The poor man's dread, and dangerous reſort,
A growling maſtiff, from a tender pup
With all the fondneſs of a brute brought up,

His

(Affuetum imperio, teneris quem pavit ab annis

Ipfe mifer, mulcetque manu, feu voce laceffit)

Excubias agitat, tectoque fenefcit herili:

Talis agit, proprio conclufus carcere, vitam

Jam fenior: fed cruda viro viridifque fenectus.

Ut quondam, aggeribus ruptis, ruit amnis inundans,

Et cultas late jam fpes, hominumque labores

Abluit, et vivo viridantes gramine nuper,

Funeftat campos, cænoque obducit inerti:

Sic teneros animos ferventi fanguine fæpe

In pronum didicit ferri, frænifque folutis

In vitium labi, luxuque labafcere vires;

Occupat ille aditus ergo, caftæque Minervæ

Clauftra tenet, juvenumque decus morefque tuetur.

Sæpe cavos oculos nunc huc, nunc dirigit illuc,

Setigerumque

His temper fhaping, as the mafter's choice
Sooths with his hand, or rouzes with his voice,
In fturdy care and furly vigils old,
Sits the grim guardian of the hoarded gold.
So pafs his days imprifon'd; but the fage
Enjoys a raw-bon'd and a green old age.

As when a river, burfting through its bounds,
With torrents rages o'er the level grounds,
It fweeps away beneath its foamy reign
The fofter'd hopes and labours of the fwain:
The meads, late vivid in their verdant prime,
Uprooting blanches, and deforms with flime:
So well he ween'd, that tender minds mifled
By boiling blood, are wont to run a-head,
And active fpirits unreftrain'd to flide
Prone into vice, and in debauch fubfide.
He feizes hence the falutary gates,
And Alma Mater's academic ftreights,
The loofe career of wayward youth ietards,
Immures their honour, and their morals guaids.

Oft roll his hollow eye-balls to and fro,
Widely they glare, tremendoufly they glow:

Portentous

Setigerumque quatit, vifu mirabile, mentum,

Inque dolos fabricare dolos parat, infidiifque

Subftruit infidias: abfentes pectore præfens

Urget, et a tergo fugientes præcipit hoftes.

At fi forte patres Almæ genetricis in atrum

Cogere concilium, dirafque indicere pœnas,

Heu! miferis, mœftifque reis, et fcripta referre

Nomina collibuit; fi perfidus extulit antro

Cerbereum caput, et referentes Gorgona vultus,

Ac, veluti prædam fpirantes, naribus auras

Captavit, fibi quifque timet fugitivus: at ille

Sanguineis oculis fubridet trifte, fremitque

Ore gravi, fera labra movens, et fpumeus ira,

Qualis aper, dentes acuens in prœlia fævos,

Horrefcit fetis, et agreftes fertur in hoftes.

Quo fe cunque movet, terror comitatur euntem;

Nec

Portentous omen! with what grifly grace
He wags the meteor of his nether face!
Dark fchemes to baffle, darker he defigns,
And deep deceits with deeper countermines:
His mind ftill prefent eyes his game, and, lo!
Quick from behind prevents the flying foe.

But if perhaps the Board-preceding man
Convenes the fathers into black divan,
If pitilefs his pleafure fhould incline
To brand offenders, or impofe a fine,
Ah lucklefs lads! and with ill-boding look
Return them, noted in his Friday-book;
If from his den the Stygian dog fhould fteal,
And all the Gorgon in his face reveal;
Keen on the breezes as he fnuffs his prey,
Each guilty caitiff trembles with difmay.
With flaming eye-balls ghaftly fmiles the fire,
And growls, and bites his lips, and foams with ire.
The boar thus foaming, when purfu'd a-far,
New-whets his tufhes for approaching war,
With briftles horrent, for the battle glows,
And rufhes headlong on his ruftic foes.
Where'er he turns, where'er the monfter walks,
Surprize purfues, attending terror ftalks.

Nec tantos avibus trepidifque, Priape, timores
Furibus intuleras, quantos trahit ille Noviftis.
Ipfi etiam infontes, quorum mens, confcia recti
Officiique diu, meritos fibi pofcit honores,
Hujus in occurfum pallent, hunc pectore toto
Concipiunt, frontifque minas orifque trementes
Barbatum imperium, et nondum commiffa luenda.

Vestibulum ante ipfum primoque in limine bini
Stant famuli, mandata quibus cuftodia portæ eft,
Ulterius ne forte pedem proferre fugaci
Tyroni liceat ficta fub imagine cuiquam:
Quinetiam ante alios longe folertior ipfe
Patricius, ftrictamque aciem per cuncta volutans,
Dum fedet, et liquidas exficcat hauftibus urnas,
Egreffus fignat tacitos, tacitofque regreffus.

Ecce viri vigilantis, opes! en illius arma!
Lurida tela locos retinent, fortita decenter,
Quodque fuum, nimiumque oculis, heu! nota novellis,

Clepfamothos,

Not thou, Priapus, who art set to fright
The timid birds by day, and thieves by night,
Can'st half infuse the panic, though a God,
That Freshmen suffer at his angry nod.
The very youths, observant of the laws,
Whose long deportment merits fair applause,
Wax pale at his approach with icy fright,
Their inmost vitals shudder at the sight.
His baleful front, his awful beard combin'd,
And all the tyrant rushes on their mind,
This for the present, and for future times
The vengeance due to yet unacted crimes.

Before the lodge two trusty vassals wait,
Assistant guardians of the bolted gate,
Lest any fugitive disfigur'd roam
Beyond the wooden barriers of the dome:
But Paddy, much more vigilant and wise,
Darting around his unremitting eyes,
Notes, as he sits and drains his liquid urns,
Their silent exits, and their sly returns.

Behold then all the porter here complete,
And strictly mark his implements of fate,
Decently rang'd each find a proper class,
Ah, too well known to novel eyes! his glass,

Vol. I.   D

Clepſamothos, calami, tum ſeria, charta; dolores
Charta levis genitura graves! nec ſeria guttis
Purior infernis! calami livore loquaces!
Clepſamothos, nimium perituri nuncius ævi!
Dividit hoc pronas caute moderator in horas
Tempus arenoſum, vaga nomina denotat iſtis.

CASIBUS hinc duris obſeſſi noĉte dieque
Mille revolventes animis excudimus artes,
Mille dolos, multique adeo, ceu ſtamine duĉti
Dædaleo, varias, vigilem queis fallere poſſent,
Invenere vias, quorum pars læta triumphis
Surreptis gaudere ſolent, ſibi denique plaudunt,
Viĉtoies tanquam rediiſſent, hoſte ſubaĉto,
In patriam poſt longa feri certamina Martis.

Tunc

Pens, ink, and paper; paper light, but lo!
The pregnant harbinger of heavy woe,
His ink, whofe drops like Stygian waters fall,
His pens, that fpeak in characters of gall,
His monitory-glafs, that ftands to fhow,
How fleet the moments of duration flow:
With this he regulates his portal pow'rs,
And meafures out the fand-devolving hours;
With thofe, refpective to the various times,
Denotes delinquents, and records their crimes.

Hence, hem'd with rocky perils night and day,
A thoufand wily ftratagems we lay,
Revolving hence our fabricable parts,
We beat our brains, and forge a thoufand arts,
And many hence, as guided by the clew
Of Dædalus, their mazy paths purfue,
Inventing methods to deceive his ken,
And mock the ftrictures of his rigid pen.

Such as efcape with rapture bound abroad,
Triumphant felons, and themfelves applaud,
As if, victorious from the tedious toil
Of Mars, returning to their native foil.

Then

Tunc totos impune dies confumere fas eft;

Seu trivias, Eblana, tuas, finuofa, pererrant,

Seu dulces auras et florea ruris aperti

Dona petunt; curis vacui, fufique per herbas,

Indulgent geniis, et lactea pocula libant,

Ardenti feu grata fiti pomacea vina;

Dulcis inæquali ftrepitu dum perfonat aures

Sylvarum pennata cohors, et fpiffa viretis

Umbra tegit ftratos, folifque refrigerat æftus.

Seu potius pictis comittunt corpora cymbis,

Et pictis pariter picta cum vefte puellis,

Liffæumque fecant remis luctantibus amnem:

Leniter increpitant velis volitantibus auræ;

Leniter horrefcunt auris volitantia vela,

Leniter et velis fufpirant voce puellæ,

Et juvenum afpirant votis volitantia circum

Vela, leves auræ, leviores voce puellæ.

Then free they rove, unfetter'd fcud away,
Joys ufher in, and circling clofe the day;
Whether each winding ftreet they traverfe o'er,
Eblana, rifling thy promifcuous ftore,
Or, more tranfported with a rural fcene,
They court calm pleafures on the flow'ry plain,
Supinely ftretch'd along the tender grafs,
Forget their cares, and quaff the genial glafs,
With fnowy fillabub revive the heart,
Or flake inclement thirft with cyder tart;
While all the fongfters of the foreft greet
Their ears with notes, irregularly fweet,
And arbours arch with interwoven fprays
A grateful gloom, and cool the funny rays.
Or, if they truft to painted gallies gay,
And painted nymphs with painted loofe array,
And, gliding down the Liffey's glaffy tide,
With bending oars the curling waves divide;
The breezes gently chide the flying fails,
The flying ftreamers to the chiding gales
Re-murmur gently; wanton as they fly,
The nymphs as gently to their mufic figh,
And foft, to fan the lover's youthful fire,
The fails, light gales, and lighter nymphs confpire.

BUT

JAM vero, pulfura polos, Academica furgit
Tempeftas, puerique vibrant in prælia linguas,
Pulmonefque agitant, ac tenfo pectore rumpunt;
Nec mora: turpiloquis convicia plurima nautis
Infpeigunt, nautæque illis graviora retorquent,
Jamque iterum ardefcit duplici difcordia flamma,
Atque venenatæ volitant hinc inde fagittæ,
Et nautis, et rauca procul ftrepit unda Noviftis.

Sic, poftquam Æthiopum concretis montibus olim,
Æftivis tandem refolutæ folibus, altæ
Defluxere nives, jamque Ifidis arva futuras
Pervolvunt meffes, crefcentis ad oftia Nili
Concurrunt hinc, inde feræ, fremituque frequenti
Horrifonas avidis edicunt faucibus iras,
Et feptemgeminis refonant ululatibus undæ.

UNA fenum facies, eademque effæta cupido eft:

Quo

BUT now a rifing College-tempeſt rolls
A vocal peal, enough to rend the poles,
The boys for battle point their brandiſh'd tongues,
And heave, and ſtretch, and burſt their lab'ring lungs:
Quick they diſcharge their water-wit : each tar
With keener taunts retorts the wordy war:
And now the double diſcord kindles high,
From ſide to ſide the poiſon'd arrows fly ;
Boatmen and Freſhmen all tumultuous roar,
The mingled din reſounds along the ſhore.

So, when from frozen Æthiopian hills
The genial ſun unbinds the ſnow, in rills
To run, and roll through Ægypt's thirſty plain
The future harveſts of her golden grain,
Thick to the banks of ſwelling Nile a-pace
From various quarters ruſh the ſavage race;
Thick as they ruſh, their yawning jaws preſage
Portentous diſcord and inſatiate rage;
From coaſt to coaſt the frighted billows bound,
And hoarſe re-murmur to the dreadful ſound.

ONE common fate attends decrepit ſires,
Doleful their aſpect, and extinct their fires :

Quot varii vero vultus juvenumque colores,

Tot variæ fpecies animorum hinc, inde vagantur.

Hic, vix elapfus foribus (ceu Phœbus ab alto

Aureus, exoriens bigis lætatur Eois,

Ætheriamque viam vorat igneus axe furenti)

Impiger immenfos ardefcit carpere curfus;

Acria jamque vocat fociam in certamina pubem,

Spumantem jamque urget equum, ftimulifque laceffit

Ignipedem, pronufque jubis in verbera præceps

Tendit iter, rapidoque retro ruit impete tellus.

Mollius ille fuos artus et crura movere,

Atque choros agitare leves prægeftit: at alter,

Heu! latebras nimium blandas, mortique propinquas,

Sirenum explorat: latices interritus haurit

Lethæos, gaudetque malis, fruiturque veneno,

Ante

But youths, as various in their features gay
And mien, so various in their fancy stray:
One scarce has glided through the narrow gate,
When big with transport, and with pride elate,
(As clad with golden majesty proceeds
The Sun, exulting on his eastern steeds,
Through plains ætherial with impetuous force
Rolls the mad axle, and devours his course)
He glows to traverse o'er the distant plain,
In keen contention with his youthful train,
And panting now for dusty glory strives,
Impatient now his foamy courser drives
With knotted lash, with goring fury plies,
While from his heels the living light'ning flies:
Redoubled speed incessant he provokes,
Prone on the mane, and stretches into strokes;
He presses headlong, swims the giddy space,
And rushes back beneath the rapid race.

This longs to figure, as the fair advance,
His pliant limbs, and skim the mazy dance.
Another swain explores the downy seat
Of soothing Sirens, and the deathful gate,
Their fatal cups he perseveres to drain,
Exults in ruin, and enjoys his bane,

Ante oculos necdum fulgentes perspicit angues.

Hinc rari repetunt, seris hortantibus umbris,

Ferratas jam jam claudendæ Palladis arces,

Desertofque lares, intacti casibus; ut si

Quos dubios Castor ducat, Polluxque reducat

Clauftra per, et scopulos, et hiantes funere Scyllas.

Ne, pueri, ne tanta animis assuescite flagra,

Neu famæ primas in nubila vertite luces,

Aut læto fisi campo male pinguis amoris,

Heu! Patriæ meffem in viridi succidite culmo.

Nonnulli, quorum mentes alit incola virtus,

Quos rerum accendit pulchrarum nobilis ardor,

Præmunitque pudor, famæ morumque satelles,

Furtivam fine labe diem clausere soluti,

Illæsique suos noctu tetigere penates

Æris ad undantes monitus et signa sonora.

His

Nor yet perceives, though full before his eyes,
The ftingy ferpents in their bright difguife.

HENCE few, though caution'd by the midnight hours,
Revifit, ready to be barr'd, the towr's
Of Pallas, creaking with her laft alarms,
And empty manfions, free from hoftile harms:
As if fome doubtful mariners were veer'd
By Caftor on, and back by Pollux fteer'd
Through ftreights and rocks, where foamy Scillas rave,
And deep deftruction gapes in ev'ry wave.
Ah! never, youths, indulge the guilty flame,
Nor cloud the dawnings of your future fame,
Or fhear, by love's luxuriant foil betray'd,
Hibernia's harveft in the verdant blade.

BUT fome, whofe minds exalted virtue feeds,
And ftings with luft of honourable deeds,
Whofe reputation modefty fecures
From outward taint, and guards the moral doors,
Have freely fpent the furreptitious day
Serenely calm, and innocently gay,
And, duly fummon'd by the nightly bells,
Befought uncenfur'd their peculiar cells.

E 2   Benigner

His afpiravit melioɪ natura Noviſtis,
Eɩ felix potiore luto præcordia finxit.
Hos ubi naſcentes ſtupuerunt luminis oras,
Hauferuntque auras, proprio puriſſima Virgo
Proſpexit cœlo, radiiſque refinxit alumnos:
Eloquii furtique Deus per dura jocoſam
His indulſit opem, dedit et ſpecioſa Laverna
Perſonas, mollique manu ſub carcere triſtes
Permulcere canes, vigileſque ſopore dracones.

Ipse autem dudum memini vidiſſe recentem,
Infana poſtquam lucem contriverat urbe,
Ad portam tandem fera ſub noᵉte reverſum.
Jamque triumphantem tacita dulcedine caſus
Evaſiſſe omnes, et inani fraude tumentem.
Aſt ubi ſignatum fatali codice nomen
Senſit, et ad pœnas tali pro crimine ſe mox
Venturum, obſtupuit viſu, riguitque pavore.
Tum triſti vultu, tum blanda voce petebat
Patricium, duplices tendens ad ſydera palmas,

Judicium

Benigner nature thofe difpos'd to play,
And form'd their hearts of better temper'd clay;
Thefe, at their birth, when they began to ftare
At infant light, and draw celeftial air,
Unfpotted Virgo, thefe her pupil kind
View'd from her orb, and with her beams refin'd:
To thefe, of other paffing means bereft,
The graceful God of eloquence and theft,
Beftow'd his pleafant aid, Laverna gave
The fpecious mafk, and tutor'd to deceive,
With foothing hand to lull their fnarling foes,
And watchful dragons into foft repofe.

A CERTAIN Frefhman, who had fpent the day
In the loofe freaks of ev'ry idle play,
From town returning in the evening late,
With filent rapture fmiling pafs'd the gate,
Miftaken hugg'd himfelf with fecret pride,
That, as he pafs'd, he had re-pafs'd unfpy'd.
But when to view the fatal book he came,
And found in fable characters his name,
Aghaft he ftood, quite thunder-ftruck with fear,
The baulk was inftant, and the mulct was near.
With fpeeches bland and deprecating face
He fues to PADDY, and bemoans his cafe;

Judicium ut quocunque modo revocaret amarum;
Olli fubridens, contracta eft fronte minatus
Patricius, capitifque dein concuffit honores
Incomptos, graviter frendens, ac talia fudit.
Nos adeo cæcos, ftupidos adeone putafti,
Clam quos exires? Te vincula nulla coercent:
Judicio, quo dignus, abi contentus; et olim
Forte gradus, generofe, tuos meliora fequentur.

DIXIT, et in terras vultum deflexit: at ille
Infandas iterum eft orfus renovare querelas,
Aggrediturque iterum dictis, numenque tyranni
Supplicibus pofcit votis, et munera fpondet.
Aft ingens veluti rupes, porrecta profundo,
Ionius licet hinc æftus bacchetur, et illinc,
Infultans lateri, fractifque remugiat undis,
Mole fua confixa manet, tumidæque ruinas
Indignatur aquæ: fecus haud immota manet mens
Patricii, vanæque preces funduntur in aures.

Quo

To Heav'n uplifting both his hands and eyes,
Some way reverſe the cruel doom he cries.
PADDY contracts his brow, then grimly leers
Both at the Freſhman's poſture and his fears,
Shook the rough honours of his matted head,
Snarl'd an enormous grin, and mockful ſaid:
What could you think me ſuch a ſtupid aſs
To let your worſhip unregarded paſs ?
What break through all reſtraints, theſe bars deſpiſe,
Nor dread the ſearches of theſe piercing eyes?
Submit with patience to the mulct aſſign'd;
The next elopement more ſucceſs may find.

HE ſaid : his fiery eye-balls on the ground
He ſternly fix'd: the Freſh in mournful ſound
Anxious renews his heavy tale again,
And begs, and prays, but begs and prays in vain.
The potent argument of bribes he try'd
With ſuppliant vows to bend the tyrant's pride.
As o'er the deep ſome huge extended rock
Reſts on its baſe, and firm againſt the ſhock
Diſdains the billows of Ionian tides,
That roaring laſh its hoarſe-reſounding ſides:
So fixt is PADDY's unrelenting mind,
And pray'rs and preſents to his ears are wind.

The

Quo fuper invidia juvenis commotus et ira,

Qualis mufca levis, jam jam giaffantis Aiachnes

Irretita dolis, moribundo murmure muffat,

Talis, nequicquam fato obluctatus iniquo,

Fiacta gemit, gelidaque tremens formidine pectus

Triftis abit, bilemque fovet fub corde: perit vox

Imperfecta---Lupi mœrin. videre priores.

At quem non unquam lachrymæ mollire fluentes,

Nec miferæ potuere preces, oblata neque ulla

Munera, Patricium quendam fuperaffe recentem,

Qua non arte alius, memini: dum pervigil aftat

Veftibulo, demum nullo comitante miniftro,

Extemplo verfutus adit, lævaque caniftrum

Protendens, crudele nefas involvit amicis

Vocibus, aggrediturque incautum, ac talibus infit.

Hic Peti pulvis, quali non illa probofcis

Eft

The youth, enrag'd with indignation, boils.
As, thick entangled in Arachne's toils,
The feeble fly repeats its piteous moans
In broken buzzes, and in dying tones:
So fad he murmur'd in defponfive plight,
With horror trembling, and congeal'd with fright;
The brooding choler, fmother'd in his breaft,
Confus'd the fenfes, and the voice fupprefs'd,
Without a word abafh'd he fneak'd away;
The wolves ill-boding faw him firft that day.

But Paddy, whom nor tears, nor pray'rs could move,
Nor proffer'd gifts e'er foften into love,
A wily Frefhman, mafter of his part,
Subdu'd with more than Machiavelian art.
Keen as he ftood, attentive at his poft,
At length divefted of his ufual hoft,
The traitor comes: the cruel mifchief lies
Deeply conceal'd beneath a fair difguife:
His hand protends a canifter of fnuff,
And friendly terms accoft the monfter rough.

Inclos'd in this is fuch a fragrant ftore
Of fnuff, as never fed your fnout before,

Eſt epulata prius, qualem non Scotia jactat,

Clauditur: anne velis tantum ſuffimen ab inde

Sumere? Siqua fides, nemo mihi gratior alter,

Quocum partirer quicquid bene ſpirat odoris:

Tende manum; ne parce, precor, tibi rite paratis,

Muneribus: te plura manent; eſt copia cornu

Pulverulenta domi, ſunt et mihi nuper ab Indis

Tortilis, et pariter fragrantia ſectilis herbæ

Pabula.   Patricius, ſceleratæ neſcius artis,

(Omnigenis ſolitus formis inhiare tabaci,

Seu naſo ſufflare, fero ſeu prendere morſu,

Seu per clauſtra tubi fumum ductare ſequacem)

Protinus exclamat: tali pro munere grates

Permagnas equidem dederim.   Tum perfidus ille,

Naribus

Let faucy Scotland match it, if fhe can:
Wilt take a pinch ? if there be faith in man,
No mortal breathes, with whom thy faithful boy
Would fooner fhare fuch aromatic joy.
Hold out your hand----come, take it piping hot,
'Twas made for you, and prythee fpare it not.
More grift awaits thee; for my horny mill
Domeftic teems with dufty plenty ftill ;
And I have lately gotten huge fupply
Of leaf for pig-tail, and for cut-and-dry.

PADDY, ne'er dreaming, that the leaft device
Could lurk beneath a compliment fo nice,
Rejoic'd to find he could relieve his want;
For ftill tobacco was his darling plant,
Whether voracious with uncommon guft
He fnuffs the prurient particles of duft;
Or twifted weed with grinding jaws invades,
Or through the ftreights of tuby-chimney leads
The fmoak obfequious----I fhould give, he cries,
A thoufand thanks for fuch a dainty prize.

THE faithlefs Frefhman with revulfive fhocks
Rends the clofe cover from the full-fraught box

Beneath

Naribus admotæ, magna vi tecta revellit

Pyxidis, et subito fertur glomeratus in auras

Pulvis; in obliquos oculos pars volvitur, inque

Naïes pars patulas, et rictus pars in hiantes :

Tum vero, infandum nimium testata dolorem,

Ignea suffuso liquuntur lumina fletu,

Irrorantque genas; exundat faucibus humor,

Atque laboranti sternutant culmina naso.

Interea juvenis, nullis obstantibus, exit

Magno cum risu victor, lachrymisque subacti

Lætatur, pedibusque petit pernicibus urbem.

HAUD secus, ut perhibent, quondam Laertius heros

Immanem Cyclopa cavo cæcavit in antro,

Effugitque vafer sociorum fata cruenta:

Nec secus in terras misit Saturnius olim

Mente dolos agitans, Pandoram, occulta ferentem

Dona deum : postquam claras venere sub auras,

Gentibus occubuit variorum turba malorum

Advena,

Beneath his nofe, and, fudden as he rends,
A curling globe of cloudy duft afcends;
The fleeting particles, difpers'd in air,
His noftrils thefe, and thofe his eye-balls fhare;
The fiery eye-balls lamentably pour
On either gutter'd cheek a briny fhow'r,
While through his mouth a mucous torrent flows,
And all the dome re-echoes to his nofe.
The youth, loud laughing with difdainful fcoff,
Triumphant marches unobftructed off,
Joys in his tears, as thick they trickle down,
And flies like lightning to the noify town.

Thus in his dreary cave the monftrous wight
Huge Polyphemus was bereft of fight,
And thus the crafty Greek, as fame relates,
Efcap'd the crude deftruction of his mates:
Thus once, deep-pond'ring fraud, Saturnian Jove
Difpatch'd Pandora from the realms above;
A box fhe bore, and in that box confin'd,
The contributions of the Gods combin'd;
The cover foolifh Epimetheus drew,
In various forms the pent contagions flew:
'Till then unknown, a formidable band
Of evils pofted through the peopled land

Advena, morborumque cohors, triftifque feneĉtus.

Tum furor exarfit belli; tum, fævior enfe,

Mollities otiumque animos fregere viriles,

Tarda prius, rapidi ruit inclementia fati,

Conclufitque diem fpatio breviore fupremum.

PATRICIUS vero, ftimulis agitatus acutis,

Lumina læfa fricat, madido turgentia luĉtu;

Quo magis ille fricat, teneros magis acriter orbes

Irritant atomi: pedibus contundere terram

Incipit, horrendifque replet mugitibus antrum,

Attonitum, trepidumque imis a fedibus antrum!

Qualis ubi in circo latrantes cominus hoftes

Taurus fronte premit, dentes fi forte tenaces

Naribus infixit catulus, dum pendulus hæret,

Ille boat, pedibufque leves difpergit arenas.

HAS inter pœnas, quantum fremit æthere fulmen,

Patricium

In black proceſſion, with diſeaſes drear,
And ſad old age, ſlow-lagging in the rear.
Then flam'd the rage of baneful war, and then,
More fell and fatal to the race of men,
Licentious joys and indolence reclin'd
Unbrac'd their nerves, and womaniz'd their mind :
Inclement fate exerts auſterer pow'r,
And with a quicken'd pace precipitates the hour.

PADDY, through pungent pain, without relief,
Rubs his tormented eyes, ſurcharg'd with grief,
The tickling atoms, darting through the pores,
His agonies aggrieve: he ſtamps, and roars,
So loudly roars, with ſuch an hideous yell,
As ſhook the center of his hollow cell.
Thus when a bull, whom circling crowds incloſe,
With butting front provokes his barking foes,
If at his noſe a keen aſſailant ſprings,
And tugging gripes, dependent as he clings,
The lordly beaſt with bellowings profound
Fills the vaſt void, and ſpurns the ſandy ground.

AFFLICTED thus he rings redoubled cries,
Loud, as when thunder murmurs through the ſkies:

Convuls'd

Patricium tonat ore gravi Divumque Columbam,

Et quæcunque colit fimulato numina ligno,

Marmoreofque deos, divafque ex ære recifas,

Seu tabula pictas, et quos rubrica notavit

Pontifices, Miffæque duces: hos pronus adorat,

Effufis precibufque piis dirifque malignis.

    Gentes Ierneæ vos, O clariffima quondam

Lumina, grande decus, rerum tutela mearum!

Tu pie, cœlicolas inter numerande, Columba,

Quem vitreis veneror fphæris, in vota vocatum

Virginea cum Matre Dei! tu fignifer olim

Maternæ cuftos, et adhuc fpes maxima Romæ,

Cui data jampridem eft radiantis janua cœli,

Cujus et aufpicio Matris non degener Almæ

Occludo, referoque fores, et limina fervo:

Tuque adeo, facro cujus de nomine nomen

Ipfe meum duco; merito quem dignor honore;

Annua cui noftris fumant altaria donis;

Natalis

Convuls'd with pain, outrageous as he bawls,
On PATRICK much and COLUMB-KILL he calls,
Paternal faints, and, what he rates as good,
. Invokes his houfhold Deities of wood.
Trumps all the Rubric heroes of the Mafs,
And Gods in ftone, and Goddeffes in brafs,
Or mimic paint; to thefe devoutly bends,
And pious pray'rs with bitter curfes blends.

YE Worthies, once HIBERNIA's radiant hoft,
My graceful honours, and my guardian boaft:
Columba thou, for pious acts of old
Far-fam'd in legends, and with faints enroll'd,
Whom with the Virgin-mother I adore,
With vows replenifh, and with beads implore:
Thou Peter, whilom Rome's unerring guide,
And yet her hope, and high pontific pride,
To whom were granted by divine demife
The golden portals of the blifsful fkies;
Beneath whofe awful patronage I wait
To fhut, and open Alma Mater's gate;
And thou, from whofe inviolable name
I date my title, and derive my fame,
Whofe fhrine with homage I approach, to whom
Load annual altars with divine perfume,

Natalis per me cui nunquam ficcus abivit,

Quin, et Shamrogis redimitus, fancte, galerum,

Te, veniente die, te, decedente quotannis,

Spumanti patera et dapibus venerabar opimis:

Et vos mendici fratres, divinitus aucti

Divitiis, celebrefque patres per fæcula, quorum

Reliquias veneror fupplex, atque ofculor offa!

Nequicquam has fraudes alto fpectatis Olympo?

Jam fceleratus abit, noftrorum caufa malorum,

Perfidia lætus.   Vifu fuperabor adempto.

At vos, O Divi! veftrum exaudite clientem,

Inque caput meritas damnatum effundite pœnas::

Fulmine correptam jam jam flagrante, fororum

Dirarum ad fedes animam depellite fontem,

Aut faltem æthereis perftringite lumina flammis,

Barbara quæ mœfto deducunt gaudia fletu:

Sentiat

Whose natal day was never known to pass
Without the tribute of my votive glass;
For whom displays thy reverential PAT
The tufted Shamrogue in his high-cockt hat:
Propitious as the years revolving run,
Whom with the rising, whom the setting sun
He duly hails, and spreads the table round,
With foaming cups, and dainty dishes crown'd.

YE begging brotherhood, a vagrant race,
Poor in good works, but very rich in grace.
And fathers fam'd, whose reliques I revere,
And bones I kiss on marrow-bones as bare.
Behold ye now with unaffected eyes
These bold impostures from your lofty skies?
Exulting in his fraud the faithless foe
Escapes in triumph, and derides my woe:
But hear, O hear! ye tutelary saints,
My just petitions, and my sad complaints:
My wrongs redress, your angry bolts make red,
And hurl vindictive thunder on his head.
His body blast, with rapid rage impell
His guilty spirit to the shades of hell:
At least with lightning dim those orbs of light,
That view my tortures with malign delight;

Mad

Sentiat ille meos, agitata mente, dolores
Mordaces, medioque die nigrefcere folem:
Erret inops, nec fune canis veftigia paffim
Cœca regat: quin ipfe viam per fola locorum
Prætentet digitis, nec torto pollice peti,
(Quod fic eft aufus puer impius invidiofa
Inceftare manu, et rapidis difperdere ventis,)
Soletur fauces, nec odoro pulvere nares.

Hæc ubi dicta dedit, tumido de pectore, tanquam
Ilia ducturus, fingultum expirat anhelum:
Tum, ter Ave blaterans, pugnis cava pectora pulfat;
Ter crucis effigie fefe præmunit, et ora
Ter fancta confpergit aqua de fonte vetufto
Patricii, atque oleo perfundit luminis orbes
Accenfos, oleo, pulla quod pyxide dudum
Ille magus, medicufque fagax, ac dentifricator,
Carminibus (quamvis verborum nefcius ipfe)
Circeis, herbifque potens, opiferque per urbem,
Haud alii penetranda, patent cui myftica rerum,
Hiffernanus ei, tantum tribus affibus emptum,

Signatum

Mad let him feel my pricking pangs, I pray,
And find no dawn amid the noon of day:
Poor let him wander, nor a cur by thong
Conduct his blind inſtable ſteps along:
Through dreary places let him lonely mope,
And with his hands a doubtful paſſage grope:
Then for tobacco, which the wicked boy,
Puff'd with the winds, could wantonly deſtroy,
O! may he never with a twiſted inch
Regale his jaws, or noſtrils with a pinch.

He ſaid, and ſighing with a piteous moan,
Deep from his belly breath'd a broken groan:
Three Aves then he jabbering expreſs'd,
And with each Ave thump'd his hollow breaſt,
Thrice croſs'd himſelf, beſprinkl'd thrice his front,
With Holy-water from St. Patrick's font,
And lacquer'd over, to complete his toil,
His flaming eyes with mitigating oil,
That oil, which cook'd with chymical device
In ſable box, and three-pence but the price,
Great HIFFERNAN, that mirror of the ſtage,
Profound magician, and phyſician ſage,
The prime reſtorer of conſumptive teeth,
Who ſeeth ſuch ſecrets, as no ſecond ſeeth,

And

Signatum dederat, Stygiaque facraverat arte

Geftandum, quo non aliud præfentius ullum

In cafus morbofque graves: at protinus omnis,

Cui modo fana fides haud fallax ante reperta,

Labitur in gremium nequicquam lubrica virtus,

Et ferrugineos tunicæ funeftat honores.

Flumina falfa cadunt oculis, effufa per ora,

Flebilis et rictus, et nafi vifcidus imber

Dedecorat penitus menti venerabile fignum.

O miferas hominum curas! heu credula fronti

Pectora! fi liceat parvis componere magna,

Sic manibus cecidit malefidi Cæfar amici:

Sic Phario cecidit Magnus; fic arte Sinonis

Arx Priami cecidit, ceciderunt Troes et ingens

Gloria Teucrorum folius fraude Sinonis,

Quos

And knows (although unknowing of his verbs)
The force of noftrums, and the feats of herbs,
Conferr'd on him, and, ftroking with his palm,
With Stygian art, indu'd the myftic balm,
Than which was never a more potent fpell
Againft mifchances and difeafes fell.
But, lo ! what never had before deceiv'd
A man, unlefs of faving faith bereav'd,
The lubric virtue, trickling down his breaft,
Blots the brown honours of his thread-bare veft.
Mean-while the falty tears, diftill'd a-pace,
Bedew the channels of his fluicy face;
The ropy phlegm and driveling fnivel flow,
And deep degrade the reverend beard below.
Unhappy ftate of man ! what cares, what ftrife,
What wiles, what treacheries attend thy life!
Thus (if great villanies we rank with fmall)
A faithlefs friend wrought mighty Cæfar's fall,
And Cæfar's rival, once firnam'd the Great,
The Pharian butcher'd by a bafe deceit.
By Sinon's art thus fell the lofty tow'rs
Of royal Priam, and the Phrygian pow'rs;
By Sinon's fraud alone, diffembled well,
Their pride, their empire, and their glory fell,

What

Quos neque Tydides, vires animofque Deorum

Afpirante Dea, nec belli fulmen, Achilles,

Non anni domuere decem, non mille carinæ.

F I N I S.

MURPHÆIDOS.

What not Tydides could atchieve, infpir'd
With rage celeftial, and by Pallas fir'd,
Nor yet Achilles, thunder-bolt of war,
Wide fpreading terror, and deftruction far,
Not ten years leaguer, not the martial throng,
That mann'd the fleet, that fleet a thoufand ftrong.

The END of the FIRST BOOK.

MURPHÆIDOS.

LIB. II.

PATRICIO dudum fuso, foribusque reclusis,
   Ac nullo custode gradus per aperta tuente,
Jam victrice fuga metam tetigisse, meoque
Insignem capiti palmam rapuisse videbar:
Quum geminus mihi montis apex et gramine circi
In medio apparent virides, ubi MILTON Homero,
MILTON inhonesta rythmorum compede liber,
Virgilio LAWSON, STANHOPUSQUE minantia Flacco
Tela manu quatiunt, et amico carmine pugnant.

THE

MURPHÆID.

BOOK II.

THUS Paddy routed, and the doors difclos'd,
  My fteps no more to fcouting eyes expos'd,
By flight victorious now I feem'd to feize
The ftated goal, and fnatch the glorious bays:
When, lo! a mount majeftic to be feen
With double front, and graffy lifts between,
In profpect rofe ; where MILTON, undebarr'd
By Gothic rhimes, affails the Grecian Bard;
Where LAWSON Virgil, and where STANHOPE braves
Melodious Horace, and his weapons waves:
The chiefs oppos'd exert their native might
In rival ftrains, and urge the friendly fight.

THUS

Hɪ feptem, ærifono tremulas difcrimine, chordas
Leniter attingunt, et amores flebile-fuaves
Auribus inftillant; aut læto pectora pulfu
Pertentant: illi certatim accendere fervent
Magnanimos in bella duces, numerifque canoris
Armorum ftrepitus animafque ciere tubarum.

Sᴛᴀɴᴛ rofeo circum pubentes flore Camœnæ
Jamque his, ᴊamque illis mira dulcedine plaudunt,
Ancipitemque pari diffindunt munere Martem.
Per loca texta rubis, pendentibus afpera faxis,
Huc me celfus honos, huc ipfa pericula raptant
Ardentcm, ac toto ftimulatum Pæone mentem.

Nᴇ fidi vero comites, vocefque viarum
Fallaces, abfint extrema in parte laboris.
Te vocat Alma Parens, hederas tibi culta juventus

Decerpit

THESE gently touch their foft refponfive lyres,
The notes ftill changing with the trembling wires;
Still, as they change, through raptur'd ears they roll
Love's mournful fweets, and fink into the foul;
Or tun'd to glee the living ftrings employ
In fprightly ftrains, and fwell the heart with joy.
Thofe glow to kindle with intenfer heats
Heroic fpirits into martial feats,
Bid armours clafh, in brazen fongs a-far
Awake the trump, and rouze the foul of war.

THE Mufes wait, with rofy beauty bright,
Around, amaz'd, and fmitten with delight,
Now thefe, now thofe applaud, and fplitting calm
The dubious conteft with dividual palm.
Through caverns prickly with perplexing fprays,
Rough pendent horrors, hither lofty praife
Invites my fteps: the very perils charm,
And facred raptures all my bofom warm.

LET faithful friends attend my laft effay,
And focial converfe, to deceive the way.
Thine Alma thee, thy letter'd mother calls,
Her youth pluck ivy from the verdant walls,

Her

Decerpit muris, celebrique in limine fternit,

Neu ferum hoc pigeat jam te fumpfiffe, DELANY,

Pignus amicitiæ, Fidei fortiffime duĉtor,

Infpirante Deo, qui fandi fulmine Paulum

Ore refers, gentefque doces agnofcere Chriftum,

Inque plagas humiles demiffum lumen ab alto,

Cujus in afcenfum capita aurea fydera condunt;

Ipfe procul Titan ftupefaĉtus imagine languet,

Morte triumphata, vinĉtifque furoribus Orci,

Unde falus orbi redit, immortale parentis

Dum repetit folium, et cœli fibi vindicat arces.

    Quo vero mortalis agor? nimis obruor unda

Lucis inacceffæ; quis enim bibat Omnipotentis

Luminibus radios, aut Majeftatis Alumnum,

Cujus ab arcano procedunt omnia nutu,

Unigenamque Dei? Traĉtus pete, Mufa, patentes

                                 Inferiore

Her youth, embellifh'd by thy toils await,
And ftrow frefh garlands at the crowded gate,
Nor thou, DELANY, late addrefs'd, refufe
This pledge of friendfhip from the grateful Mufe;
Thou dauntlefs guide, who fummon'd by the call
Of God, canft thunder with the voice of Paul,
And rebel nations with conviction awe,
To hail their Saviour, and revere his law,
To hail that light, that everlafting light,
Sent down to vifit this abyfs of night;
At whofe afcent the planets veil their blaze,
The fun far pines at his reflected rays;
Whilft he, triumphant over death fuftain'd,
Hell's portals batter'd, and her fiends enchain'd,
Redeems the world, refeeks his Father's throne,
And high afferts the Heav'n of Heav'ns his own.

BUT whither mortal would I rufh? my fight
Sinks, overwhelm'd beneath a flood of light,
Light inacceffible: can vifual fenfe
Imbibe the radiance of Omnipotence,
Or HEIR of MAJESTY, the SON, whofe nod
Moves all in all, the HOLY ONE of GOD?
Ambitious Mufe, through fields of ambient air
Expatiate free beneath an humbler fphere,

Rap

Inferiore polo, luces vifura minores

Lactanteifque vias, crebroque fatellite lunam

Regnantem, et pronos ducentia fydera menfes:

Seu potius libeat cernentem cuncta tueri,

Ore alterna facro moderantem froena diei,

Cunctaque pafcentem genitali lampade, folem,

Et, cinctas oriente auro, coeloque natantes

Coeruleo nebulas, variumque coloribus arcum,

Imbriferum nitido fignantem tramite tractum:

Sive per ima fequi paffim veftigia, formis

Divinis rerum variarum impreffa, fupremum

Artificem, rivifque vagis exquirere fontem

Æternum; fpeculare facra ratione furentem

Oceanum, et vivo ridentes gramine campos,

Fronde nova fylvas, pudibundis floribus hortos.

Aufa nec hæc fine mente pia, fine numinis aura

Attentanda reor, nec honeftæ culmina laudis.

Nos

Rapt with aftonifhment, purfue the maze
Of beamy leffer orbs and milky ways;
The Moon night-regent with her ftarry throng,
And figns, that lead the rolling months along:
Or if thou covet rather to furvey
The Sun, all-feeing ruler of the day,
As round the globe he travels in his turn,
Reviving all things from his parent urn,
And fleecy clouds in azure fkies behold
Floating aloft, and edg'd with orient gold,
Nor lefs the radiant bow, which circles wide
The watry pole with many-colour'd pride,
Or through the loweft veftiges divine,
Imprefs'd on nature's various forms benign,
Explore the bright artificer fupreme,
And fount eternal from the paffing ftream:
View the vaft ocean, difciplin'd to wage
War within limits, and with reafon rage:
Mark, how the meads with verdure fmile, the bow'is
With leaves, the gardens blufh with virgin flow'is
Nor are fuch objects to be dar'd in rhime,
Nor fuch the points of honeft fame fublime,
Unlefs devotion awful thoughts infpire,
And godlike fpirit breathe celeftial fire.

Nos autem, a cœptis longe jocularibus aɛtos,

Calliope crebris revocat clamoribus: audin',

Ut tonat ad portas? fremit, increpitaque morantes.

Feſtum iter ingredior.   Plebes procul eſto profana,

Immodulata procul.   Tu vero dulcis amice,

‒‒‒‒ ‒‒‒‒ chare diu, dubio ſuccurre labori,

Atque vagos dignare gradus efferre per arɛtos

Parnaſſi calles, doɛtoſque accedere fontes,

Atque haurire modos, inſanas arduus unde

Deſpicias hominum curas, humiliſque coaɛtas

Ambitionis opes vel vi, ſeu fraude, malorum

Materiem, peſtemque malis: virtutis at arma

Sunt, manibus comiſſa piis, ac dona deorum,

Intemerata tuis, Phœbi non degener hoſpes,

O Patriæ venturɛ decus, Britonumque voluptas!

Ecce! iterum Murphæus adeſt, nec, ut ante, videbis

Luminibus

But, lo! Calliope recalls amain
Our fteps wide-wand'ring from her fportive ftrain :
Hark, how fhe thunders at the gates ! away,
She fretful cries, and chides our long delay.
The road is hallow'd, hence, ye herd profane,
Avaunt, inconfcious of the tuneful ftrain.
But ──── ──── thou my pleafurable friend,
And long endear'd, the doubtful toil attend
Through narrow mazes, tracing, as I fing,
The mufeful mountain and the myftic fpring;
Whence you may view the defpicable fhow,
The crazy cares of bufy men below,
Or mean ambition's ill-fufficing wealth,
By rapine wrefted, or compil'd by ftealth,
Inglorious wealth, procur'd with anxious pain,
The fource of evils, and the bad man's bane :
Yet this, committed to fuch hands as thine,
Is virtue's weapons and a gift divine,
Accomplifh'd patron of the tuneful quire,
Whom Phœbus vifits, and his beams infpire,
O born to rife thy native country's boaft,
And waft new glories to the Britifh coaft.

Lo ! Murphy comes again upon the ftage,
Nor fhall you fee the recollected fage

As

Luminibus captum, nec nota fraude petendum;

Quo quare tibi cunque Recens, exire neceſſe eſt,

Si ſuperare libet, contempto carcere, poſtes

Clauſtrorum horriſonos, et amantes limina valvas;

Fabula Mendici ſeu ſit referenda theatro,

Quum ridere velis; ſeu ſit caſurus iniquis

Cæſar amicorum manibus, lachrymiſque decoris

Virtutem plorare velis, non digna ferentem:

Haud præceps, inſane, foras exire monerem,

Nec tibi cœnandi veniat tam dira cupido;

Namque prius vigilanda tibi ſunt plurima portu

Prudenter, pelago quam pandas vela patenti;

Eja! ergo, ſi forte minus per te ſapis, audi

(Et memor ipſe mali miſeris ſuccurrere diſco)

Eludendus erit quibus artibus iſte ſatelles.

Dum

As lately robb'd of optic ken, or twice
Prone to be baffled by the fame device.
If therefore, Frefhman, thou wouldft fain unbend
Thy graver ftudies, to my lays attend:
Where e'er it fuits thy genius beft to roam,
Indignant of the gate and guarded dome;
Whether the bold Macheath's difafters move,
And Polly charm thee with unequall'd love;
Or mighty Cæfar to the ftage fucceed,
Doom'd by the hands of hollow friends to bleed,
And thou, in pity to the murder'd chief,
With real tears adorn the pictur'd grief:
Ah! rufh not headlong, nor with eager guft
Do thou fo much for any fupper luft:
Though keen your appetite, your thirft fevere,
Your tackles in the harbour firft prepare,
Ere to the fmiling main and tempting gales
You truft the veffel, and expand the fails.
If void of precept, and reftrain'd through fear,
You doubt your own abilities to fteer,
Attend; for I with fympathifing breaft,
In evils vers'd, would fuccour the diftreft:
Then hear what arts, what ftratagems defeat
The prying guardian of the dreadful gate.

THE

Dum reliqui diftent, folo cuftode relicto
Patricio, tunc necte dolos, Ithacique vagantis
Infidias imitare duplex ; tunc undique cautus
Profpiciet, qualis ferpens Epidaurius, ille,
Immanis qualis ferpens, haud promptior hoftem
Exploiare vagum, quam diro figere morfu :
Quin quanto vigilare magis fpecularis acutum,
Deceptare magis tanto contende paratus.

Ergo duos fi forte olim fpectabis amicos,
Os habitumque rudes, tractandis partibus aptos,
Addictofque tibi, patrio fermone jubeto
Compellare virum : quota, fodes, hora diei
Exquirant, eademque fibi cognomina fingant,
Communefque patres et ab una ftirpe nepotes,
Murphæi fublime genus, qui regia quondam
Momomiæ fceptra, et populos ditione tenebat,
Inque diem hofpitibus mactabat mane bidentes
Ter denos, totidemque fues, flammaque cremabat,

Et

The reſt apart, that lucky minute catch,
When the rude monſter ſtands alone to watch:
Like ſage Ulyſſes, oily to deceive,
Then all your wiles and artifices weave.
Paddy with ſerpent ken will ſtare around,
And ſtrictly traverſe all the hoſtile ground,
True Epidaurian ſnake in double ſkill,
Not more acute to ſee, than prompt to kill:
But thou, the more he darts a piercing glance,
The more in ſubtle ſtratagems advance.

If haply therefore you ſhould ſpy a pair
Of friends, diſtinguiſh'd by their awkward air,
Their Teaguiſh tone and clownly garb, engage
Theſe, thy beſt actors for the doubtful ſtage.
In Attic Iriſh let them greeting pray
To know with favour but the time of day:
By compliments like this, when grown more free,
Let them cull out his birth and pedigree,
Aſſume his name, recount their fathers o'er
And ſons, deſcended from O Murphy-more,
O Murphy-more, who held the regal reins
Of Munſter fair, and rul'd the vaſſal ſwains,
Who daily ſlaughter'd, for his gueſts to dine,
Thrice ten fat wethers, and as many ſwine,

His

Et Vitæ fundebat Aquam, ceu fluminis undas.

Jamque novo læti cognato, lumina cœlo

Attollant, fimul aftra canant felicia, tanquam

Argenti immenfa ftupuiffent mole reperta.

Tum gravibus pugnis contundant terga benigne,

Ut valuitque diu, rogitent, dextræque viciffim

Conjungant dextras, et inungant ofcula labris.

Ille, fuam prima repetens ab origine gentem,

Magnanimos jactabit avos, heroas Iernes,

Carnificis quos atra manus, proh fata nefanda!

Dulcibus e fociis, nequicquam flentibus infra,

In fuperas auras et non fpirabile cœlum

Suftulit ante dies, ac jam florentibus annis

Vota patrum patriæque fimul fpem gentis iniquis

Aptavit laqueis, animafque ita turbine torto

Projecit miferas, et nodo vindice folvit.

                                        Interea

His whiſky burn'd with purifying flame,
And pour'd, like water from the running ſtream.
Proud of their couſin, let them lift their eyes
With ſudden rapture to the vaulted ſkies,
And bleſs their happy ſtars, as much aſtoun'd,
As at a pot of bury'd treaſure found;
With fiſts full heavy let them then attack,
And kindly thump him on the brawny back,
Shake hands alternate, and with eager dint
Ambroſial kiſſes on his lips imprint.

PADDY will ſtraight on this occaſion run
Through all the tribe from father down to ſon,
Sum all his anceſtors with gallant pride,
Hibernian chiefs, in feats of arms well try'd,
Whom, Oh ſad ſentence and ſevere decree!
Jack Ketch's hand with dire dexterity
Exalted, rapt from weeping friends beneath,
To dance in æther, which they could not breathe,
To ſwing, alas! before the ſtated time,
Green in their years, and blooming in their prime,
With art adapted to the nooſy rope,
Their parent's comfort, and their country's hope,
With twirling jerk their vital thread, I wot,
Toſs'd, and cut off with ſoul-abſolving knot.

　While

Interea greſſu præter-labere loquentes.

Exiliens vero foribus circumſpice, ne te

Quis cernat cuſtos : clauſtris egreſſus iniquis,

Ibis ovans, laxoſque pedes et libera tolles

Colla jugo, nymphaſque inter ſpirabis odores

Fragrantes, quos rura tibi peperere Sabæa,

Pulvereaſque comas, juvenum de more ſoluto

Pone redundantes, vento jactabis inani.

Qualis avis, ferrata diu quam tecta coercent

Luctificam, ſi forte fores pervaſit apertas,

Læta alis plaudit, cœloque potita patenti

Sylvicolas inter ſocios modulatur amores.

Illi colla modis tendunt, ſimul ore loquaci

Cantus dulce rudes iterant, reducemque coruſcis

Excipiunt pennis : reſonant arbuſta triumphis.

Palladiis miſſis, Cythereia leniter arma

Indue,

While thus they hold the monſter at a bay,
Clear as the coaſt appears, then ſlink away:
But flying cautious caſt a backward eye,
Leſt any porter ſhould your ſteps eſpy.
When you have paſs'd the pinching gates, employ
The flying moments in exceſs of joy;
Freed from the galling yoke, and Paddy's beck,
Uſe pliant limbs, and bear aloft your neck:
Exhauſt the ſpirit of Sabæan blooms,
To wound the nymphs with breezes of perfumes,
And give with graceful negligence behind
Your duſty locks to wanton with the wind.

THUS, long confin'd within the wiry grate,
And pining ſad, if haply through the gate
The bird elopes, he claps his joyful wings,
Exults in open air, and ſweetly ſings:
His woodland mates extend their warbling throats
In ſongs, love-labour'd to his liquid notes:
Him late reſtor'd they gratulate around,
With feather'd triumphs all the groves reſound.

WHEN you have caſt Minerva's badge aſide,
Array yourſelf with Cytherea's pride;

Indue, et in pugnas prodi, velut alter Adonis.
Qualis papilio volitans impune per hortos
Vere novos, lufuque procax, et prodigus alis
Nugatur lepide, florefque innoxius ambit:
Audax fœmineas inter tenerafque cohortes,
Et nitidus plumis, ac torto fquameus auro,
Signa feres, referefque decus palmamque pufillam.
Tum demum, nulla cohibendus lege nec arce,
Vive tui juris; moderetur fræna voluptas.

Sin fortuna vetet, fraudem quo fæpius iftam
Exercere queas, minus aut exercita juftis
Succedat votis, alienas quærere veftes,
Depofitis propriis, multum fortaffe juvabit.
Ergo toga monuiffe velim te cingere picta
Affeclæ, quam forte placens ancilla tuendo
Depereat: tutus tali velatus amictu
Ingenio licet Arcadius, tardufque pedum vi,
Effugies, nullaque ex te ratione coacta,
Spectabis fcenas fumma de parte theatri.
Quicquid agunt infra, meritorum maximus inde
Arbiter ingemines plaufus, aut fibila tollas;

Infulfifve

The counterpart of foft Adonis, fine
Advance, and arm'd for execution fhine.
As through the gardens in reviving fpring
Defportive, pert, and prodigal of wing
The butterfly light flutters o'er the bow'rs,
And toying wooes, nor hurts the blooming flow'rs:
Among the tender, female forces bold
So bright with plumes, and fcal'd with twifted gold
Shalt thou difplay thy trophies to their eyes,
Bear off applaufe, and reap the puny prize.
Then let your fancy, by no ftatutes ty'd,
Become the rule, and pleafure be your guide.

BUT left the ftratagem, propos'd above,
Cannot be practis'd oft, or, practis'd, prove
Succefsful, much may fecond thy defire
To drop the gown, and feek a ftrange attire:
Then take the footman's parti-colour'd coat,
On which fome charming chamber-maid may doat:
In fuch a garb, although as dull an afs,
As ever lagg'd, fhall you fecurely pafs,
From upper gallery fublime furvey
The fhifting fcenes, nor for your pleafure pay:
Whatever parts are acted, hit, or mifs,
Be thou the critic, and applaud, or hifs;

Infulfifve petas falibus juvenes bene cultos,

Qui fuggefta premunt, caveaque licentius errant.

Ufque adeo fervilis erit munimen in arctis

Veftis, et ex humero dependens teffera nodo.

Hæ tibi erunt comites, his clauftra per afpera pronam

Experiere viam, ventofque fequere fecundos.

Sic Anchifiades, fumptis infignibus olim

Graiorum, conferta ruens per tela, per hoftes,

Scæarum intactus portarum limina tranfit.

Quod fi forte dolos humiles innectere cordi

Sit minus; ingenuæ fi longa volumina tractu

Hinc atque inde togæ, crebrifque horrentia criftis,

Virgatumque auro tunicarum, ac textile fignis,

Admirere decus; longum fi ferre laborem

Mufarum

Or on the beaux difcharge your witlefs wit,
Who throng the ftage, and flutter in the pit.
Such fafe protection fhall a fervile drefs
Procure its dapper wearer in diftrefs,
And knot, depending from the fhoulder, prove
A current ticket for the realms above.
Let thefe become thine ornamental pride,
By thefe attended fhalt thou fmoothly glide
Through ftreights difaftrous, and with fwelling fails
Cut thy prone courfe, and gain upon the gales.
Æneas thus, that venerable don,
A Grecian liv'ry for his own put on,
Exactly mantled in the grave difguife,
Untouch'd through all the Grecian hoft he flies,
Through darts and fpears erect: the Scæan gate
At laft completes the hero's fafe retreat.

But if your fpirit foar above the feats
Of fervile fhifts and pitiful deceits,
If you would trail ambitious up and down
The long-roll'd honours of the tufted gown,
And fet your heart on gaudy garments, brac'd
With fpriggy gold, and woven figures grac'd:

Mufarum indocilis, partefque fubire minores
Dedignere, potens atavis, opibufque beatus :
Continuo pullus generofo de grege fies,
Cui veteres nefcire artes, habitufque recentes
Noffe datui : tum difce graves contemnere leges,
Ingeniumque fequi, fociifque accumbere menfis.

Sin minus impenfis durus pater annuat æquis;
Si tibi jam dubium tenera lanugine mentum
Florefcat, puerique notet propiora puellæ
Ora rubor, ne te molli cum vefte fororem
Induere auricomam pudeat, neu, vertice celfum
Et jactare caput, frontemque aperire protervam.

At mihi vultus, ais, torvus, faciefque viriles
Horruit in fetas : animofi militis ergo
Aptetur lateri gladius, capitique galerus,
Caftrenfi de more minax, auroque trilici

Ardeat

If you, defcended from a ftock of 'fquires,
Renown'd for wealth, and happy in fuch fires,
Difdain to labour through the ring of arts
Againft the grain, and act inferior parts,
Commence a gentle commoner, unbred
In antient books, but neweft fafhions read;
Defpife pedantic rules, with fair fuccefs
Purfue your genius, and with Fellows mefs.

    But fhould your father niggardly not nod
To grant the juft expences of a Cod; *
If callow down your doubtful chin array,
And yet the rofes of your cheeks betray
More maid, than boy; endow'd with equal bloom,
Your florid fifter's flowing robes affume,
Nor blufh to tofs the lofty head alert,
And perk with coming airs the forehead pert.
But you reply: my vifage, grim with feams,
And briftling into beard, the man proclaims.
Then ftrut a captain, and with gallant pride
Adapt the pendent weapon to thy fide,
Toledo trufty to thy fide, and fhock
The peaceful porters with a martial cock.

    * A cant word, fignifying a Fellow-commoner

Ardeat ornatus, bis poto fulgeat oftro,

Fulminei Mavortis honos et fanguinis omen.

His iter indutus fpoliis, horrendus et armis,

Nocte fub obfcura perages; tibi cominus acres

Cuftodcs cedent, et eunti porta patebit.

　　At multis varianda modis pro fydere rerum

Militiæ ratio eft.　Urbanam carpere cœnam

Si cupias, nec non ea cura remordeat alvum;

Si modo tranfverfos ingenti pondere vectes

Nocturna refilire manu, refilire diurna,

Difficilefque vias facili tibi cardine pandi;

Si Iani ferale caput curafque bifrontes

Expugnare velis; ne, jam deprenfus in arcto,

Obfequiis invade virum: neu retia tende,

Retibus implexus temere, pacemve duello

Mifce mifer: premit, ecce, lupus graviore trementes

Dente feras! informe nefas! amplectitur urfus

　　　　　　　　　　　　　　　　Arctius

Of triple tiffue let thy garments blaze
With gold embroider'd, and emit the rays
Of purple, twice imbib'd, the trophy fhrewd,
Of flaming Mars, and harbinger of blood.
In thefe bright fpoils and awful arms array'd,
An eafy paffage in the dufky fhade
Thou fhalt explore; the porters to thy 'fcape
Shall yield compliant, and the wicket gape.

BUT as things vary by their guiding ftar,
So muft you change the ftratagems of war:
If from a cit a fupper you would draw,
And that concern affect your empty maw;
If you, by nightly and by daily hand
Revolving, would the maffy bolts command,
And glad accomplifh through the guardful gate
With eafy hinge the difficult retreat;
If Paddy's pate you would inveft in form
And double-fronted vigilancy ftorm;
If peradventure you fhould be trapann'd,
Attack him not with fupplications bland;
Spread not your nets, entangled in his toils,
Nor fue for quarters, while the battle boils;
For, lo! the wolf with unrelenting fway,
And feller fury rends his panting prey;

L 2

The

Arctius imbelles, rabieque jacentibus inftat.

His adeo in rebus dictum tibi tolle Maronis;

" Una falus victis nullam fperare falutem."

Fæminlum ad gemitum divifque effufa finiftris

Vota parum cauti, circum ftridentibus undis,

Et laceram Borea puppim jactante, recurrant :

Tu procul a terris venturos profpice cafus,

Et feris ocurre malis: tu pace ferena

Arma fagax in bella para, tenebrifque reconde

Ante memor. Strucrefne cavas, penitufque latentes

Infidias? genialis hyems, haud irrita fraudi,

Signa dabit; quum jam Liffæus flumine vincto

Conftat iners (Boreæ gelida fi fævit ab arce

Acrior ira Jovis) vitreo dum marmore pectus

Undique collucet, liquido remeabile lapfu,

Miraturque vagos cives, et non fua plauftra:

Dum concreta cavis dependet ftiria tectis,

Et veteres referunt Saturnia tempora ludos.

Tun

The fhapelefs Bruin, hugging out of breath,
Preffes the proftrate animals to death:
Hear Maro's leffon then, if overthrown,
" Your only refuge is to hope for none."

Let frantic men recur to female cries,
And feek in vain protection from the fkies;
While to and fro the roaring billows reel,
And howling tempefts tofs the fhatter'd keel:
Thou far from land the brooding ftorm furvey,
And fage prevent the perils of the fea:
In downy peace prepare the proper arms
For horrid war, nor give thy foes alarms,
But deep conceal them.   Would you fcoop your mines?
The genial winter fhall afford you figns;
When Liffey ftands, in icy fetters bound,
With current frozen into folid ground,
(If from the region of Riphæan fnows
The keener breath of bitter Boreas blows)
While, now repaffable by fcating lines,
With glaffy breaft the liquid mirror fhines,
And wonders wide at fpectacles unknown,
And vagrant cits and waggons, not its own;
From hollow domes while icicles depend,
And youths in games the Saturnalia fpend.

Then,

Tum, dudum in medias deductum lampade noctes,

Cecropiæ folenne Deæ, Phœbique canorum

Mufeis pendet vacuis opus interruptum.

Bacchus ovat: raptim portis bipatentibus unda

Nigra ruit juvenum, variamque effufa per urbem

Græcatur: fimul ipfe, fpecu, rigidique relicto

Carceris officio, fapientem demetit ore

Canitiem cuftos, genioque begnignior atras

Solatur curas, et formidabile ridet.

Nec non et digitis, et equino pectine crines

Horrentes perarans, hircique indutus olentis

Duras pelle manus, hirtos meditatur amores,

Et, pofitis novus exuviis, feftaque decorus

Vefte, fenex fentit veteris veftigia flammæ,

Jam tremulæ Veneris lippique Cupidinis hofpes,

Divinas

THEN, lately lengthen'd into midnight damps,
And watch'd ferenely by the folemn lamps,
The works of fages, who divinely fang,
In empty ftudies interrupted hang.
Boon Bacchus triumphs: forth a fable tide
Of ftriplings rufhes through the portals, wide
Difplay'd on either hand, and, up and down
Effus'd, gay revels through the mazy town:
Ev'n Paddy, fam'd for quick-difcerning ken,
Forfakes the limits of his difmal den,
The rigid duties of his office drops,
And from his face its hoary wifdom lops,
Then, to his genius more benign, beguiles
His gloomy cares, and formidably fmiles;
With forky nails, and comb, compos'd for mares,
He plows, and harrows his horrific hairs,
And, hands incafing with uncurry'd gloves
Of he-goat-hide, preludes his rugged loves.
Stript of his old habiliments, all gay,
And new-bedeck'd with coat of holiday,
The fage feels, creeping through his vital frame,
The gentle traces of his former flame,
And longs to languifh in the wither'd arms
Of blear-ey'd love and paralytic charms,

Refolv'd

Divinas vifurus anus, quæ fternere lectos

Pierios juvenum, thalamifque averrere fordes

Pulvereas, plumafque vagas, et, fulphure pingues,

Inftaurare focos flammis, atque ilice rafa

Mane folent.   Obliquat iter per devia curvum

Ancipitefque vias ambagibus, ad pia donec

Limina nympharum et cafta in penetralia ventum eft.

Tu cœcos vero motus ne quære doceri,

Arcanofque locos: oculos averte fequaces,

Idaliæ neu facra Deæ fub luce maligna

Contemplare: diu deprenfi vulnus amoris

Fervet atrox, tacitoque dolor fub pectore glifcit,

Nec læfum precibus, nec multo thure pudorem

Placaris, dum te fpectat, vigilantior Argo,

Janitor, ultricefque fedent in limine Diræ.

Huic adeo, quoties manifefta luce videndum

Se

Refolv'd to vifit thofe Pierian hags,
Who make the beds of academic wags,
With brufhes wont to fweep away from rooms
The duft offenfive, and the vagrant plumes ;
Whofe mattin breath officioufly confpires
With match and fhavings to revive their fires.
Through devious paths he winds his crooked ways,
And alleys, doubtful with meandring maze,
'Till he has reach'd the pious lofty feats
Of nymphs nectareous, and their chafte retreats.

But feek not thou to trace the puzzling roads,
His hidden motions, and their dark abodes :
Avert thy dogging eyes, nor mark a–fkance
The rites of Venus with malignant glance :
The wound of love expos'd with fecret fmart
Glows in the foul, and rankles in the heart,
Nor fhall intreaties, nor the copious flame
Of incenfe pure appeafe offended fhame,
While Pat, more keen than Argus, at the hatch,
And at his gate the vengeful furies watch.

As often then as in the face of day
The hero fully would himfelf difplay,

Se prodit, lentoque gradu metitur arenas,

Te comitem adjunge, et lateri concrefce; fubinde

Egregias fidei fancto fub fœdere nugas,

Atque aliquid prægrande Nihil ftillabis in aurem

De Patre Romano, jam jamque frementibus arma

Francigenis, et mox redituro nefcio-quodam

Scotorum in fines, et aviti munia fceptri

Vocibus ille tuis mirantes fubrigit aures,

Arreptamque manum, duro ceu forcipe prenfam,

Quaffat ovans; adfint cœptis ingentibus, orat

Multa Deos, inhianfque genis, immane benignus,

Heu! teneris, roftroque ferox, rabida ofcula mordet:

Nec te pro meritis, tanto pro munere judex

Audiet orantem non exorabilis olim :

Solventur fubito portæ : tu miffus abibis.

Ut feriæ fugere leves, labentibus alis,

Et gravis ingratæ fucceffit cura Minervæ,

Contractique rigor ftudii ; fremebundus ad antrum

Trifte

And pace the courts with flow majeſtic pride,
Hail fellow walk, and faſten to his ſide,
Then by the bye, and under ſacred ſeal
Of ſolemn faith, ſome big romance reveal,
Some pompous nothing of the Pope of Rome,
A French invaſion, and I know not whom,
In Scotland landing, to maintain by fight
His antient ſcepter and paternal right.
He, greedy feaſting on the tales he hears,
Pricks up in rapture his aſtoniſh'd ears,
Your ſocial hand affectionately takes,
As preſs'd by pincers, and exulting ſhakes,
Implores the Gods to back the great deſign,
Then yawning wide, and ſavagely benign,
Your tender cheeks with beariſh beak o'erpow'rs,
And gummy kiſſes bitingly devours:
Nor for ſuch merit, ſuch a piece of news
Shall he, juſt judge, your future ſuit refuſe;
With pliant hinges ſhall the porter ope
The yielding portals, and his friend elope.

WHEN light the feſtivals, too light to laſt,
On gliding pinions, have ſerenely paſs'd;
When ſad Minerva's heavy toils ſucceed,
And lads, contracted in their ſtudies, lead,

M 2

Tremendous

Trifte redit, calamumque vibrat, folitumque fatelles

Induit horrorem.　Tum læto lumine folem

Arrififfe fibi puer augurat, obvius heros

Quem minus irato dignatur cernere vultu;

Cujus Pierides afflarunt pectora flammis,

Cui mulcere trucem Pallas, cui Suada tyrannum

Ingenio dictifque dedit : fed gratior olli eft,

Qui pictis abacis didicit colludere furtim,

Et, prope jam victor, vinci, nec velle videri.

Tum vero fenior, claufo certamine, dextros

Ipfe fuos jactus agilefque recolligit artes,

Et palma et fpoliis pariter tumefactus inemptis

Impletur dapibus, fufoque liquefcit Iaccho:

Milefii

Tremendous Paddy, circumfpectly grave,
Returns with murmurs to his tragic cave,
And wields his grey-goofe weapon, and anon
Puts all the horrors of the porter on.

THE boy then fancies, that the Sun hath fhone
On him propitious, and on him alone,
On whom the hero condefcends to ftare
With looks lefs angry, than he wont to wear,
Whofe breaft the Mufes have inflam'd, whofe tongue
Minerva fafhion'd, and perfuafion ftrung
With all the graces of her claffic page,
To move the tyrant, and appeafe his rage.

BUT he finks deeper into Paddy's heart,
Who plays Back-gammon with the fage apart,
And, on the point of beating, learns to yield
The mock-fought honours of the checker'd field.

THE conteft clos'd, the fenior acts agen
His dextrous throws, and movements of his men,
And, puff'd alike with conqueft and with fpoils,
Reaps the full harveft of his table-toils,
His tunny paunch with unbought difhes fills,
And with full-flowing tides of claret fwills :

Milefian

Milesii sine fine sales, sine fine cachinni

Ingeminant : peti distillat faucibus humor

Lentus; at hærescit semesi copia morsus

Fida, nec indecori sordescunt pulvere nares.

Nec vero illius longo post tempore noctis,

Valvarum stridorem inter tractumque fragorem

Vinclorum et curas claustrorum, hinc inde volantes,

Quæ mentem in diversa trahunt, et lumina versant,

Immemor, obliquis oculis nutuque loquaci

E tota veterem convivam gente togata

Sevocat immunem, portaque emittit amica.

Sin tibi non alia valvæ ratione patescant,

Adversoque minax obsistat limine Janus;

Ipse viam, facilemque fugam, lætumque per urbem

Hospitium expedies victor, nec flebis inultus

Lynceos

Milefian wit is bandied o'er and o'er,
And jokes on jokes fet all the board a-roar;
While fiom his lips, diftilling down his chops,
The ropy nectar of tobacco drops;
But to his jaws the faithful plug adheres,
And graceful duft his purple nofe befmears.

Nor he foigetful of the paft delight,
And entertainment of that happy night,
Amidft the griding door's harfh-giating ftrains,
And draggy crafhes of difcordant chains,
Amid the crowding cares on either fide,
Which pofe his prudence, and his looks divide,
Culls his old mate, with partial wink a-fkew,
And vocal nod, from all the gowny crew,
Without a fine, without a bribe enfures
A pafs, and flips him through the friendly doors.

But if no better means the gates difclofe,
And Paddy's menaces your fteps oppofe,
You for yourfelf fhall fhifting expedite
A ready paffage, and an eafy flight,
And fairly compafs your determin'd end,
A cheerful fupper from fome city-friend:

Nor

Lynceos oculos, dextramque Recentibus atram,

Cenfuramve gravem, patriis nec fero luendas

Ex loculis pœnas; lictor fi perfidus olim

Finibus excedat propriis, pedibufque profanis

Aufit humum fcelerare facram, aut fi, longius æquo

Errantem a ftabulis, nigrantem Palladis agnum

Occupet, et rapiat, bibulafque propellat ad ædes:

Tunc Almæ contactus honos, tunc læfa gemifcit

Majeftas: furibunda volat, ceu flamma, per arces

Fama fuas.   Ut apes, ubi cerea regna laceffit

Vefpa ferox, roftroque bibax agit undique prædas

Hyblæas, hoftem denfo circum agmine ftrident,

Exacuuntque iras: ita turbine vindice pulfi

Pro lare Cecropio, rapto pro fratre juventus

Bella fremunt horrenda, faces et funera jamque

Tela

Nor ſhall you rue his hawking eyes, and hand,
So blackly fatal to the novel-band,
Or heavy cenſure, nor atonement worſe,
Late to be render'd from your father's purſe.

If any bailiff ſhould tranſgreſs his bounds,
And taint with impious feet the ſacred grounds,
Or ſable lamb, far ſtraying from the fold
Of guardian Pallas, with arreſtive hold
Tap on the back, and, griping by the pole,
Coercive hurry to ſome ſponging hole,
Stain'd by the touch, then Alma's honour ſmarts,
Then wounded moans the majeſty of arts:
Indignant fame, like lightning from the ſkies,
With rage tempeſtuous through her turrets flies.
As when a waſp invades the waxen toils,
And rending revels on Hyblæan ſpoils,
The buzzing bees in circling bands engage
The felon foe, and whet their honeſt rage:
So for the freedom of their houſe attach'd,
Her trophies tarniſh'd, and their brother ſnatch'd,
The youth incens'd with univerſal ire
Breathe horrid battle, faggot-flaming fire,

Tela vibrant, foribufque ruunt, peftemque rapacem

Corripiunt avidi pavitantem, et multa precantem

Voce, tremore, piis oculis, ad fydera palmis

Nequicquam tenfis; ac, non indebita funi

Jamdudum, infeftis invadunt unguibus acris

Colla cohors, prenfantque manus, pedibufque retractum

Per terram ardentes ad frigida balnea raptant,

Ora luto, et multo maculatum fanguine, monftrum.

Omnibus unus amor tetrum genus Harpyjarum

Exercere odiis, milvumque abolere voracem:

Tormenti fed quifque novas excogitat artes,

Ingeniique moratur opus difcrimine: tandem

Convenit, et pœnas Majorum more repofcunt.

Hi circumcifis male fraudant auribus æquum

Carnificem; hi ferro candenti crimen inurunt

Fronti

And fell deſtruction : now, renown'd for feats,
They wave their blades, and, ruſhing through the gates,
Now panting ſeize with horrible delight
The peſt rapacious, thunder-ſtruck with fright,
Imploring mercy with repeated cries,
With trembling limbs, with ſupplicating eyes,
And hands, to move the bum-compelling pow'rs,
In vain extended to the ſtarry tow'rs.
With keen-ſet nails his gullet they purſue,
His gullet, long not to the rope undue :
His hands they fetter, and with glowing wrath,
And rapture ſweep him to the frigid bath,
Dragg'd by the heels, a monſter plaiſter'd o'er
With kennel-eſſence, and defil'd with gore!

ALL, all conſpire to perſecute with ſpite
The harpy-brood, and rend the rabid kite :
But each invents new racks, and in the maze
Of various wits the work at hand delays.
At length, concurring to chaſtife his crimes,
They vote the laws of antecedent times :
Theſe circumciſe his forfeit-ears, and rob
The honeſt hangman of a ſhilling-job;
Thoſe on his front with ruddy flaming brand
Imprint the late pollutions of his hand:

N 2

His

Fronti turpe recens : vultu memorabile, T. C.

Altius horrefcit.   Juvat exantlare fed illos

Pierios latices, capitique infundere, donec

Infectum fcelus eluitur luftralibus undis.

Jura tacent: vindicta, fragor, furor, ira, tumultus

Mifcentur : dulces difcordi voce forores

Dira canunt, fciffaque toga Tritonia fævit.

Ne vero, juvenes, nimium ferventibus, oro,

Indulgete animis : immanem tollite ludum.

Extinxiffe truces lymphis ultricibus iras

Sit fatis: heu ! tædis funeftis parcite, ferro

Parcite fatifero, neu fœdo fanguine puras

Commaculate manus, miferamve abrumpite vitam.

Criminibus ruat ipfe fuis, et penfilis olim,

Nec fine lege, graves perfolvat gutture pœnas.

Surdior

His hideous vifage frowns with grimmer hue,
And deep T. C. ftands legible to view.
But others joy with pumping hands to heave,
And on his forehead difembogue the wave
Of fpring Pierian, 'till with foamy play
The pure libations wafh his guilt away.
Dumb are the laws: through Alma's wide domain.
Noife, fury, wrath, promifcuous tumult reign:
The Nine their notes in direful difcord drown,
And Pallas riots in her tatter'd gown.

But, gentle youths, your glowing wrath allay,
Ah! banifh, I befeech, the favage play.
Suffice it fully to have quench'd the flames
Of hot refentment with revengeful ftreams:
With-hold your torches, livid through the fhades,
With-hold the gafhes of your fatal blades:
With blood ignoble in unfeemly ftrife
Foul not your hands, nor fnap the wretched life:
Ripe let the culprit fall in after times
Beneath the load of his enormous crimes,
And bear, with gullet in a twifted ftring
The noofe of juftice and dependent fwing.

Surdior et fcopulis undifque prementibus actam.

Interea vigiles dudum, intentique miniftri,

Prodigiis moniti tantis et cardine rerum

Jam verfo, ut quondam pavidi, furgente procella,

Cuftodes ovium fugiunt de rupibus altis,

Arboreafque petunt imis in vallibus umbras,

Deferuere fores : cedit pater ultimus ipfe

Patricius throno, portæque relinquit habenas.

Tuque puer, cui lene pati mala non fua pectus

Jam didicit, trifti captivo nec tamen audet

Præfidio fieri, fluvioque obftare ruenti,

Horrendum fuge confpectum, teque eripe turba

Infana fapiens, et, qua via ducit ad urbem,

Flecte gradus, placidoque procul contende Lyæo.

Egrediendi

In vain I beg : they rage with wild uproar,
Deafer than rocks, and furges on the fhore.

MEAN-WHILE the porters lately wont to wait
With eyes attentive to the crowded gate,
Warn'd by fuch omens, difcipline infring'd,
And prefent pofture of affairs unhing'd,
Defert their pofts : as fearful, when a ftorm
Begins to rife, and clouds the fkies deform,
From lofty rocks the fhepherds fly like hail,
And feek the bufhy coverts of the vale.
Laft Father Paddy from his throne, with pains
Retreating flow, refigns the portal reins.

AND thou, gay youth, whofe gentle bofom flows
With tender pity for another's woes,
Yet dares not fhield the captive in extreme
Diftrefs, and ftem the torrent of the ftream,
Avoid the rueful horrid fight; endow'd
With cool difcretion fly the raging crowd;
Thy fafer paces to the city bend,
And, far from frays, with Bacchus boon contend.

Egrediendi artes hæ funt, hic lubricus ordo:
Tu vero tentare vias, et fpernere clauftra
Incipies, audaxque olim fine cortice nabis,
Poftquam longa dies, variis exercita curis,
Reddiderit dextrum meliores nectere fraudes.

Interea forfan mea te præcepta juvabunt,
Et, Mufa monftrante viam, veftigia tendes
Tuta per obftantes hoftes, et ferrea portæ
Vincula; nec penitus ftudiofi carmina vatis
Excedent animo: circum mea tempora nectes
Victrices hederas, doctarum infignia frontum.

Jam longum permenfus iter, fub fine laborum
Sifto gradum plaufu cœtum, palmaque decorum

Mufarum

THESE are the myfteries, the gliding train
Of arts, that teach you glad egrefs to gain:
But you, fuccefsful in each enterprife,
Shall find a paffport, and reftraint defpife,
Shall boldly venture through the flowing tide,
And, buoying without cork, the billows ride;
When length of time and practice in extremes
Have tutor'd thee, to plot profounder fchemes.

MEAN-WHILE perhaps thefe documents of mine
May much facilitate thy prone defign,
And thou, beneath the Mufe's guiding hand
Safe fteer thy progrefs through the planted band
Of eyeful foes, through difficulties ftreight,
And barricadoes of the bolted gate:
Nor fhall the labours of the Mufe depart,
In dead oblivion, from thy grateful heart;
My temples fhalt thou crown with green rewards,
Victorious badges of melodious bards.

THUS having meafur'd fuch a lengthy fpace,
I triumph now to terminate the race,
And at the pillars of the tuneful quire
Sufpend my folemn quill and votive lyre,

Muſarum ad poſtes et Phœbi mœnia feſtum

Suſpendiſſe tholo plectrum, citharamque dicatam

Rite juvat.   Siquid veri præſagia pandant,

Me læti paſſim pueri per aperta viarum

Sæpe canent, recinentque ſenes, me, carmine ſacro

Indomitas arces auſum oppugnare Minervæ,

Et reſerare fores, famæque recludere portas,

Extremumque fugax nomen deferre per orbem.

F I N I S.

SPECULI

Faſt by the walls of Phœbus.   If the page

Of divination aught of truth preſage,

Me ſhall the youth in open ſtreets rehearſe,

And ſages echo with reſponſive verſe ;

Me, who relying on the magic pow'rs

Of numbers, dar'd to brave Minerva's tow'rs,

Unbar the doors, unfold the gates of fame,

And through the diſtant globe diffuſe my flying name.

THE END.

SPECULI POETICI

LIBRI QUATUOR.

AD VIRUM EXCELLENTISSIMUM

PHILIPPUM, Comitem de CHESTERFIELD,

HIBERNIÆ PROREGEM, &c.

THE

POETICAL MIRROR

IN FOUR BOOKS.

To His Excellency

PHILIP, Earl of CHESTERFIELD,

Lord Lieutenant General, and General Governour of

IRELAND.

AD LECTOREM.

PRÆMONITUM velim Lectorem, Authorem totius hujufce Poematis effigiem animo conftruxiffe, Comite de Chefterfield Regias apud Hibernicos gerente vices, et flagrante per Scotiam Rebellione; literis vero non nifi quinquennio poft mandaffe.

QUANTI fit apud omnes, rei ludicræ ftudiofos, JOHANNIS PHILIPS opufculum, neminem latere cenfeo, qui minimum modo Romanæ puritatis et falis Anglicani fapit.

ILLIUS ergo veftigia nos arctius initio fecuti, tandem latius evagati fumus, quodque ARGUREIDA ftatueramus appellare, perductis quatuor ad finem libris, alio titulo, magis
operi

operi confentaneo, defignari voluimus. Integros autem verficulos PHILIPS Appendici fubjungi curavimus, ut inde quid in melius, pejufve mutavimus, pateat.

UTILE dulci mifcere mihi mehercule fuit in votis: quod fi quidpiam orbi literariæ vel emolumenti, vel voluptatis attulerim, fatis erit operæ pretium.

SPECULI

SPECULI POETICI

LIBER I.

MAGNUS in angusto labor est, nova carmina pango,

Verba sequens aliena meis, gazamque Britannam

Vertere in Ausoniam, Phœboque sacrare per orbem

Accingor. Tu primus ades, tuque annue cœptis,

O decus Aonidum, STANHOPEI sanguinis hæres

Inclyte, quem gremio nutrici Pallas alumnum

In patriæ spem fida tulit, Divæque decentes

Finxerunt;

THE

POETICAL MIRROR.

BOOK I.

GREAT is my toil, though narrow be my theme,
  New ſtrains I ſing, through devious paths explore
Harmonious treaſure, ſtudious to refine,
To ſtamp the Britiſh into Latian coin,
And conſecrate it to the God of Day
Wide o'er the globe. Thou firſt attend, and thou
Inſpire my lays, O glory of the Nine,
Accompliſh'd STANHOPE of illuſtrious blood,
Whom faithful Pallas in her genial breaſt
Divinely cheriſh'd, and the graces form'd,

VOL. I.   P   Thy

Virtuti dum lingua fuit; cui gratia fandi

Cecropiique fales! Auguſtæ fperne beatas

Urbis opes, procerumque epulas, et leniter audi

Pierides, doctamque fitim, efuriemque canoram,

Et mecum arcanos jam nunc afcende receſſus.

Ne tamen ipfe tibi moveat faſtidia vates

Æris inops, caſſuſque penu, fi plena fideli

Reddiderit fpeculo rerum fimulachra, fluentes

Deliciis epulas variis, nulloque lepore

Conditas, tardofque viris ducentia fomnos

Pocula, mufarum veſtrique haud confcia Phœbi.

At mox ingenii pennis fugientibus udam

Spernet humum, cœtufque humiles, et, concitus æſtro

Nobiliore Dei, perſtringet carmine victor

Geſta ducum, heroafque fuis interferet aſtris.

FELIX,

Thy country's hope! whofe dignity might fwell
The Roman fenate, while her voice was free,
The voice of virtue: thou with elegance
And Attic wit adorn'd, defpife the wealth
Of proud Augufta, fly the coftly feafts
Of pamper'd nobles, and indulgent hear
The plaintive Mufes; hear their letter'd thirft
And tuneful hunger, and with me afcend
The myftic chambers of their high retreats,
Nor let the Poet, void of current cafh,
And vital food, provoke thy pure difdain,
If he prefent, as in a faithful glafs,
The round refemblance of material things,
Grotefque and rude, profufe luxuriant fcenes,
Difhes, unfeafon'd with delicious wit,
And flowing goblets, which incline the guefts
To lazy naps, unconfcious of the Nine,
And active God, that animates thy breaft.

But foon, the Mufe, on foaring pinions borne,
Shall fpurn inglorious earth, the groveling crowd
And, ftung with Pæan's nobler heat, difplay
The deeds of chiefs triumphant, and infert
Heroic fouls among their natal ftars.

Happy

FELIX, qui curis, felix, qui litibus atris

Ætatem femotus agit, lautumque crumena

Contexta folidum, feu pelle tuetur ovina!

Non illum fpes alma, fides non deferit audax,

Non trepidum formido premit, raptoris adunci

Nec facies inopina ferit.   Non edita voce

Oftrea viva vorax bibit auribus, invia labris,

Ambrofiafve fagax nequicquam naribus auras

Artocreæ captat, nec Zythi gaudia ficco

Deperit ore mifer: quoties quin humida triftes

Nox umbris terras operit, ftipatus amicis

Flectit ad infignem veftigia læta tabernam,

Feftivofque choros, liquidofque inftaurat honores.

Nec minus ille memor nymphæ, quæ dulce videndo

Pectus perftrinxit tenerum, placidumque venenum

Implicuit venis, animamque accendit amore,

Ingenuam agnofcit venerem : redeunte culullo,

Ut valeat, Divos orat, jugique fruatur

Lætitia

HAPPY the man, who, void of cares and ſtrife,
In ſilken, or in leathern purſe retains
A ſplendid ſhilling! him nor bounteous hope,
Nor daring faith deſerts : no guilty fear
Purſues him trembling, nor the Gorgon face
Of hookful bailiff unexpected ſmites.
Not he voracious with inſatiate ears
Ingulphs new oyſters from the diſtant cry
ALIVE! ALIVE! impervious to his lips,
Nor with ſagacious noſtril ſnuffs in vain
The fumes ambroſial of hot mutton-pies,
Noɪ melancholy ſighs for chearful ale
With arid lips; but when the beldam night
With ſable mantle overſpreads the face
Of earth, day-widow'd, uſher'd with his friends
To club-frequented tipling-houſe he ſhapes
His joyful ſteps, and carolling renews
The liquid honours of the ſocial board.

HERE mindful of the nymph, whoſe vivid eye,
Sweet-glancing, deep transfix'd his tender breaſt,
And, pleaſing poiſon through his manly veins
Infuſing, fir'd his captive ſoul with love :
He frank avows his honourable flame,
With each returning glaſs invokes the Gods,

To

Lætitia, pueroque pari, fociifque propinat.

Interea, trepido fumantes thure, vapores
Ore haurit, redditque: cavis ruit India buccis
Denfior, et circum redolentia tempora fpirat:
Nafus ovat medius, fufofque reforbet odores.
Proximus ille foco, perpendens abdita rerum
Fronte gravi, nutuque loquax in fede curuli
Confilium regit obfcurum: fin blanda moretur
Fabula prodigiis, fin lætas defricet aures
Ambiguii falis, aut verborum lufus amœnus,
Solvitur in rifum: fremitu laquearia plaudunt.

Ast ego, quem, ftimulis agitans, penuria cingit,
Atque comes malefuada fames, hærentia pelli
Arctius offa traho, corpus exangue minutis
Suftineo fruftis et aceto, parcius haufto,
Umbra viri! vacua fpatior tum folus arena,

Dormitove

To grant her health, and joy, and equal love,
And recommends the bumper to his mates.

MEAN-WHILE with mouth alternative he draws,
And thick emits the tepid vapours bland
Of unctuous, odorific weed: in wreaths
Forth India globous from his bellow-cheeks
Rushes, and round his aromatic brows
Successive breathes: amidst the lambent maze
His nose exults, and drinks the floating fumes.
He next the fewel'd hearth with solemn front
Deep matter cons, in magisterial chair
Important lolls, and with a nod controuls
The dun Divan.   But should a merry tale
Tickle his ears, or should a pun escape,
A pun ambiguous, or conundrum quaint,
He laughs: the roofs resound with loud applause.

BUT I, whom griping penury surrounds,
And hunger, sure attendant upon want
Ill-prompting, drag a length of skin and bones,
With scanty offals and small acid tiff,
Wretched repast, my meagre corps sustain,
Shade of a man! then solitary stalk

Through

Dormitove domi, Phæbo vicinus et aftris.

Hic ultra nubes leviori perfruor aura,
Et, macie tenues, et acuto frigore pigros,
Afflatu foveo digitos, perque horrida tetri
Clauftra tubi (neque enim laribus fuligine.cedit
Hiberna tinctis, ebenove nigredine lævi)
Refpiro peti, graveolentem flamine, fumum.

Haud nigriore tubo Cambrus, breviore nec unquam
Utitur antiqua clarorum nomine regum
Arthuri tum gente fatos, tum Cadwaladeri,
Heroas longa doctus deducere virga ;
Per vaftos quoties nec amicos frugibus agros,
Perplexifque rubis et acutis afpera fpinis
Per juga, per curvas valles tardafque paludes,
Et rapidos fluvios et jam fine tramite tractus,
Rupibus horrentes et verticibus præruptis,
Preffo lacte potens, patrioque inflatus honore
Urget equum, patulaque toga fublimis obumbrat,
Quo vafer in triviis merces exponat emendas
Arvonii, feu vult Mariduni, five vetuftæ

Brechiniæ,

Through lonely walks, or moaping doze at home,
Aloft, contiguous to the Sun and Stars.

HERE, perch'd above the groſſer clouds, I draw
Empyreal air, and with a warming puff
Regale my wan, my lady-finger'd hands,
Numb'd by keen Boreas; or through tube, as black
As winter-chimney, or well-poliſh'd jet,
Exhale Mundungus, ill-perfuming ſcent.

NOT blacker tube, nor of a ſhorter ſize
Smoaks Cambro-Briton (vers'd in pedigree
Sprung from Cadwallader and Arthur, kings
Full famous in romantic tale) when he
O'er barren plains, wide, deſolate, and hills
Perplex'd with brambles, rough with prickly thorns,
Through mazy winding vales, through lazy lakes,
Impetuous rivers, pathleſs wilds and tracts
Horrid with craggy cliffs and pendent rocks,
Upon a cargo of fam'd Ceſtrian cheeſe,
His country's pride, and honour of his houſe,
High over-ſhadowing with broad ſurtout,
Beſtrides his beaſt, with ſage intent to vend
His curdy venture at Arvonian mart,

Brechiniæ, aut refluis ludens ubi flexibus hortos

Lambit Ariconios Vaga, dites ubere glebas,

Fructibus unde rubent frondes, laticefque quotannis

Lenæi manant, quales·non vicerit uva

Maffica, nec Setina potens; haud acre Falernum,

Se licet heroum crepet eloquiique parentem,

Pontificumque decus, vatumque Helicona piorum.

Dum fic ingratæ ducendo tædia vitæ

Tabefco, torvo vultu greffuque filenti

Aeriam afcendens arcem, me creditor, ecce!

" Nec vifu facilis, nec dictu affabilis ulli,"

Importunus adit, proh formidabile monftrum,

Invifum pariter Diis, ac mortalibus imis!

Vocali ter calce gravi portæ intonat atrox;

Ter diras aperit fauces; ter gutture·rauco

Me vocat invitum: jamdudum exofa vocantis

Verba recognofco, vacuo velut edita bufto,

Infauftumque

Or Maridunum, or the antient town
Brechinia clep'd, or where the filver ftream
Of Vaga, fportive with meandring arms,
Encircles Ariconium, fruitful foil!
Whence orchats blufh with fruitage, and in rills
Nectareous juices flow, that well may vie
With Maffic, Setin, or renown'd Falern,
Campania's purple pride, although it boaft
Itfelf the parent of heroic worth
And flowing eloquence, the rofy grace
Of Pontiffs plump, and Helicon of Bards.

THUS while my joylefs minutes tedious lag,
With looks demure and filent pace a dun,
Horrible monfter, hated by Gods and men,
Shocking to fight, implacable of ear
To fofteft note of pity-moving tongue,
To my aerial citadel afcends!
With vocal heel thrice thundring at my gates,
He opens thrice his hideous jaws: my name
He thrice invokes from hoarfe-refounding throat,
And lengthens out a deeper groan.   Too well
I recognize the long-detefted tone,
As utter'd from a Cœnotaph, too well

Q 2

The

Infauftumque fonum, et ferales omine cantus.

Heu! quid agam? vel quo fugiam conterritus, expes?

Pulvere commixtos, iterumque iterumque cremandos,

Per cineres, minimis atro carbonibus, antro

Sublabor, penitufque cava me noɗte recondo.

At, qua rara fluunt per clauftrum lumina fiffum,

Qualis erat, quantufque nefas! adverfa tuenti?

Hei mihi! quot fcelerum facies graffantur in uno,

Gorgones, Harpyæque truces, jam jamque Chimæræ,

Spirantes flammam, et cinɗæ ferpentibus Hydræ?

Obftupui, riguique metu: ftant vertice crines

Arreɗi; tremulo ftillat de corpore fudor

Frigidus; aftriɗo concrefcit lingua palato,

Vocis inops; genua ægra labant: difcrimine feɗæ

Abjetis exanimem feclufus, obambulat auceps!

Nos omnes auræ, fimul ipfa filentia terrent.

ARIDA

The voice ill-boding and the folemn cant,
A deadly dirge.   Arrefted with furprife,
What fhould I do? or whither turn? aghaft ·
Amaz'd, confounded, through the mingled mafs
Of afhes, cinders, twice to be reviv'd,
And flack fulphureous, to the black recefs
Of coal-hole fugitive I flink, and couch
Reptile, intomb'd beneath the celly gloom.

BUT, where through chinks a dubious gleam pervades,
How huge and dreadful to the peeping eye
His port appear'd ? how many baleful forms
In one upflarting rag'd? what Gorgons grim,
Harpies obfcene, Chimæras breathing flames,
And hiffing Hydras, girt with fnaky folds ?
I fhrunk aftounded, ftiffen'd with affright ;
My hairs erect ftand briftling on the fcalp;
A chilly fweat bedews my fhudd'ring limbs;
My tongue, clofe-cleaving to the vocal roof,
Forgets her faculty of fpeech, my joints relaxt:
The Hawk, excluded by a thin-flit dale,
Hovers, and gapes, and for his quarry pants!
Me ftings each breeze, the very filence damps.

HIS

Arida frons, rugis perarata, et conica menti
Canities, textumque decus venerabile colli
Sanctis ora viris fatorum infanda minantur.
Solenni prolixa manu membrana volutat,
Horrendas testatà notas, memoresque figuras,
Visu terribiles oculis mortalibus ægris.

Ecce ! autem a tergo tardis se gressibus infert
(Diique Deæque piis tales avertite pestes !)
Monstrum aliud, paribusque ferox accingitur iris,
Cujus ab officio nomen deducitur Harpax.
At superi obscœnas occultis viribus olim
Et magica virtute manus (mirabile dictu!)
Imbuerunt.   Humero palmam si forte siniſtro
Vatis obærati lethcam injecerit ultor,
Nec mora, nec requies : contactu flexile, corpus
(Quales olim equites) malefacram fertur in arcem,
Vis ubi multiplici clausum tenet objice ferri,
Robustæque fores, donec conversa Minerva
In Plutum redimat captivum.   Debitor æris

Ergo

His faded front, entrench'd with many a frown,
And conic beard, and fpreading band, admir'd
By modern faints of Abrahamic air,
Difaftrous acts forebode: in his right hand
Long fcrolls of parchment folemnly he waves,
With characters and figures dire-infcrib'd,
Grievous to mortal eyes.   Behind him ftalks
(Ye Gods and Goddeffes, avert fuch plagues
From righteous men!) with felon fteps and flow
Another monfter, not unlike himfelf,
Sullen of afpect, by the vulgar call'd,   ·
A Catchpole, fitly from his office call'd,
Whofe hands polluted delegating Gods
With force incredible and magic charms
Erft have endu'd: if he his ample palm
Should haply on ill-fated fhoulder lay
Of debtor, ftrait his body to the touch
Obfequious, rapt (as whilom knights were wont)
To fome enchanted caftle is convey'd
Where bars impregnable, Ætnean files,
Cyclopean temper, and coercive chains
In durance ftrict detain him, 'till in form
Of Plutus Pallas fets the captive free.

BEWARE,

Ergo cave, fi quando velis exire, caveto;
Omnia tuta timens, huc, illuc lumina torque.

Sæpius hic oculis longe veftigia fignat,
Et bivio latet obliquo triftive caverna
Perfidus, incautum quo tactu rite nefafto
Fafcinet. Haud aliter felis (meminere poetæ)
Lucifugis inimica feris, et acuta per umbras
Hinc atque inde tuens, exefis incubat antris,
Horrefcitque pilos, tenditque madentia crebris,
Cladibus arma pedum, funeftos muribus ungues.
Aula non aliter laqueata, five culina,
Vifceribus deducta fuis, extendit Arachne
Retia rara, ftruens errantibus obvia mufcis.
Illa fpecu, meditata nefas, latet abdita texto
Pendula: præda procax, fatorum improvida, fraudes
Proruit in medias, et inextricabile lethum,
Rauca canens; neque tela juvant intorta neque artes
Obnixæ, aut, varia refplendens iride, forma.
Infidiofa cavis nequicquam implexa repugnat
Vefpa plagis, fucufque gemens, et, prodigus alis
Papilio, maculis, et vivo difcolor auro.
Illa levi tacitoque frequens ad ftridula lapfu

Signa

BEWARE, ye debtors, when ye walk, beware:
The coaſt is clear, the ſky ſerene ; yet dread
Impending ſtorms, be circumſpect; for oft
This caitiff eyes your ſteps aloof, and oft
Lies perdue in ſome nook or gloomy cave,
Prompt to enchant ſome inadvertent wretch
With his unhallow'd touch.   Grimalkin thus
(As poets ſing) to light-avoiding mice
Quick-ſighted foe, with unremitting eye
Lies nightly brooding o'er a chinky gap,
Protending her fell claws, diſtain'd with gore
Of thoughtleſs vermin, and Arachne thus
In vaulted hall, or ſteamy kitchen hangs
Her ſubtile, filmy, diſembowel'd web,
Obvious to vagrant flies: ſhe pendent lurks
Within her woven cell: the humming prey,
Regardleſs of their fate, ruſh on the toils
Tenacious and inextricable death,
Nor aught avail their native arms, nor arts
Auxiliar, or their forms of Iris-hue:
The waſp inſidious, tangled in her nets,
The buzzing drone, and gaudy butterfly,
Proud of expanded wings, diſtinct with ſpots
And gloſſy gold, in vain reſiſt.   Aloft

Signa ruit, trepidifque cohortibus horrida raptim
Involat, et roftro pedibufque tenacibus inftat.
Nec mora, quin, calido ftillantem fanguine vitam
Sæva reluctantem potat, fpoliifque fuperba
Corpora tarda trahit dirum in penetrale retrorfum.

His equidem auguriis fatifque frequentibus icti,
Haud ultra fines pimplæi carceris arctos
Ferre pedes, vultus nec aperto credere cœlo,
Audemus, cauti quin ftricto corpora vallo
Munimus, claufafque domos, atque invia caftra,
Pieria tanquam refidentes rupe, tenemus
Eminus, et crudis meditamur prælia chartis.

Huc pauci afcendunt comites, quos æquus amavit
Delius: accipimus paucos, quos ardua Clio
Perfpexit fidos, digitoque vocavit aventi.

HINC

Light, foftly gliding to the fignal-buzz,
She rufhes, horrid on the trembling band
Precipitately darts, and keen affaults
With feet attractive and retentive beak
The murmuring victims, then with eager jaws
Envenom'd, leechy drinks the fanguine life
Of foes reluctant, and with backward ftrides,
Elate with fpoils, into her loathfome cave
Their bulky carcafes triumphant diags.

WARN'D by thefe omens and repeated fates,
We bards effay not idly to furpafs
The narrow limits of our prifon-houfe,
But, ever on the watch, our bodies guard
With airy rampiers, barricade each pafs,
And pitch our camp, as on the forked hill,
High, inacceffible, and meditate
On papers crude imaginary wars.

HITHER but few, whom Phœbus hath belov'd,
Afcend accepted, but a few, whofe faith
The lofty Mufe from tryal hath approv'd,
And hail'd with beck'ning finger to afpire.

Hinc procul, undantem turba, fremituque furentem,

Per trivias plebem, cives hinc mercuriales,

Qui nunquam æthereæ pretium didicere Camœnæ,

Despicimus, terræ soboles, quas alta tueri

Astra poli, Phœbumque piget! speculamur et æris

Hinc quæsitores, et, amantes curva viarum,

Exploratores, oculis venantibus acres,

Legitimumque nefas, et ineluctabile vati

Strativago, manibus metuendos Harpagas uncis.

Hi procul intactos gelida formidine stringunt;

Quem vero tetigere, tenent, rapiuntque, trahuntque,

Nequicquam Divumque fidem, populique precantem

Auxilium, et misero ferientem sydera planctu.

Ast illi subjecta premunt jam colla triumpho

Horrifero, tristisque canunt præludia fati,

Carceris antrum ingens, et opacum fornice clauftrum,

Pervigilumque canum excubiis·ferrique rigore

Heu! circum septum, gravis incunabula luctus,

Mordacisque

HENCE far we view the wavy multitude,
With mingled murmurs mad'ning through the streets:
Indignant hence with pity we look down
On mercenary cits, who never learnt
The worth of fong cœleftial, fons of earth,
Whofe vifual orbs have ficken'd to furvey
The firmamental ftars and orient Sun.
Hence we defcry remorfelefs duns afkance,
And fcouting fetters, keen with hunting eyes,
That coaft the crooked paffes of the ftreets,
And legal fiends, by ftreet-pervading Bard
Inevitable, odious Harpies, hook'd
With forky talons.   At a diftance they
Strike frozen panics into wights untouch'd;
But whomfoever they have touch'd, they hold,
They fnatch, they drag, imploring ufelefs aid
Of Gods and men, and piercing with their cries
The ftarry vault.   In horrid triumph they
Deprefs the captive neck, and fing the fad,
The bitter preludes of impending fate,
Prifons, and cells, and dreary dungeons, arch'd
With ever-during night, and thick befet
With rueful vigils of infernal hounds,

Blood-

Mordacifque domum curæ, vivifque fepulcrum,
Diis etiam invifum Stygiis! quali impete dextras
Clavigeras tollunt, et querno pondere firmant!
Ut capto illudunt! vos O, quibus Harpagis horror,
Inftantifque timor famis, aut divinitus ardor
Spirandi fuperumque diem, folemque tuendi,
Præcipitate fugas.   Alieni confcius æris,
Quifque cavet monitus, refugitque exterritus auras.

   Sic, ubi venatu fero juga rupibus alta
Luftravit lupus, et furiis exarfit acutis,
Hinnuleum impaftus dumofo in monte vagantem,
Tondentemque comas Cytici florentis, acerba
Fauce premit, prædæque inhians infævit: at illa
Corde tremit, vallefque cavas ululatibus implet
Flebilibus: fugere leves per devia longe

Blood-fcenting, durance within durance, fenc'd
With hammer'd rigour, maffy bolts and bars,
The flinty cradles of defponding woe,
The difmal dome of gnawing care, and grave
Of living Lazars, by the very pow'rs
Of Hell abhorr'd.   With what Herculean might
They wave their club-compreffing hands, and arm
With weight of oaken argument! how fteel'd
They fport with anguifh, and infult the wretch
Attach'd! O ye, who dread the Harpy-claws,
And inftant want, or would divinely breathe
Pure upper day, and greet the joyful Sun,
Fly quick as lightning.   At the loud alarm
Each mortal, confcious of a bond or note,
To covert hies, and fhuns the face of day.

THUS, when a prowling wolf, in tedious queft
Of prey, hath rang'd the rugged hills, and, ftung
With rabid rage, efpies a tender fawn
Defportive, vagrant on the fhaggy brow
Of mountain fteep, cropping the flow'ry fhrub,
With ruthlefs jaws wide-yawning he invades
The proftrate animal, that beats at heart,
And fills the hollow vales with plaintive cries:

Far

Lustra feræ, ac denfos nemorum petiere receffus.

Vos vero, quos firma tenent cœnacula dudum
Conclufos, ærifque reos cum fœnore fumpti,
Ne, nimium tutis confifi rebus et auræ
Spiranti, infidias contemnite defuper imas,
Raptorumque dolos, et iniquos vatibus ungues.
Hi nempe in triviis nudoque fub ætheris axe
Algentes hyemant; at propugnacula vatum
Sufpiciunt avidi, et dubiæ mercedis avari,
Infomnes agitant noctes, et poftibus altis
Incumbunt, foribufque hærent; fi forte facultas,
Si qua viam fraus inveniat, lucemque ftruendo
Multa terunt: illi dociles, quo retibus hoftes
Alliciant pavidos, et fub ditione morentur,
In varias fefe didicerunt fingere formas.

Rusticus hic fiet, pede, veftibus, ore, capillis
Horridus incomptis: hic militis induet arma
                                        Nobilis,

Far through their haunts the savage tribes retire,
And seek the deep recesses of the woods.

    But ye, who, pent in airy forts, assert
Your freedom, bound in sum-creating sums,
Trust not to fair appearances, nor scorn
The wiles of bailiffs, undermining wiles,
And hooks, destructive to the tuneful fry;
For they, detach'd through mazy streets and lanes,
Winter beneath the naked copes of Heav'n
Congeal'd, but note the capitols of Bards
With upcast eyes, and, lur'd with scent of gain,
Lead sleepless nights: on pillars unobserv'd
They rest incumbent; and adhere to doors,
If haply fraud admittance find, nor less
They waste the night in many-woven plots,
And, subtle to seduce their wary foes,
Ensnare, and hold in tributary bonds,
Convert the Catchpole into various forms.

    WITH hobbling gait, garments uncouth, and hair
Matted and frizz'd, this gapes a rustic clown;
That frowns a captain, with Toledo girt,
And, grandly marching with mavortial port,

Nobilis, et gradiens auroque ardebit et oftro.

Ille facerdotem præ fe fert impius atrum,

Mentitus rofeafque genas patulumque galerum,

Et, cœli fumptis infignibus, augur Averni

Labitur in caulas, et prenfos opprimit agnos.

Ufque adeo vigiles ludunt infomnia fenfus,

Et recti capimur fpecie, virtutis et umbra.

Sæpius at lecto meretrix elapfa tepenti

Sopitos perjura finus elufit amantis,

Et rapto fceleris pretio, foribufque reclufis,

Anguimanam infudit mifero fub nocte catervam.

Proditus ille Deos Hecatenque Erebumque Chafofque

Ore tonat, dirafque vomit, furibundus: at illa

Condit opes, ridetque dolis, immota, repertis.

Haud fecus in fomnis, gremioque infida jacentem

Aufa virum conjux violare, et, robore tonfo,

Sæva

Blazes with broider'd gold and Tyrian dye:
Another impious, borrowing the prieſt,
Belyes the roſy cheeks and broad-brim'd hat;
The fiend of Hell uſurps the badge of Heav'n,
Glides through the fold, and ſeizing rends the lambs.
Such fond illuſions mock our wakeful eyes;
So much are we the dupes of fancy, caught
By ſemblances of truth and virtue's garb.

 But oft, elopen from her tepid bed,
The perjur'd nymph abandon'd hath betray'd
The void embraces of her ſleepy ſwain,
Receiv'd the guilty bribe, unbarr'd the gate,
And in the dead, the ſilent mid-night hour
Pour'd on the wretch a ſnaky-handed band.
Betray'd he ſtorms, enrag'd invokes the Gods,
The Furies, Chaos, Erebus, and rings
A peal of curſes: but ſhe ſinks the pelf,
And ſmiles, unſhock'd at her detected crimes.

 The faithleſs wife thus dar'd to violate
Her wedded love, diſſolv'd in ſleep, and, lock'd
Within her Siren-arms, his manhood ſhore,

Sæva Philiſtæis ridendum tradidit: ardens
Ille comis viduus conatus tollere dextram
Eiſætam, at ſolitam ferratas frangere turmas,
Ingemuit, ſenſitque jugum mœſtiſſima volvens
Lumina jam, cœlum jam nunc hauſura ſupremum.

Tanta viii virtus adeo, Solomonis et ingens
Mens, altum complexa polum ter aſque profundas,
Fœmineis cecidere dolis.   Fuge pellicis artes
Illecebraſque procul, quæ jam ſeſe implicat almam
Virginis in ſpeciem teneræ, quæque ore pudico
Auroram rubet, et, fandi velut inſcia, votum
Suſpirat, quo mox imis illapſa medullis
Inſideat victrix, et te tibi ſurpiat ipſi:
Hæc neque amicitiæ neque ſanctum fœdus amoris
Reſpicit, obſcœno jamdudum dedita lucro.
Mollibus illa modis lymphatas alligat aures
Attamen, et mentem attactu ſuper aurea raptat
Aſtra levis, placidaque quatit formidine pectus:
Illa tuas onerat cœnis haud ſordida menſas,

Et

And him deliver'd cruel, to be ſcoff'd
By proud Philiſtines: widow'd of his locks,
He mad in vain eſſay'd to raiſe his hand,
Barren of deeds, but whilom wont to break
The brazen files of war: he roll'd his eyes,
To drink the lucid, laſt farewel of Heav'n.

Thus not the vigour of Sampſonian arms,
Nor depth and heighth of Solomonian ken
Immenſe, capacious both of heav'n and earth,
Withſtood the ſtronger wiles of woman weak.
Avoid the weening harlot's pliant arts
And luring baits, who perſonates the maid
Soft, ſweetly ſimple, and with artleſs airs,
Auroral bluſhes, innocence, and ſighs,
As from an heart untutor'd, into thine
Would ſlide, and ſteal thee from thyſelf away.
Nor ſacred friendſhip ſhe, nor plighted hand
Of vow regards, to lucre-loving luſt
Alone eſpous'd: yet, ſhe can bind thine ears,
Attouch the ſtrings, that animated wing
Seraphic thoughts, and vibrate into love,
And ſhake thy ſoul with melting agony.
Thy daily board with delicacies rare
She decks unſparing, and invites thy foes

Her

Et fcelerum focios inimicos pafcit heriles :
Tecta nitent epulis : Bacchus fluit undique rivis
Spumeus, heu! rebus retro labentibus æftu.

INTEREA patrias per venas fœda futuros
Jam tetigit natos: natorum lethifer ictas
Angor agit foboles, et avita germinat ira.
At tibi pro cœnis, pro dulci nectare tandem
Abfynthi latices, fellifque immifcet amaras
Luxuriæque feces, laceratæ verbera mentis!
Quinetiam invehitur meritis ingrata peractis,
Et maculis tradit famofis nomen in ævum
Trifte revolvendum fenibus, præcepta daturis,
Ridendum pueris imberbibus atque puellis.

Sic memini tardam cœno fub colle paludem,
Vernantem in prati morem, veftirier herbis,
Et, liquidam lapfu fcatebrarum præpete, lympham
Haurire, et late letheos reddere odoies,
Unde venena bibit cœli fragrantior aura,
Quæ circumludit, fontemque refrigerat alis.

DIRA

Her bofom-friends.   Thy ftately chambers fume
With fplendid banquets, and thy liquors flow
In ftreams redundant, as thy fortunes ebb.

MEAN-WHILE fhe vifits through thy parent veins
Thy future fons.   The deadly bane afflicts
Their fons, and fprouts with patrimonial rage.
But, lo! for banquets, dulcet draughts, at laft
She mingles in thy cup wormwood and gall,
The lees of luxury, the bitter dregs
Of mad profufion, anguifh and remorfe,
Maligns thy favours with ungrateful breath,
And blurs thine honour through the book of life,
A fcape-example fad, to be revolv'd
By commentary fages, and propos'd
The gaze and taunt of beardlefs boys and girls.

So have I feen beneath a pleafant hill
A quaking bottom, rank with lazy mud,
Yet mantled like a mead with living green,
Suck in the current of a cryftal fpring,
And in return emit a deadly ftench :
Infection hence imbibes the fragrant breeze,
That fportive fann'd, and cool'd the fountain-head.

                                        CONTAGIOUS

DIRA premunt aditu faciles contagia vates,

Pœnituitque fidem multos habuiffe profanis,

Agninaque lupis fub pelle latentibus olim.

AT qualis prætor, concuffam glandibus, urbem,

Atque, diu cinctos numerofo milite, muros

Occlufis retinet portis, atque arce tuetur,

Nec tantum, belli jam jam fervente tumultu,

Tela ferox telis atque ignibus objicit ignes,

Quinetiam infidias, tacitis haud fraudibus impar,

Subruit infidiis, cunctafque recolligit artes,

Quo tegat ipfe fuos, quo ruptos diffipet hoftes.

Nec minus ufque tuis hoftes inftare feroces

Mœnibus, et membris intendere bella nefanda

Rere vigil, cæcofque dolos motufque futuros

Præcipe mente procul, peftemque repelle rapacem:

Aut

CONTAGIOUS ills affault unwary bards,
Of accefs eafy; many have deplor'd
Their faith, repos'd in fycophants profane,
And very wolves, in fleecy forms array'd.

BUT, as a leader with compacted gates
And tow'ring battlements maintains, and guards
Some antient city, thunder-ftruck with Mars,
And walls, long vefted with affailing bands,
Nor in the tempeft of tumultuous war
Hurls only weapons againft weapons hurl'd,
Flames againft flames with hiffing, red rebuff,
But, not unequal to the rival chief
In latent mifchief, deeply countermines
Each plot with plot, and fummons all his arts,
His men to cover, fafe entrench'd beneath,
And diffipate aloft his blafted foes:
So thou, not lefs obfervant, apprehend
Fierce foes approaching, to befiege thy walls,
And ever and anon to levy war
Accurs'd againft thy members: in thy mind
Anticipate a-far their dark defigns,
Their future motions, and repel the peft
Rapacious: or if evil Dæmon fmite

Aut fi calce fores irato pulfat inertes,

Terque quaterque quatit caput atrum, et fremit ore,

Sæviat in ventos: at anhelam comprime tuffim,

Confule rimofum monitorem, et vulneris expers

Obliquis oculis vultus jaculare minaces.

Ne vero, miferande puer, ne crede colori;

Nulla falus oculis vitreis, fiducia fronti

Nulla, putrem, aut vacuam celanti pectore mentem.

Egregia tenuis forma, vultumque puellæ

Puniceum intactæ propior, fœdiffimus hofpes,

Qui fuit in ganeis, et flecti nefcius Harpax,

Quem vigil irrifum fublimi Barrus ab arce

Afpexit, plaufitque diu fibi, virginis arma

Affumpfit, traxitque ftolam per ftrata fluentem.

Jam Dea prodit ovans, nymphis jamque altior extat,

- Nuda finus niveos, oculifque nigrantibus ardens,

Ventilat ora levis, gemmifque auroque refulget.

Hanc

Thy patient door with angry heel, and ſhake
The Gorgon-head, and give the prowling tongue,
Loud let him rage againſt the winds: but thou
Mean-while reſtrain thy wheezing cough, conſult
The dun-ſcope, and, exempt from hoſtile glance,
With eyes oblique the ſurly phantom ſhoot.

YET yield no faith, unhappy youth, to forms;
Eyes are falſe mirrors, faces painted tombs
Of rotten minds, or hollow hearts at beſt.
A certain bailiff, elegant of mien,
And fluſh'd with Maia's bloom, the vileſt he
Of brothel-rooks, inexorable imp,
(Whom Barrus watchful from his lofty dome
Eſpying baffled, and applauded long
Himſelf) aſſum'd a virgin's potent arms,
And ſailing trail'd a flowing length of robe.

A GODDESS now triumphant is reveal'd,
And, ſoft-advancing, over-looks her nymphs
Attendant: ſhe, with ſnowy boſom bare,
And ebon-eyes, reflecting liquid fire,
Fans her fair face, and irreſiſtleſs flames
With poliſh'd adamant and figur'd gold.

Her

Hanc videt, aftantem proprio fub culmine, Barrus

Jam captus, vifumque trahit per membra venenum;

Afpectu propiore frui, alloquioque morari

Ardefcit, turrique ruens decurrit aperta:

At fubito horrendis amplexibus hoftis amantem

Cingit atrox, pofitaque Dea, bacchatur Erynnis,

Attractuque tenax fremit horridus unguibus Harpax.

Sic olim in Lybiæ campis arentibus æger

Sole gravi, ficcaque anima, fi forte viator

Confpexit varios autumni munere ramos,

Deflexitque via greffum, jam brachia tendit,

Deliciis inhians, avidufque revellere fructus,

Cum fubito elapfus foliis ruit anguis, et artus

Implicat immani multoque volumine ftringit

Sibilus: ille haurit perculfo pectore demens

Serpentem horrorem, tortaque in morte rigefcit.

VATIBUS

Her Barrus views beneath his caſtle fix'd,
Already captur'd, and imbibes the bane,
Shot through his limbs: he, panting to enjoy
A nearer aſpect, and with gentle ſpeech
Detain the charmer, blindly glows, and prone
Deſcending ruſhes from his fort relax:
But ſudden fierce the metamorphos'd foe,
With horrible embraces circling, hugs
The frighted ſwain: ungoddeſſed the fiend
Irrumpent rages, inſolent he ſtorms,
And all the vulture pounces in his claws.

THUS in the wither'd plains of Lybia drear,
If haply ſick'ning with the ſolar beam,
And ſoul a-thirſt, the traveller hath 'ſpy'd
A leafy tree, with vegetable gold
Diſtinct, and wander'd from his path : he feaſts
His eyes, and, luſting to poſſeſs the fruit,
Extends his arms; when lo! a wily ſnake,
Soft-gliding from the verdant ambuſcade,
Darts, baleful, hiſſing, and enwraps his limbs
With ſcaly zone voluminous : he ſucks
The ſerpent horror through his chilly breaſt,
Aghaſt, and ſtiffens in the folds of death.

To

VATIBUS ufque adeo, quorum juvenilibus undis

Feivefcunt venæ, quorum malefida voluptas

Coida iapit, fluitantque vagis jam pectora votis,

Haud minimum intererit, ftimulos abolere dolofos

Infanæ Veneris cæcique Cupidinis ignes,

Et partem noftri meliorem, munere cœli

Conceffam, motus animæ, quibus afpera pectus

Peiftringunt aliena tuum mentemque gemellam.

Tu foli tibi difce pati; nam fignifer ater,

Et modo quem cecini, vectore immanior ipfo

Umbrarum, tactuque gravi cane turpior Orci,

Poftquam fe Proteus varia in miracula rerum

Multarum optata mutaffet devius a re,

Infani fpeciem nimium male-fanus arufpex

Præbuit, et, fracta ceu fpe, ftetit ante feneftras

Eugenii, reftimque ulmo fufpendit opacæ,

Et laqueum aptavit collo, ramoque prehenfo

Projecit rapido contortum turbine corpus

Ima

To poets then, whofe veiny channels glow
With youthful tides, whofe hearts dilated pant
For faithlefs pleafure, and whofe bofoms float
With vagrant wifhes, little will it not
Avail to banifh the deceitful ftings
Of madding Venus, the bewitching flames
Of eyelefs Cupid, and the very gift
Of Heav'n irradiate, better part of man,
Thofe tender pulfes of the foul, by which
The pains of others penetrate thy breaft,
And twin-affection.   For thyfelf alone
Learn thou to fuffer; for the black, the foul
Comittal-bearing herald, whom I fang,
More favage than the ferry-god of fhades,
In touch more odious than the dog of hell,
When into various prodigies he chang'd
His mimic fhape, but wander'd from his mark,
Too rational in augury malign,
Put on the madman, as in deep defpair
Before the windows of Eugenio ftood,
And high fufpended from an umbrous elm
An hempen halter; to his worthy neck
The noofe he fitted, feiz'd a branch, and off
He caft his body with a fudden jerk

Centripetal,

Ima petens: gemit alta comis horrentibus arbor,

Ceu male librati sceleris jam confcia, jamque

(O utinam jugulo recte perpendiculari!)

Fraude duplex foedaque tenax erroris iniqui

Dependet dextra: sed tanquam litera longa,

Fatifero appenfus filo, per inane coactor

Hinc atque inde natat, membrifque rudentis alumnus

Luctatur trepidis, humilefque recalcitrat auras.

Horruit Eugenius, visu perculfus iniquo,

Oblitufque suæ perituro ferre falutem

Decurrit fpecula, vix rapta vefte, petitque

Trifte malum, captumque manu fuffulcit: at ille

Defilit in terram, et multa vi prenfat amicum

Attonitum, colloque trahit, raptatque fub umbras,

Cimmerias umbras, lapidofa cubilia vatum,

Vincla

Centripetal, the living gallows groan'd,
Horrent its leaves, as confcious of the guilt
Unduly weigh'd, and now (O had it been
Right by the gullet perpendicular!)
In guile a Janus, and of error foul
Tenacious, by the right-inglorious hand
He fwings dependent, like a long jot-j,
As meet appendix to the fatal thread,
From fide to fide the fell collector high
Floats waving, and the rope's difciple apt
With writhing limbs, as through convulfive throes,
Reluctant quakes, and kicks the nether air.

    Eugenio fhudder'd at the fhocking fight;
He felt the man within him, and (alas!
Forgetful of himfelf) to fave the wretch
Scarce feiz'd a garment, from his trufty tow'r
Down errant ran; he fought the dangling dog,
And found, fuftain'd with hand humane; but he
Springs to the ground, and with collected rage
Grappling invades the charitable friend
Amaz'd and fpeechlefs, by the collar drags,
And hurries headlong into vaulted fhades,
Cimmerian fhades, the ftony-matted beds

Vincla recufantum, horrifono ftridentia tractu,

Eumenidumque fpecus et non remeabile clauftrum.

SED quid plura loquax raptorum arcana referrem?

Quid varias artes, cæcique incendia belli,

Et fcelerum facies, et adunci tela furoris?

Hæc data virtuti merces, ea reddita dextræ

Dona piæ moneant, habitantes æthera, vates

Afpectu miferis oculos avertere monftris,

Et munire manu, munitaque tecta tenere.

ERGO foras prodire nefas debentibus æra?

Nulla dies animos mœroribus eximet atris

Curarum immores, celebrefque impune jubebit

Perluftrare locos, lætofque revifere cives?

SEPTIMA lux, fuperas conceffa tenentibus arces,

Exoritur, cœcaque monet fine fraude per urbem

Phœbigenas errare pios, atque ora tueri

Harpagis

Of Bards, abhorrent from ear-griding jars
Of clanking chains, and lamentable dens
Of howling furies, irrepaſſable!

But why prolixer ſhould the Muſe reveal
The myſteries of manucaptors? why,
The multifarious arts, the magazines,
Infernal trains of deep-concerted war,
And forms and weapons of arreſtive rage?
Theſe wages, paid to meritorious deeds,
Such meaſure meted to the pious hand,
May caution tuneful denizens of air,
To turn their eyes from ſpectacles of woe,
Well guard their forts, and guarded well maintain.

Shall debtors never venture then abroad?
Shall no bright period of revolving time
Unbend their minds, from gloomy cares releas'd
By balm oblivious, and indulge to range
Frequented walks, and glad reviſit friends?

To thoſe, who tenant high abodes, the ſeventh
Devoted Sun auſpicious beams, and bids
The blameleſs race of Phœbus rove ſecure

U 2

Through

Harpagis impavidos, frontique obſtare minaci.

Cerberei ſiluere canes.   Tum civibus ægris

Aſpirant Zephyri, et fugiunt toto æthere nubes

Solis in adventum ſancti: labor improbus, artes

Quærendi ceſſant, occluſæ cardine fraudes

Dependent, placidoque quies illabitur orbi.

Ipſe etiam in triviis occurrit vatibus ultro,

Atque prior ſalvere jubet, precibuſque benignis

Proſequitur, jungitque manus, atque oſcula figit

Creditor, haud auſus perituros hiſcere nummos.

At prius, infames ubi prædam cunque locorum

Conſpexere lupi, duro ſub pollice prenſam

Raptores agitare, revellere, trudere in antrum

Monſtriferum, bibulum, captis ubi triſte relucent

Anguſtæ, et ferro ſtabiles hinc, inde feneſtræ.

Hic miſeris extorquet opes, tenebraſque minatur

Carceris,

Through city-mazes, undifmay'd behold
The face of Catchpole, and confront his frowns
With brave defiance.   Hufh'd are all the dogs
Of war Cerberian: then to fainting hearts
Cool Zephyrs breathe, and through the pure expanfe
Thick clouds retreat before the radiant face
Of holy light.   Difhoneft labour, arts
Of fordid lucre halt: inglorious frauds
Hang on the hinges, and on downy wings
Sweet quiet gliding lulls the peopled globe.
The very dun, obfequious in the ftreets,
Accofting poets, gives the firft good morn,
Purfues with fhow'rs of benifons benign,
Joins hand to hand, and fixes lip to lip,
Nor hints one word of perifhable pence.

   But human wolves, wherever they beheld
Their booty whilom, with rapacious clutch
Tormented, ravifh'd, cramm'd into a den
Portentous. fpongy; where to captives coop'd
The narrow windows pal'd on either hand
With rigid bars monaftically gleam.
This, coin extorting from the wretched, threats
Profounder durance, darker jail, and glows

                                        Impetuous

Carceris, ignefcitque iris, atque intonat Orcum.

Ille diu claufos campi fpe pafcit aperti,

Irretitque dolis, loculofque evifcerat : inde

Aurumque argentumque fciens enucleat imum,

Et miferos tandem miferos prædator inanit

Æie vago, Cereris pretio Zythique fupremo,

Heu! quod, turpe fugax liquidoque volantius Herme,

Aftreæ, digitos perlabitur, irrevocandum.

Quinetiam in templo fanctas cum ftaret ad aras,

Vota ferens, laticefque facros in vefte facerdos

Candenti, cœloque manus oculofque precantes

Tenderet, horrendum dictu, vifuque nefandum!

Gens infefta viris, Divifque invifa, ruebant

Per fcelus audaces, deprenfaque membra trahebant

Ex adytis, nec jam, violato numine, turbæ

Vindicis horrebant rabiem, nec tela flagranti

Miffa polo; tanto lucri præfentior ardor

Exacuit furiis, et pectora vinxit aheno.

Concusso,

Impetuous with red rage, and thunders Hell:
That feeds his vaſſals, long immur'd, with hope
Of open field, and with deluſive ſleights .
Paunches their pockets, thence enucleates
Their gold, their ſilver, and piratic clears
Their inmoſt holds of bread-procuring braſs,
The final purchaſe of a pot of ale,
That baſely recreant, and more volatile
Than liquid Hermes, through their fingers glides,
By chymic juſtice not to be recall'd.

Ev'n in the temple when the prieſt of old,
Veſted in white, at th' holy altar ſtood
Bearing oblations in the ſacred cup,
And rais'd to Heav'n his ſupplicating hands
And precant eyes, Oh, horrid to be told,
And ſinful to be ſeen ! an impious race
Noxious to men, and hateful to the Gods,
Ruſh'd unappall'd through barefac'd wickedneſs,
And dragg'd arreſted members from the ſhrines;
Nor, having with polluted hands profan'd
Religious homage, dreaded they the rage
Of vengeful multitudes, nor weapons hurl'd
From flaming Heav'n: ſo much the luſt of gain,
More ſacred, ſtung, and bound their breaſts with braſs.

A r

Concusso, demum luſtris labentibus, orbi
Emicuit Gulielmus, avis ingentior altis,
Lux hominum, demiſſa Deo, ſceptrique poteſtas
Legiferi: qualis curru ſublimis in auras
Raptatus quondam aligero, domitorque draconum,
Triptolemus latis arriſit gentibus infra,
Et divina manu diffudit ſemina glebis
Virgineis, cultuque feros mollivit agreſtes.

Talis ad aſtra, potens animi, perque ardua tendens,
Naſſovus patefecit iter, triplicique potitus
Imperio, æquatas rerum tractavit habenas,
Et paſſim inſevit ſubjectis aurea terris
Jura parens, docuitque truces miteſcere gentes.

Ille ubi crudeles proſtravit Marte tyrannos,
Flagra virum, tumidaſque minas effregit et iras,
Victorem edomuit ſeſe, mediiſque triumphis
Fræna modumque animis ardentibus obtulit Heros,
Et magnum inſtituit ſancto ſub fœdere regnum,

Jam

At length in procefs of appointed time
Immortal WILLIAM to the drooping world
Shone greater than his godlike fires, the light
Of men divinely fent, and legal foul
Of fceptred power.   As in chariot wing'd
Sublimely rapt Triptolemus, and fam'd
For dragons vanquifh'd, fmil'd on realms beneath
Extenfive, and with genial hand diffus'd
Celeftial grain to fructify the womb
Of maiden earth, and foften brutal hinds
By fhapely culture: ample thus of heart,
Through deeds of arduous enterprife, NASSAU
Explor'd a paffage to his kindred ftars,
And, circled with a triple diadem,
Suftain'd the regal reins with equal hands:
Through fubject kingdoms golden rights he fow'd,
And favage nations manner'd into men.

He, when the vigour of his arms deprefs'd
Tyrannic fcourges of their kind, and broke
Their menaces and rage, fubdu'd himfelf
Victorious; in the midft of triumph he
Set reins and bounds to his heroic mind,
And founded majefty fupreme on league

Jam rerum fubiturus onus, populique minifter
Regius, at major votifque potentior æquis.

Tum patei armifonis inflari cantibus æra,
Inferrique manus vetuit certamine victis.
Tum paci impofuit mores, enfefque nefandos
In, cereale decus, falces curvavit agreftes.
Semirutas urbes, everfa refurgere juffit
Mœnia, et immenfum fulcari claffibus æquor
Thuriferis, gravibufque auro, quafque abfcidit olim
Undarum rabies, longoque interluit æftu,
Alternis reium connecti mercibus oras,
Hinc, ubi purpurea nafcentem lampade Phœbus
Te, vitæ fpes alma dies, accendit, et inde,
Serus ubi adverfis extinctum fubruit undis;
Qua medio furit igne polus, quaque afpicit arctos
Ardua, concretos æterno frigore, campos.

TUM

Inviolable, willing to fupport
The weight of empire, to the public weal
Menial, but, monarch of his people's heart,
More great and mighty in their juft efteem.

THE father then forbade the brazen fong
Of war to found, and violence to crufh
The proftrate foe, then morals gave to peace,
And into fickles, rural armament,
And pride of Ceres, bent the deathful blade;
Then cities half-demolifh'd, walls eras'd
Bade re-arife, and floating forefts plow
The watry wafte, to bear Sabæan gums
And teem with orient gold.   He bade thofe coafts,
Which oppofite the mad, indignant waves
Had rent, and bath'd with interlunar tides,
By mutual commerce re-united meet,
Here, where the Sun, in pledge of active life,
Kindles the day with purple dawn, and there,
Where late he drowns it in the furgy weft,
Where maddens with meridian flame the pole,
And where aloft the polar bear beholds
Vaft regions, chain'd with ever during ice.

X 2

Tum fera barbaries, aftrifque advecta tyrannis,

Cladibus Hibernas toties bacchata per urbes,

Et germana comes, gremiumque armata colubris,

Fœda fuperftitio Stygias fugere fub umbras.

Horruit ipfe viris referatum limen Olympi,

Immiffafque faces, animarum raptor et auceps.

Annua tum primum funt aufi credere vota

Telluri agricolæ, fortiri jugera faxis,

Molirique domos, et cingere fepibus arva.

Securi demum, et læti pubentibus herbis,

Erravere greges, propriaque fub arbore cultor

Poma manu carpfit, ramis pendentia textis,

Religioque recens cœlo caput extulit alto;

Propugnavit enim princeps fidiffimus aris,

Et, vindex fcelerum, prifcæ pietatis honores

Reftituit, fraudefque adytis, cultuque furores

Expulit:

THEN lawless fury, sanctify'd misrule,
That rag'd with havock through Hibernian towns,
And her twin-sister superstition sad,
And arm'd with snakes imbosom'd, murm'ring fled
Appall'd, and routed to the Stygian shades.
Th' infernal bailiff, ravisher of souls,
Abhorrent started at the gate of Heav'n
Unbarr'd to men, and living light effus'd.

THEN first the swains laborious dar'd to strow
Their vows, entrusted to the cultur'd glebe,
With stony bounds appropriate acres, plan
Mansions, and gird with guardian hedge the plain.

AT length secure on bloomy pastures, gay
Stray'd fleecy flocks: beneath his foster-tree
The joyful planter with rewarded hand
Pluck'd autumn pendent from the woven boughs,
And undefil'd religion rear'd aloft
Her awful head; for, opulent in faith,
The prince undaunted for her altars fought,
And, guilt avenging, piety restor'd
With antient honour, and expell'd from fanes
Imposture base, and persecution foul

From

Expulit: ille etiam, vates miseratus egenos,

Reddidit edicto per gentes libera passim

Sabbata, nec passus temerari sancta profanis,

Harpagas obstrinxit, rabidosque coercuit ungues.

FINIS LIBRI PRIMI.

SPECULI

From adoration.   He, in pity too

To Bards infolvent, through the nations round

The Sabbath-days edicted to be free,

And, holy things difparting from profane,

Harpies reftrain'd, and clench'd their clutchy claws.

The END of the FIRST BOOK.

T H E

SPECULI POETICI.

LIBER II.

SALVE, ſumma ſalus hominum, ſuperumque voluptas!

Reſpice nos tandem, et, cœlo delapſa ſereno,

In terras riſura veni cantantibus, auro

Et gemmis potior, vitali charior aura,

Libertas! quid enim lætum ſine numine veſtro

Per campos late pingues, urbeſque potentes ?

Tu

THE

POETICAL MIRROR.

BOOK II.

HAIL, health of men and bliſs of Gods refin'd!
    At length behold us, from thy ſeat ſerene
Ethereal gliding, deign to viſit earth,
And temper by thy ſmiles our choral ſong,
Sweet Liberty! to be prefer'd to gold
And ſtarry jewels, dearer than the breath
Of life; for what without thy balm divine
In life is joyous through the vernal wealth
Of rural ſcenes, and lordly cities fair?

Tu, fatus Japeto poftquam deduxerat heros

Lampade Phœbea præclarum et nobile furtum,

Ingeniique ferax agiles infudit inerti

Materiæ radios, flammis melioribus olim

Magnanimum generofa virum, comes aurea Divom,

Corda refinxifti, et liquidi fuper ætheris axem

Raptafti mentes, patriæ pietatis amore

Accenfas, famæque avidas poft fata perennis.

Te veniente, dies illuxit lætior: auræ

Afflarunt animis vires labentibus: ipfa

Nubila tum vario clarefcunt lucis amictu,

Et patefacta procul fubridet janua cœli.

Dulcior in fylvis avium concentus amores

Paftorum infpirat, fidofque refufcitat ignes:

Ipfe tibi ftridens rapidis aquilonibus, undis

Efferus infanis, gratatur pontus, et altis,

Imperiofa fremens, fubfternit claffibus iras,

Frugifera feu pace tument, feu marte rubefcunt

Velivolo.

When bold Prometheus artful had convey'd
Down from the day-diffusing orb his bright
And glorious theft, and fruitful in the lore
Of quick invention, into dead terrene
Æthereal souls infus'd, with better flames
Thou, prime attendant on the Gods, of old
The glowing breasts of heroes didst refine
And wing aloft, above the pure expanse,
Their spirits, kindled by the patriot-ray
And, after death, interminable fame.

At thine approach more beautifully bland,
The day rejoices: fresh to languid hearts,
The breezes breathe refection: sullen clouds
Brighten, embroider'd with the various robe
Of streamy light, and, open from a-far,
All glorious laughs the golden gate of Heaven.

The feather'd folks with softer notes inspire
The loves of swains, and wake their faithful flames:
The deep, remurmuring to the boistrous howl
Of polar tempests, mad with angry waves,
Thee gratulates, and bows the hoary head
Of anarchy beneath thy naval oaks
Majestic, nursing in their ample wombs
Commercial peace, or flagg'd with crimson war.

Y 2

Dame

Velivolo. Tibi, purpureos induta colores,
Pandit opes, nemorumque comis horrefcit, et effert
Uberiore finu turgentia femina rerum
Terra parens, montefque feri pacantur in arva,
Concretafque diu per faxea vifcera venæ
Paulatim abjiciunt fordes, inque æra liquefcunt.

Te Themis alma præit, gladioque accincta tuetur
Diva Deam, nectitque Ceres tibi flava coronam
Triticeam, et pinguem prætendit Pallas olivam.
Te circum Aoniæ, certantes carmine, Nymphæ
Colludunt, choreafque ineunt hinc, inde frequentes
Sylvicolæ in numerum Fauni Dryadefque puellæ.

Ceu verno fub fole viget nutrita patenti
Arbor agro, viridefque comas, et florida fœtu
Brachia tendit ovans: ita latum clara per orbem,
Aufpiciis inventa tuis, monumenta priorum
Increvere virum, et famæ tetigere cacumen.

HINC

Dame earth, array'd with purple beauties gay,
Unlocks her treasures, roughens with the gloom
Of stately groves, and from her bosom pours
Profuse the swelling seeds of various fruits.
Hence savage mountains into furrow'd fields
Are soften'd, miny magazines, conceiv'd
Long through the bowels of impregnate earth,
Purge off their drofs, and into metals melt.

Fair Justice thee precedes, and girt with sword
Defends her sister goddess, and for thee
Plump yellow Ceres binds the wheaten crown,
And Pallas bends her olive-bearing branch.
The tuneful sisters in alternate strains
Around thee sport, and in the fairy maze
Shepherds and nymphs innumerable dance.

As blooms a tree beneath an April Sun,
And, foster'd in some open field, displays
Its verdant foliage, and expanded boughs
Florid with fruitage: through the spacious earth
Thus cherished beneath thy brooding wings
The deathless arts of antient sages rose
Illustrious far, and reach'd the mount of fame.

Achaia's

Hinc decus Argolicæ gentis, pater altus Homerus
Sydereum superavit iter, penitusque supremo
Concilio admissus tulit in certamina turmas
Cœlicolum, et vario decoravit numine bellum
Dardanium, decimumque sagax deduxit in annum
Arma Deosque canens; hinc innarrabile finxit
Volcano fabricatum opus, et gestamen Achillis.
Hinc Jovis, horribili fulgentem Gorgone, prolem,
Et ferro rigidem, et, spirantem funera, Martem,
Rectoremque Deum, terras, maris æquora, cœli
Astra supercilio quatientem, aut vindicis iræ
Fulmine flagrantem nebularum in nocte minaci.

Hinc et equos, Neptune, tuos per summa secundo
Cœrula labentes curru, quo præpete sensim
Aerii trepidant montes, sylvæque corucæ,
Trojugenumque domus, Graiumque in littore puppes.
Nereidum agnoscit regem chorus. Alta dehiscunt
Lætitia,

ACHAIA's glory, father Homer hence
Unrival'd ſhot above the ſtarry flight,
And, mingled with Saturnian ſynods, rous'd
Celeſtial forces into mortal ſtrife,
With partial Gods diverſifying grac'd,
And lengthen'd to the tenth revolving year
Dardanian wars by ſtratagems divine.
The work of Vulcan hence in fancy's forge
Ineffable he form'd, to ſhield the ſon
Of azure Thetis: hence ſublime pourtray'd
Jove's daughter, fronted with refulgent fate,
Gorgonian horror, ſteely Mars array'd
With adamantine mail, and breathing death,
And thron'd the regent of the Gods, who ſhakes
Earth, Ocean, Heav'n's wide circuit with a frown,
Who ſpeaks the terrors of his vengeful wrath
In thunder, flaſhing through the night of clouds.

HENCE Neptune's courſers, bounding o'er the main
With wingy chariot, by whoſe rapid wheels
The lofty mountains, Ida's waving woods,
The Trojan tow'rs and Grecian ſhips at bay
Convulſive tremble.   All the briny nymphs
Confeſs their king: the billows gape for joy,

And

Lætitia, lufuque rudi fimul excita fundo,

Immenfos volvunt moles immania cete.

Te duce, Libertas, pariter tam pacis Athenæ,

Quam belli, fpoliis viguerunt ditibus : audin'

Æmathium pulfura ducem, Dcmofthenis arma ?

Ut fonat ore Deum ! patriam ut, virtute labantem,

Erigit arte potens ! ut acerbos impiger hoftes

Obruit ingenio, et tonitru rapit omnia linguæ !

Nec minus ille Deam te, te, lux æmula fandi,

Romanofque tuos fancto fub pectore fenfit,

Qui conjuratos patriam fubvertere cives

Unus in audaces eft aufus tendere vocem

Fulmineam, et flammas trepidanti reppulit urbi.

Occidit ille tamen Romæ pater optimus, ingens

Occidit Hefperiæ lumen: ruit ardua gentis

Romuleæ

And whales emergent from the vaſt profound,
In uncouth meaſures to the dancing waves
Gambol, enormous with unwieldy bulk.

BENEATH thy radiance, Liberty benign,
Not leſs triumphant for the ſpoils of peace,
Than war, old Athens to her grandeur ſoar'd.
Hark, with what force Demoſthenes diſplays
His oral arms to ſhock Æmathia's chief!
He ſpeaks a God! with what Atlantic art
He props his falling country, with what tide
Of eloquence he overwhelms his foes
Incens'd, and bears all oppoſition down,
Struck by the rapid thunder of his tongue!

NOR leſs that rival ornament of ſpeech
Thee, Goddeſs, and the rights of lofty Rome,
Thy ſanctities, beneath his pious breaſt
Imprinted felt, who dar'd alone to point
His blaſting voice againſt her rebel ſons,
Combin'd to broach her ruin, and repell'd
Approaching flames from her devoted roofs :
Yet he, the father of his country fell,
Her beſt good man, the light of Latium fell;

Romuleæ virtus, nec quifquam, confule rapto,

Aut cæcos populi motus æftufque tumentes

Placare, aut vires animofque accendere dictis

Suftinuit, felix divini muneris hæres.

Nam velut, extincto Phœbeæ lampadis igni,

Quicquid in orbe vago et fubter labentia cœli

Sydera confpicitur, naturæ, hominumque labores,

Et color, et fpecies vaiiarum dædalæ rerum

Horrefcunt tenebris, et eadem nocte premuntur.

Sic quicquid pulchrum, quicquid laudabile, magnum,

Et fublime cadit, fublata te, Dea, terris,

Nec fuperis audent demiffæ fedibus artes

Prodire ulterius, patriumve revifere cœlum.

Inde per Æmoniam et pharetratæ Perfidis urbes

Niliacafque oras, blandafque Amphionis arces,

Ille, Deo qui fe genitum jactavit, et orbis

Victorem,

Down funk the polar ftar of Rhea's race
Extinct, nor rofe a fecond heir to wield
The godlike gift, to calm the fwelling tide
Of popular fedition, or inflame
Heroic ardour with exalted words.

For, as deferted by the lamp of day,
Whatever wondrous through the copious world,
And fair beneath the rolling fpheres we view,
The works of nature and of men, the forms
Of things and beauties in their various tribes,
Are loft and bury'd in one common night;
So what we prize for elegance, or woith
Sublime or noble, when thy rays retreat
From earth, fets clouded, nor effay thofe arts,
That boaft celeftial origin, to trace
The ftars, and· re-affert their native fkies.

Hence through the regions of Æmonia wide,
The ftates of quiver'd Parthia, letter'd coafts
Of myftic Ægypt and the magic walls
Of fweet Amphion, that ambitious boy,
Who fondly vaunted, that he was the fon
Of Jove, the monarch of a conquer'd world,

Z 2

And

Victorem, divumque puer fibi facra popofcit,
Evictus luctu, et cineri proftratus Achillis,
Ingemuit nullum, vacui fub fine triumphi,
Heu! vatem geftis reperiri ingentibus æquum.

Discite juftitiam, et fævos cohibete furores,
Terrarum domini, quorum fub pectore glifcit
Laudis amor, quos alta juvant præconia Phœbi,
Pieridumque labor venienfque in fæcula fama;
Indignantur enim natæ Jovis, horrida dictu,
Vincla pati: folitæ per apricos ludere campos,
Et paffim injuffæ fpirantes carpere flores
Heroum celebrant laudes et libera lætæ
Dona Deum, Cirrhamque vetant afcendere alumnos
Degeneres, longeque arcent Heliconis ab umbra.

Tum demum imbelli ftupefiunt pectore fenfus
Mæoniufque calor tacita formidine friget,
Mufarum quoties miles, cultorque Minervæ
Signa movens, et jam fpoliorum accenfus amore
Et palmæ ftudio, premit obfidione tyranni

And claim'd divine pre-eminence, fubdu'd
With grief, and proftrate at the folemn tomb
Of great Achilles, in the barren clofe
Of empty triumph wept, alas! no Bard
Was found proportion'd to his matchlefs deeds.

    LEARN juftice, and appeafe your cruel rage,
Ye lords of earth, beneath whofe bofom glows
The love of praife, who pant for Pæan's lay,
The Mufe's plaudit and eternal fame;
For, lo! the daughters of indulgent Jove
Difdain reftraint: through funny meadows they
Wont to difport, and pluck unbidden flow'rs,
Frefh-breathing, hymn the memorable feats
Of honour'd heroes and free gifts of Heav'n,
But interdict unworthy fons to climb
Their hill, and banifh from the facred fhade.

    BENUMB'D and feeble is the Poet's breaft,
And chill'd the rapture of Mæonian flame
Through filent awe, when militant he moves
Minerva's enfigns, and, already fmit
With luft of laurel and reward, befets
The tyrant's palace, unfubdu'd by ftorm,

                           And

Jamdudum indomitas, nec apertas vatibus ædes,
Aggrediturque modis præduras mollibus aures.

Sic vis ingenii, numerorum Diva creatrix,
Languet, hebetque; animæ primo sic impetus ortu
Deficit: ingenuus fœdo sub carcere vates
Serpit humi, et veneres inculto carmine sordent
Ut, tener in cunis, natu pulcherrimus, infans,
Hinc atque inde artus corpusque astrictus iniquis
Succubuit vinclis, et degener increscendo
Consenuit, lumbos distortus, et horruit in se
Pygmæos mentitus avos, patriamque pusillam.

Impius ille fuit, sævisque immanior ursis,
Durior et scopulis, et atroci surdior austro,
Qui prius, innocuum Phœbi genus! impete raptos
Damnavit tenebris, et olenti carcere dulces
Conclusit vates; fidei cœlestis inanem
Qui mentem in terras turpes defixit, egenis

And barr'd for ever againſt claſſic feet
Obſequious, and mellifluous aſſails
With ſofteſt cadence his obdurate ears.

Thus edge of genius, the creative pow'r
Of ſong ſublime is blunted, and deprefs'd:
Thus in its birth the particle of air
Æthereal ſickens.   Couch'd in ſordid cell
The ſoarer grovels, and his mental charms
Bewray'd and horrid hobble into light.
As, beautiful in birth beyond compeer,
A cradled infant with his members crampt,
And body bound conformal to his chains,
Diſtorted lies, degenerate in growth,
And crabb'd, and, ſhrunk into himſelf, belyes
A pigmy lineage and a puny ſoil.

Impious was he, more mercileſs than bears,
Harder than rocks, and deafer than the roar
Of rending blaſts, who firſt to gloomy ſhades
Damn'd, and inclos'd in peſtilential hold
Seraphic warblers, violently ſnatch'd,
A blameleſs race! who, void of heav'nly faith,
Prone fix'd his heart upon the brutal earth,

                                              And,

Signandas manibus tabulas ceramque premendam,
Nodofos legum laqueos, qui finxit, et æra
Carminibus vetuit mutari rauca canoris.

A r vos mortales, quorum præcordia turpi
Squalefcunt fcabie ftudioque immane ruendi
Æris et argenti, divinis parcite mufis,
Et cæcos prohibete dolos famulofque rapaces;
Omnia cœlicolis quoniam fuper aftra beatis
In commune jacent, et nullo fœnore crefcunt
Divitiæ, inque vicem fefe fine fine fruuntur;
Carminibus vero gaudent, et carmina crebri,
Seu cithara, feu voce libet, gratiffima reddunt.
Perpetuo varii labentes ordine menfes
Se fugiunt, choreaque premunt revolubilis anni,
Compofitofque vagi dant motus orbibus orbes
Ad numerum, et magni refonat concordia mundi.

UMBRARUM

And, framing bonds in judgment to be fign'd,
And feal'd by needy hands, the penal gins
Of knotty laws, forbade the fair exchange
Of jarring copper for melodious lays.

  But, O! ye mortals, whofe diftemper'd fouls
Ruft with an itch infatiate and the luft
Of piling filver, upon filver heap'd,
Brafs upon brafs, yet fpare the facred nine,
And check your black deceipts and rav'nous imps;
Since all things lye in common with the Gods,
And riches without intereft increafe;
While they each other in eternal round
Reciprocal enjoy, but moft rejoice
In blifsful ftrains, and blifsful ftrains return
From harp, or voice attemper'd, as befeems
Angelic concert.   In perpetual orb
The various months each other fhun, and chafe,
And fill the chorus of the circling year;
The fpheres to fpheres in meafur'd motions keep
Refponfive time, whence jubilant refult
The concord pure and univerfal fong.

UMBRARUM cuftos, ipfe alti janitor Orci
Crinitas tenuitque minas rabiemque trilinguem,
Threicio pulfante Lyram: ftupuere forores
Ultrices: Manes late filuere nocentes,
Pœnarum obliti: et rapta cum conjuge Pluto
Annuit, et plectro victum agnovere tyrannum
Dirus amor, rifufque ferox, ac torva voluptas.

Nos autem, ardentem cœli qui cernimus axem
Lucentefque polos, et celfas prendimus arces,
Gens inimica choris magis implacabilis urget,
Mille petunt fraudes, et, hiantes faucibus, hoftes
Nocte dieque fores circumftant agmine denfo.

DUM loquor, ecce! venit tandem cum gente togata
Ipfe, fui quanto, fuperi, fub pondere! Prætor.
Ut, non indecori tumefactus pectora faftu,
Prominet in ventrem! viden' ut fe copia-cornu
Diffundit capite, et circum cava tempora glifcit?
Ut criftæ furgunt! ut majeftate rotunda

Ora

THE very keeper of unbody'd shades,
Deep hell's grim porter, while the Thracian Bard
Awak'd the lyre, with-held his bristled threats
And three tongu'd ire.   The vengeful sisters paus'd,
Amaz'd through blandishment: the guilty ghosts,
Unconscious of their pains, attentive hark'd,
And tyrant Pluto with his ravish'd bride
Assented: him, by song subdu'd, confess'd
Dire love, and savage smiles, and stern delight.

BUT us, who view the flaming arch of Heav'n
And starry poles, and people turrets high,
An hostile race, untuneable of soul,
Assail ; a thousand frauds and foes a-gape
Thick night and day besiege our gates imbarr'd.

Lo! whilst I speak, with gowny Myrmidons
The lordly May'r approaches, furr'd with pow'r,
Beneath, ye Gods, what luggage of himself!
With what becoming pride of puffy chest
He bulges into paunch ! his head a-down
What plenty streams as from her fountain horn,
And glistens round his hollow temples! How
His crest uprises! how his cheeks inflate

Blush

Ora rubent, triplicique toro palearia ludunt!

Crine natat præcanus apex, Pyliumque profatur:

Fronte riget crifpatus honor, fegetefque per armos

Miratur caput undantes, et non fua tecta.

Collo vincla brevi (mihi talia nectite Divi!)

Dependent, tortoque auro pater urbis inhorret.

Tum virgam quatit: hac vates ille evocat antris

Pallentes, alios in clauftra tenacia mittit,

Net lites, dirimitque, et vocibus æra refignat.

Huic iter expediunt prælongis fuftibus atri

Lictores, populumque abigunt hinc inde prementem.

Verticibus creber tunfis cruor effluit: ingens

Fit fragor: horrifonis reboat clamoribus æther.

Ipfe

Blufh with round majefty, and underneath
His chin in triple cawls the dew-laps play!
Delug'd with hoary hairs, his pate befpeaks
A Neftor; briftles on his front erect
The curly worfhip, and, diffufive wav'd,
O'er either fhoulder, his adoptive fkull
Admires rich crops, and umbrage not its own.
From his curt neck a linky length of chain
Depends, (O, bind but fuch a chain for me,
Ye gracious Gods!) and ftiff the civic fire
Stalks horrent, wreath'd in complicated gold,
Then fhakes his wand : by this he conjures up
From darkfome durance pale enchanted Bards,
Others difpatches, long to be detain'd
In fad fojourn, irremeable ftreights,
Spins mazy fuits, or cuts the knotty ftrife,
And with a word abfolves the debted fum.

BLACK Lictor-bailiffs clear his deftin'd way
With cudgels long-projecting fhade, and drive
Aloof on either fide the preffing crowd:
From pounded pates a gory torrent flows
Faft, frequent : huge the crafhing murmur founds,
And Heav'n rebellows to the mingled roar.

He

Ipfe autem, magna medius fervente procella,

Compofitis fertur gradibus, vultuque fereno.

Sic latrare canes, inverfam flumine, Phœben,

Perque umbras ululare lupi : tamen illa, tumultum

Dedignata, regit ftellas, liquidumque per axem

Radit iter tacitum, et pleno procul ore refulget.

JAM vero ante ipfum (Prætori cedite cives!)

Cœruleam indutus chlamydem, caput exhibet altum

Armiger, argentoque gravem, ferroque rigentem,

Et nunquam viduum vagina, fublevat enfem,

Argumentum ingens, animique infigne trophæum!

PONE patres ineunt civiles ordine pompas,

Turgentefque artus, et, jam languentia motu,

Membra, diu defueta viis, et vifcera tractim

Protrudunt tardis obnixibus Aldermanni,

Spirantes adipem.   Vultus notat uva rubentes

Luxuriatque

He nathlefs, undifturb'd amidft the din
Tempeftuous, loudly raging, fagely moves
With fteps compos'd and countenance ferene.
So maftiffs at the Moon's inverted face
In watry mirror bark, and through the fhades
Wolves hideous howl; yet fhe, fublimely fpher'd,
Indignant of their difcord, rules the ftars,
Soft gliding through the liquid axle fhaves
Her pace, and fhines with full-broad face afar.

But now before his mightinefs (good folks,
Room for my lord!) his armourer, array'd
In robe cerulean, rears his caftle-head,
And wields the civil fword, puiffant blade,
Pond'rous with filver, ftiff with polifh'd fteel,
And never from the wedded fheath divorc'd,
Broad argument, and emblem of his heart.

Behind the fathers Aldermannic grace
The peaceful pomp, and puffingly project
Their bloated limbs, with motion faint, difus'd
To flinty ftreets; with fnaily pace they trail
Along the tun-circumference of guts,
Perfpiring fat.   The ruddy grape diftains

And

Luxuriatque genis. Epulis Saliaribus illis

Haud opus: at fi grex aulai limen opimæ

Antiquum attigerit, quantas dabit ille ruinas

Vervecum lumbis ? cæcis quæ funera porcis

Tergoribufque boum ? teneros cum matribus agnos

Dentibus avellet, vitulis nec parcet amatis,

Jam varias formas bipedumque in nomen ituris,

Nec volucri, Cytheræa, tuæ. Non anfer edacem

Heu! rabiem effugiet, quanquam fe candidus hofpes

Haud cætu indignum arguerit, majoribus ortum,

Qui quondam imperii, Gallis venientibus, arcem

Turrigerumque decus Romæ domitricis et orbis

Protexere caput per opaca filentia noctis,

Aufpicibus queruli pennis monituque loquaci.

JAM vero medium curfu luftraverat orbem

Phœbus,

And wantons in their cheeks.   Nor needed they
Delicious fare: if yet the burgherhood
Should reach the threfhold of their antient hall,
Enrich'd with oil, what ruin will they gafh,
What wafteful inroads into mutton-loyns
Bell-weather'd ? what fell havock will they make
On flaughter'd pigs and lufty chines of beef ?
With fangy teeth fhall feverally they
Tear tender lambkins with maternal ewes,
Nor quarter give to fatted calves belov'd,
Now doom'd to deviate into various forms
Of animals, and into bipeds rife,
Nor fpare thy bird, O Venus : not the goofe
Shall 'fcape, alas! their cormoranting rage,
Though fhe right candid might approve herfelf
Of fuch affembly not unworthy deem'd,
Defcended from thofe fapient anceftors,
Who whilom, when the nightly Gauls advanc'd,
With boding wing and monitory chant
Gaggling preferv'd the guardian capitol,
Rome's pillar'd pride, and Tholfel of the world.

    BUT now the Sun in his diurnal courfe
Had meafur'd half the globe, and headlong drove

Phœbus, et Hesperiam sitientes pronus ad undam
Egit equos, jam lora dedit fluitantia bigis:
Nec minus ardentes, et anheli strata viarum
Permensi demum, seniores læta quirites
Tecta petunt, fessosque toris in mollibus artus
Permulcent, recreantque pedes animosque labantes.

JAMQUE ministratis fumant convivia mensis,
Increpitantque moras: dentes haud segnius olli
Exacuunt epulis, atque annua vota facessunt.
Quippe dies genialis adest, urbique regendæ
Electo Prætore sacer, sibi poscit honores
Egregios, festasque dapes, et pocula fratrum
Oribus alta cavis, ac dolia ventribus æqua.

CERTATIM incumbunt operi, dextrisque coruscant
Cultra truces, furcasque vibrant hinc, inde sinistris:
Corruit horrisoni ferri nemus; atria strident.
Partes, quisque suas, peragunt: amor omnibus idem

Vescendi

His fiery prancers to the weſtern wave,
Now gave the ſteeds his flowing reins: nor leſs
The ſenior denizens inflam'd, a-thirſt,
And out of wind perambulating ſtreets,
Beſought their palace.   Now they gain the goal,
On downy couches lull their weary limbs,
And feeble feet, and fainting ſouls refreſh.

AND now the banquets fume on tended boards,
And chide delay: with expedition edg'd,
They whet their tuſhes for the prime repaſt,
And ritually perform their annual vows;
For, lo! the day, the genial day, devote
To city-ruling Stadtholder elect,
Demands peculiar honours, feſtal food,
Deep goblets, ample as their gulphy mouths,
And hogſheads, broad as their capacious weams.

THEY to their work with emulation ply
Both hands expert, fierce flouriſh in the right
Their knives, and brandiſh in the left their forks
Bidental: rude the ſteely foreſts craſh
In harſh encounter: harſh the roofs reſound.
Each acts his part: of eating without end

B b 2   Th

Vefcendi fine fine vorax, fine fine bibendi,

Durus uterque labor, fed quem tolerare Lyæus

Ipfe pater monet, atque oculis Ceres afpicit almis!

Tofta boum, lixata fuum, concocta bidentum

Membra fecant, Mavortis opus! tepidofque per artus

Sanguineum populantur iter. Non fævior Ajax

Balantum invafit turmas furibundus inermes,

Exitioque dedit. Romani nominis horror,

Nerias non fic Alpes penetravit aceto

Afer atrox. Hos dira fames, fitis acrior urget.

ALITUUM volucrumque genus, quæ denfa nigrantum

Tecta petunt nemorum, aut campo fpatiantur aprico,

Quæ vitreos fontes, viridique interlita mufco

Flumina amant, vel quæ celebrant plaudentibus alis

Horrea, plena dolo, ac, domino pafcente, feruntur

Crudeles in amicitias et fœdera mortis:

Qui liquidos tenuere lacus, qui ftagna paluftri

Tarda

The love, of drinking without end alike
Poſſeſs'd them all, ſevere the double taſk,
But ſuch as Bacchus tutors them to bear,
And Ceres views with all ſufficient eyes.
The roaſted joints of oxen, boil'd of ſwine,
Of mutton bak'd they hack, mavoitial work!
And deep depopulate their bloody way
Through tepid limbs.　Not fiercer in his rage
Ajax attack'd the weaponleſs brigades
Of bleaters, and to ſwift deſtruction gave:
Not with ſuch rapid violence the dread
Of rival Rome, the Carthaginian plow'd
His acid paſſage through the tow'ring Alps.
Theſe feller hunger, keener thirſt incites.

The various kinds of birds and fowl, that haunt
The ſhady woods, or ſunny plains prefer,
That love the pure tranſparent ſprings, or ſtreams
Skirted with moſſy green, or thoſe, who glad
With plauding wing frequent the grainy barn,
Fraught with deceit, and fed by faithleſs hands
Of ſoothing lords, are lur'd into the ſnares
Of cruel friendſhip and the leagues of death:
Whatever fiſhes cut the liquid lakes,

Whatever

Faida ulva, flexifve vagos in vallibus amnes;

Qui placidos coluere finus, quique æquoris alta,

Aut fcopulis hæfere cavis in littore, pifces,

Condimenta gulis fimul acria, dulcia, falfa

Labuntur, crudumque chaos per vifcera crefcit.

Hic libis inhiat mellitis; ille placentas

Abforbet folidas: nafo ruber alter adunco,

Immerfus phialæ, niveis barbata trophæis

Labra refert: multo fpumefcunt pectora lacte.

Ast epulas inter medias laticefque jocofos

Sors, adverfa ruens, infundit triftia lætis,

Et celeri trepidos mifcet certamine fervos:

Pectora pectoribus concurrunt, orbibus orbes,

Atque cyphis, immane! cyphi, folatia vitæ,

                                    Confligunt:

Whatever batten in the muddy pools,
Lazy with fenny weed, or thofe, that coaft
The ferpent rivers through the winding vales,
Thofe, that inhabit pleafurable bays,
And briny manfions of the main, or cling
To rocks half-eaten on the fandy fhore,
With fundry fauces, dulcet, acid, falt
Glide mifcellaneous down their channel throats,
And the crude chaos thickens in their guts.

THIS gapes on cates delicious; that abforbs
Whole quaking cuftards: into phial deep
Another dives his rubric nofe high-arch'd,
And bears a-back, with fnowy trophies barb'd,
His lips: with cream his hoary bofom foams.

BUT, in the midft of banqueting and wine
Jocofe, an ugly mifadventure, crofs
Rufhing, confounds their merriment with dole,
And giddy vaffals againft vaffals drive
In hot contention: breaft to breaft oppos'd,
Difhes to difhes clafh, and, Oh fad fate!
Cups againft cups, the joys of life, run foul,

Conflicting

Confligunt, vitreis crepat icta fragoribus aula.

Interea fenior, multa gravitate verendus,
Qui quondam, arguto percurrens pectine telas,
Dædalus omnigenum fpecies variare ferarum
Novit, et urbanos intexuit arte tyrannos,
Par opibus meritifque patrum nitet ordine frater.

Hic neque concuflus cafu, neque providus heros,
Se bene curatum tacite probat, ac veneratur
Delicias, mollique manu dum palpat omafum
Crefcentemque Deum, patinam, titubante miniftro,
Præcipitem, ingentem caput accipit: impete ftannum
Inflexum refilit: pater ingemit, ilia pulfans,
Jam primo rerum variarum flore referta.
Olli turpe tumor frontem notat ater honeftum,
Alter, et alter adhuc fuperingruit, hirfutifque
Ecce! fuperciliis horrenti prominet umbra,

Quique

Conflicting, brittle, ruinous: the dome
With glaffy din reverberating rings.

MEAN-WHILE a fage, for gravity rever'd,
Who, lengthy webs with tuneful fhuttle erft
Broad traveifing, to variegate his toils
With all the forms of animals well knew,
And city-regents laborate inwove,
Equal in wealth and corpulent deferts,
Amidft the fathers dubb'd, a brother fhines.

NOR fhock'd by chance, nor provident of thought,
This worthy filent much approves himfelf
Well-pamper'd, and adores the dainty fare;
But while he ftrokes with fofteft hand his paunch
And growing God, a vaffal tripp'd, and full
His head receiv'd precipitant a difh
Of orb immenfe: the batter'd pewter bent,
As from fuperior energy recoil'd.
The father groans, and beats his belly, ftor'd
With lufcious bits.   Indignant welts deform
His honeft front protuberant, that o'er
His briftly brows projeet a gloomy fhade,
Horrid and huge, and from the wide canals

Quique ingens torvufque tuentibus : atra cruoris

Naribus unda fluit liventibus : offa cerebrum

Dura tenent, capitifque tegit feptemplicis umbo.

At fera diluvies olei per colla, per armos

Volvitur, haudque fuis pinguefcunt membra faginis.

Pectora pifce fcatent, pifcem femoralia captant :

Tarda linunt oculos collyria, fufa venena

Inficiunt bibulamque togam, tunicamque madentem,

Natalem tunicam, tenui quam priftina lino

Deduxit conjux, fatique ignarus, et ipfe

Venturæ tum laudis adhuc, contexuit : illam

Fida domi coluit natarum maxima virgo

Pulchra diu, pulchræque dein non degener artis

Frondibus et volucres, et floribus involitantes

Finxit apes, operafque dedit (pia dona!) ferendas

Inviolata patri, nimium nimiumque beato,

Si decus ipfe domus geftaffet textile dudum,

Virgineum

Of livid noſtrils diſemboguing flows
Tartareous ichor: but the ſolid ſkull
His brains invelopes, and the ſev'n-fold targe,
To outward force impenetrable, guard
The crude conſiſtence.   But a-down his neck
And ſhoulders faſt an oily deluge rolls
Continuous, and his brawny limbs acquire
Lard adventitious.   With delicious fiſh
His boſom ſpawns; his breeches catch the fry.
The clammy ſalve bedews his ſaucer-eyes,
The trickling poiſon ſtains his ſpongy coat,
And lacquer'd tunic, birth-day tunic gay,
Which of the fineſt lint his conſort ſpun
In younger days, and he, not conſcious yet
Of hidden fortune and his future fame,
Right neatly wove: his eldeſt daughter, bright
With maiden beauty, long preſerv'd at home
The curious texture, and with beauteous art
Paternal through the level ground inwrought
Birds over boughs, and over flowrets bees,
Light hovering on the wing, and ſpotleſs gave
The pious labours of her filial hands,
As monuments of love, to grace the ſire,
Too happy mortal ! had he ſtill ſuſtain'd

Virgineum ut foboles tenuit fine labe pudorem.

ILLE ftupet, fœdafque manus et lubrica tollens
Ora, oculis imbrem lachrimarum effudit inanem,
Heu! falfis oculis, quibus afpicit incruftati
Tegminis illuviem, quibus irrita munera natæ,
Tartareas maculas ignominiamque tenacem
Multa gemens. Pudor, ira, dolor præcordia tentant.

ILLUM indignantem, et pugilum de more nitentem,
Artificum domini variorum urbifque tribuni
Laudibus extollunt male falfis, atque finiftros
Ingeminant plaufus, et inexfaturabile rident,
Et lugubre patres fubrident, ora Catones,
Triftior ut quondam per brumæ nubila Phœbus.

AT Prætor, decorifque fui, fratrifque pudendi
Haud oblitus, eum dictis permulcet amicis,

Et

The woven glories of his house, as she
Preferv'd her virgin honour undefil'd.

 AMAZ'D he ftar'd, and lifting up his hands
Polluted, and his face japan'd with oil,
Pours from his eyes a briny show'r of tears,
From aching eyes, with which he views the filth
Of veft incrufted, and embroider'd gifts
In vain of daughter fair, lamenting much
The Stygian fpots, indelible difgrace!
Shame, anger, grief diftract his boiling breaft.

 INDIGNANT him, and, like a champion brave
Anointed, shining, lo' the mafters grand
Of fundry crafts, and wardens of the tribes
Jocund extol, applaud with loud encore
Of hands, and inextinguifhable laugh,
And Cato-fac'd the Mother-Aldermen
Demurely fmile with fullen mirth, as wont
The Sun to glimmer through a wintry cloud.

 BUT, not unmindful of his own renown,
And brother foul difcountenanc'd, the Mayr
Pathetic fooths him with confoling phrafe,

And

Et jubet afferri mappas : mappæ ocius adfunt,

Hifque fupervacuum et pleno de pectore tardum

Humorem, et, craffo canas libamine, guttas

Abftergunt famuli, et lymphis luftralibus ora

Expurgant agiles.　Labes, quo fortius uda

Veftimenta fricant, inolefcunt altius ipfis.

At fronti rubicundus honos, redit, afpera gemmis,

Forma genis, Bacchique patet manifefta propago.

Sic Pelufiaco fculptum de marmore fignum

Horruit, immunda violatum afpergine cœni :

Tum, demum molli deterfum vellere, pandit

Innumeras rerum fpecies, volucrefque ferafque

Naturæ ludentis opus, venerefque fub ipfo

Sole renidentes, et venas explicat omnes.

Jamque adeo fuffecti epulis, curifque foluti,

Hofpitio effufas immittunt urbis habenas,

Purpureoque patres inftaurant flumine menfas.

Haud

And orders napkins to be brought : anon
The napkins come, and quick the waiters rub
From his full bofom the fuperfluous fat,
The clotted humour, and the pearly drops
Of grey libation, and their vigour ply
To bathe his face with purifying ftreams :
The more they curry, deeper fink the ftains,
Embody'd with his parti-colour'd robes.

　　But to his front the ruddy grace returns,
The ftudded luftre to his gemmy cheeks,
And full to view the fon of Bacchus glows
Attefted.   From Ægyptian quarry thus
A ftatue fafhion'd grimly frowns, bewray'd
With mud obfcene, but, rubb'd with fleecy wool,
Unnumber'd mimic animals difplays,
Both birds and beafts, difportive nature's work,
And, in objection to the parent Sun,
Refulgent charms and ev'ry vein unfolds.

　　And now, replete with banqueting, and free
From cares, the fathers give the flowing reins
Of city-fway to hofpitable glee,
And crown the tables with a purple flood.

　　　　　　　　　　　　　　　The

Haud moïa: ſpumantes avido de more culullos
Exſiccant, fluxuque replent, et cominus urgent,
Ac paſſim increpitant, oblitas munia, dextras.

Quin legum ultores èt libertatis avitæ
Rite duces memorant, quos inter Naſſaus ingens
Labra mero violare monet, ceu prodigus olim
Sanguinis ipſe ſui, te multa cæde, Bovinda,
Miſcuit, æternoque ſinum maculavit honore.

Tum pugnas Malbroe tuas, tua triſtia rurſus
Bella gerunt, cyathiſque acres Bacchoque potentes,
Signa movent: ſuperant montes, et flumina tranant,
Ardenteſque animis, liquidoque in Marte minaces,
Undique proſternunt (denſas ut meſſor ariſtas
Falce) catervatim repetito vulnere Gallos.

Nec

The foaming flagons inftantly they drain
With ufual flame, replenifh with a tide,
And, fift to fift engaging round, upbraid
Right hands, forgetful of their flowing tafk.

THE brave affertors of invaded rights,
And antient laws and liberty rever'd
They duly mention, amongft whom the prime,
The great Naffau to violate their lips
With wine reminds them, as of princely blood
He prodigal, thy refluent ftream, O Boyn !
In antient-day with hoftile flaughter mix'd,
And ftain'd thy bofom with immortal fame.

THY battles then, thy difmal wars they wage,
Undaunted Churchill, and with cups well charg'd
Alert, and potent in the grapy God,
Difplay their colours: over mountains high
They climb, and fwim through rapid rivers deep,
Ardent at heart, infatiable to quench
Their thirft of vengeance in the liquid fight,
(Thick as a reaper with his hook beheads
The bearded grain) they level fheer on earth
The Gauls in fquadrons with repeated wound.

Nɛc minus, accenſi viva virtute, recenſent
Teque tuumque genus, magnum decus Audenardæ,
Spes regum, regumque ſator, lux aurea ſceptri,
Et populi communis amor, quem liber ovantem
Agnovit tam marte ducem, quam pace parentem.

Tum vero ſermone graves, vultuque profundi,
Judicia expromunt regni de rebus agendis,
Atque externa ineunt aularum arcana ſagaces,
Venturoſque dolos, et ſeri ſemina belli;
Nec non Europæ volventes cardine pacem
Jam dubio ſtabilem, reprimunt, Ludovice, furores
Voce tuos, patrioſque vetant tranſcurrere fines.

Terrarum jam jam domini, qui ſæpe ſolebant
Concinnare pares dubio libramine lances,
Ac trutina penſare ſalem, prunas, piper, halec,
Zingiber, et quicquid defunctis undique ſcriptis

Vivorum

Nor lefs inflam'd with living worth fublime,
Thee and thy royal progeny they toaft,
Heroic ornament of Oudenard,
Sure hope of kings, and fire of kings unborn,
The golden light of fceptred majefty,
And happy people's univerfal love,
Whom glad they gratulate, and free confefs
In peace their father, and in war their guide.

Then, grave in fpeech, in countenance profound,
They broach their fentiments of ftate-affairs,
And deeply dive into the myfteries
Of alien courts, deceits in embryo, feeds
Of diftant war, and, on the doubtful hinge
Revolving Europe's fix'd repofe, repel
Thy lawlefs fury, Lewis, and forbid
To leap beyond hereditary bounds.

Lords of the globe, who whilom wont to trim
With doubtful poife the well adjufted fcales,
By ftated weights retailing venal falt,
Or ftony plumbs, or fpicy pepper keen,
Anchovy, ginger, and whatever fweets
Are vefted facred to the ftill remains

Vivorum vatum, Patribufque facratur inemptis,

Pendunt fata ducum gentefque bilancibus æquis,

Hefperiumque fecant diverfis regibus orbem.

Affenfere patres: Prætor, caput acre fenatus,

Annuit, humenti jam fomno femifepultus.

Exin gefta patrum recolunt præclara priorum,

Qui fociam in vitam finxerunt legibus urbem,

Moribus ornarunt, folidis ergaftula faxis

Fundarunt, triviafque cavis auxere cloacis,

Civilis decora alta togæ ! rapit æmulus ardor

Quemque fequi monumenta virum, et decerpere laudes.

Hic Aldermannis, hic fe Prætoribus ortum

Jactat; at ille, fua nixus virtute, recenfet,

Quot captiva manu commifit corpora vinclis,

Quot Veneris nymphas hefterna nocte Minervæ

Tradidit immiti, quas inter Cælia, terror

Nuptarum,

Of living Bards, and mortal tomes divine,
They weigh the fates of generals and realms
In equal balances, and canton out
The weſtern hemiſphere to various kings:
The fathers, fix'd in grand conſult, aſſent:
The Prætor, head-piece of the ſenate wiſe,
Half-bury'd now in dewy ſlumber, nods.

THEN gladly they recount the glorious deeds
Of prior ſages, who with wholſome laws
The city moulded into ſocial form,
With morals grac'd, or founded Bridewels fair
With ſolid ſtone, and winding ſtreets endow'd
With hollow ſewers, deep honours of the gown!
With rival ardour glows each doughty ſire
To trace their ſteps, and pluck eternal praiſe.

THIS boaſts his birth from Aldermen, who bore
Prætorian wand; but, on his proper worth
Dependent, that enumerates elate,
How many captives he conſign'd to chains,
How many nymphs of Venus yeſter-night
To fell Minerva's working-houſe he pack'd,
Among which radiant circle Cælia fam'd,

I he

Nuptarum, juvenumque lues, ac Diva ſuburræ,

Mollia pæduræ ſuccingens membra palæſtræ,

Et nudans non hos formoſum pectus in uſus,

Malleolum dextra tenet, averſata laborem

Terque opus orditur lentum, terque ægra reſiſtit,

Cui ſuper aſſurgit lictor tortoque flagello,

(Horrifera qualem tabula patefecit HOGARTHUS,

Et ſpirare dedit, fucique loquacis ab ore

Inſævire minis ſemperque recentibus iris)

Mente ferox, oculiſque furens, et vocibus atrox,

Cunctantem inſtigat, ſtimuliſque flagrantibus addit,

" Diſce pudicitiam monita, et non temnere linum."

JAM vero Morpheus, nebula fumante per aulam

Bacchantem cinctus, vinique adductus odore,

Concilio obrepit furtim, virgamque potentem

Prætoris, non ipſe ſuam, quatit obvia circum

Tempora:

The vagiant terror of defponding wives,
The peft of youths, and Goddefs of Duck-lane,
Girding her tender loins for hardy toil,
And baring bofom, not by nature bleach'd
For induftry profane, divinely fair,
The pond'rous mallet in her hand upheaves,
Averfe from labour, thrice effays to beat
The tough beheft, and fainting thrice defifts,
O'er whom the keeper (fuch as HOGARTH's hand
In horror-moving tablet hath difplay'd,
And taught to breathe, and from the vocal paint
To ftorm in threats and ever-glowing ire)
The tyrant rifes, and with knotted whip,
Savage in mind, in eyes outrageous, fierce
In voice, impells her lingering, and adds
With flagrant lafhes, " documented hence
" Learn continence, and not to fcoff at hemp."

BUT Morpheus now, be-mantled with a cloud
Thick fuming through the Bacchanalian hall,
And led by fteams of half-digefted wine,
Crept o'er the council unperceiv'd, and fhook
The Prætor's, not his own, enchanting rod

About

Tempora: letheo ftupefiunt lumina tactu
Ebria, in irriguum folvuntur membra foporem.

Sic, ubi Torpedo fub vaftis fluctibus efcam,
Hamatam arripuit, per longas frigida virtus
Setaram fluitat feries, cannæque ficutas,
Pifcator ftupuit, celfifque in rupibus icta
Corda repente gelu, rigidofque perhorruit artus.

Et jam finis erat græcandi : murmura ceffant :
Nequicquam tremulo fplendefcunt lumine tædæ ;
Nequicquam ingenuis redolent carchéfia paffim
Muneribus, pofcuntque manus, atque ora laceffunt.
Hic ruit in præceps ; jacet hic refupinus ; inani
Fronte capillitium, ac humeris toga defluit illi.
Hic Baccho extinguit femiuftam findona flammis
Infcius: ille, Dei impatiens, vomit ore fluentum:

Alter

About their temples: by the poppy-touch
Their drunken eyes are ftupify'd, their limbs
Diffolv'd obfequious into dewy fleep.

So, when beneath the briny waves profound
The numb-fifh hath devour'd the barby bait,
The chilly virtue circulating flows
Long through the linky line and jointed rod:
Amaz'd the fifher as a ftatue ftands
High on the rocks: a fudden horror fmites
His heart, cold, fenfelefs, and his limbs congeal'd.

AND now the revels end, the murmurs hufh'd:
In vain with trembling light the tapers flame;
In vain the goblets with ingenuous wine
Breathe odours round, the jovial hands invite,
And fmacking lips provoke. One rufhing falls
Vertiginous; another, on his back
Revolving, wallows: from the pumpion-pate
A brother's wig, and from the fhoulders broad
His mantle flips: with blufhing Bacchus this
Quenches his ruffles, half-confum'd with flames,
Unwitting: that, impatient of the God,
Pours forth a torrent from his oozy mouth.

Alter anhelanti pulmonem pectore tentat,

Ructaturque merum, pronufque in pocula ftertit,

Et perculfa gemit fomno domus alta canoro.

FELICES animæ, victu fomnoque fepultæ

Sic temere, ut pingues pifcofo in littore phocæ!

Felices animæ, vacuæ nil laudis avaræ,

Et, vigilis noftro fub pectore, mentis inanes!

Felices iterum, quibus optima munera mater

Magna parit, veftraque fovet fine parte laboris.

VOBIS vere canunt nemorum per denfa querelas,

Conjugiumque ineunt volucres, et prata pererrant

Florea apes, longeque pecus pinguefcit in herbis.

Agricolæ vobis incurvo vomere terram

Indomitam vertere, jugo ingemuere juvenci.

MERCATOR

His mefs-mate heaves with broken-winded puff
His lungy bellows, belches up a flood,
And prone, incumbent o'er his rummer fnorts;
The dome re-echoes to the tuneful fnore.

O HAPPY fouls, in full repaft and fleep
Supinely bury'd, negligently laid,
Like paunchy fea-calves on the fifhy fhore !
O happy fouls, unmov'd with empty praife,
And void of thought, that watches in my breaft!
Thrice happy Dons, for whom the fertile glebe,
Indulgent mother, bears her goodlieft gifts,
And fooths without your portion of the toil!

FOR you the birds in vernal feafon chant
Their foft complaints through thick-embower'd groves,
And airy loves in annual wedlock bind.
The bees, induftrious through the painted meads,
Inceffant roam, and cattle fatten far
On richeft herbage.   Patient fwains invert
For you the bofom of untutor'd earth,
And oxen groan beneath the galling yoke.

FOR

Mercator vobis, Borea ſtridente, per undas,
Cautibus horrendas, per conſita ſyrtibus arva
Tentat iter, ſæviſque fidem cum gentibus hoſpes
Conciliat, quem caſta domi deſiderat uxor
Cunctantem, et patrias nequicquam proſpicit oras.

At vobis molli canent lanugine ſylvæ
Æthiopum, ſaltuſque Arabum virgæque Sabææ
Thure calent, liquidoſque graves lachrymantur odores.
Heſperidum frondes Phœbus pater induit auro,
Heu! vobis pubente, ſuiſque ingrata colonis
Vinea turgeſcit, rubicundo fæta Lyæo.

Nummi qualis honos! tardi reverentia quanta
Ingenii, raucoſque modos renuente crumena
Muſarum quam curta fides atque horrida virtus!
Heu! rerum Fortuna vices ut ſemper iniqua

FOR you the merchant through the furgy deep,
Horrid with rocks, through quick, extended fands,
The tempeft howling, fteers his doubtful way,
And enters into bonds of plighted faith
With favage nations, whom his loyal wife
Long abfent pines for, and with many fighs
Mournful in vain furveys her native fhore.

BUT foft the leaves of Æthiopian woods
Whiten for you with filky down, the groves
Of Araby, Sabæan branches glow
With incenfe pure, and liquid odours weep.
Alas! for you the beamy fire of Bards
Arrays the gardens of Hefperian nymphs
With rinded gold, and lo ! the wedded vine,
Ungrateful to the pruning hand, for you
Swells genial, pregnant with the jolly God.

ALAS, what honour is imprefs'd on gold !
What homage to fubftantial dulnefs paid !
And, if the purfe remit no brazen found,
How fhort the Poet's faith, and mufic haifh !
Alas, with what iniquitous mifrule
Fortune directs the flowing turn of things,

And,

Lege regit, fortefque trahens hos improba luxu

Obruit oppletos, undafque effundit in undas:

Aft illos, remis aptos, fluctufque fecundos

Deferit orantes, nudaque exponit arena.

FINIS LIBRI SECUNDI.

SPECULI

And, drawing from her Lottery the fates
Of mortals, thefe with opulence o'erwhelms
Already gorg'd, and waves on waves impels;
But thofe, well handed for the tugging oars,
Thofe, praying for a buoying tide, deferts,
And wreck'd expofes on the naked fhore!

The END of the SECOND BOOK.

T H E

SPECULI POETICI

LIBER III.

NOS autem interea vates in turribus altis

    Nequicquam ingenii contractas pandimus alas:

Ut blandæ volucres ferri compagibus arctis

Conclusæ; dum milvus edax, atque improba cornix,

Et pica Pomonæ, et corvus Cereri vagus hostis,

Aereos tranant campos, et sole fruuntur

Jam verno, prædasque agitant impune per agros

Floriferos,

THE

POETICAL MIRROR.

BOOK III.

BUT we mean-while, in lofty turrets perch'd,
  In vain expand the pinions of our wit
Contracted, as melodious birds confin'd
In wiry prifons; whilft the greedy kite,
The croaking raven, prattling pye to fruits,
And vagrant rook to yellow Ceres foe,
Light failing through the blue ferene, enjoy
The vernal Sun, and bear unpunifh'd off

Floriferos, raucifque irritant queftibus aures.

Nos, dignos qui laude viros prohibemus opacum

Umbrarum imperium, Stygiamque fubire paludem;

Qui juffos gaudere toris, menfifque beamus

Ambrofiis Divorum epulis, et nectare vivo,

Ipfi, perpetuis exefi pectora curis,

Avulfi Phœbo, ftudioque Heliconis amœni,

Et vario rapti Fortunæ turbine cæcæ,

Jejunas agimus ferias, petimufque laborum,

Heu! finem invalidi miferæque viatica vitæ

Per fteriles artes, tortæque inventa camœnæ.

Visceribus terræ concrefcunt femina ferri,

Quæ, flammis purgata feris, finguntur adunci

Vomeris in fpeciem, flexoque aptantur aratro.

Auricomo tellus reddit cum fœnore fruges

Agricolis, paleafque toris, et pabula bubus

Haud ingrata fuis: dat fabris rafile lignum

Sylva

Their various booties through the flow'ry fields,
And grate our ears with hoarfe-difcordant cries.
We, who forbid praife-worthy men to pafs
Beneath the gloomy fhades and Stygian lake,
Who dignify them, bidden guefts to grace
Celeftial boards, and roll'd with Gods partake
Ambrofial banquets and nectareous draughts,
We pine at heart with ever-gnawing cares,
Ravifh'd from Phœbus and the mufeful fhade,
And, bandied by blind fortune's giddy whirl,
Lead fafting feftivals, and feek in vain
Of toils a period, and provifion fcant
Through the rough road of miferable life
By barren arts, and fancy on the rack.

Deep in the bowels of impregnate earth
The miny feeds of rigid metals grow,
Which purg'd by flames are temper'd into fhares,
Inflex, and fitted for the crooked plough.
The feeded glebe with golden-ear'd increafe
Repays the peafant, nor ungrateful yields
For bedding chaff, and for her oxen food.
To forming hands the foreft rude affords
Materials pliant, and profufely ftores

The

Sylva rudis, laribufque focum tædafque miniſtrat.

Sponte greges ovium candeſcunt vellere molli,

Tortilis unde labos rapida vertigine fuſi

Ducitur, et longis coaleſcunt licia telis

Paulatim, Tyriumque bibunt medicata venenum:

Quæque manus ſibi poſcit opes, et vindicat arti

Materiam in promptu, requiemque laboribus actis.

At, quos Phœbus agit lymphata mente per umbram

Pieriam, lucrique via deflexit, inanes

Ædificant arces, et lucida nubila captant.

Sedula ceu vacuo dependet Aranea tecto,

Externiſque carens opibus penſum urget, et extis

Tenuia multiplicis deducit ſtamina telæ,

Deſidioſa manu quam tandem fœmina turpi

Averrit: monumenta cadunt operoſa dierum

Multorum, et, minimo jam puncto temporis, hoſpes

Dædala,

The hearth with fewel, and the dome with light.
The bleating multitudes with fleecy coats
Spontaneous whiten, whence in heady twirl
The twisted labour of the spindle swells,
'Till by degrees the warpy threads unite
Condens'd, embody'd with the lengthy woof,
And deep infus'd imbibe the Tyrian dye.
Each menial hand demands a full reward,
Materials ready for its .proper art,
And recreation after finish'd toils:
But those, whom Phœbus hath possess'd with mind
Intoxicated through the tuneful shade,
And mad, misguided from the path of gain,
Build airy domes, and catch at gilded clouds.

    As high the spider from an empty roof
Industrious hangs, and, void of outward aid,
Pursues her task, and from her entrails draws
The slender mazes of her filmy web,
Whom some invidious lazy damsel sweeps
Away with sluttish hand: down fractur'd fall
The labour'd monuments of many days,
And, in one instant of destructive time,
The curious guest, and through the sordid house

Dædala, perque domum textæ decus omne Minervæ.

Sic vates inter terram sublimis et astra

Quærit opes, instatque operi, cerebroque repostam

Rem trahit, et gracili contexit carmina filo,

Quem tamen e castris mediisque laboribus Harpax

Impius abripuit, brutumque coegit in antrum

Divinum artificem, et risit præsagia Phœbi:

Atramenta jacent tabulis inversa: quiescunt

Prælia cæpta: leves, agitatæ turbine, quales

Cumæa sub rupe, comæ, ludibria ventis,

Hinc atque inde domus magnum per inane feruntur

Cum calamis, laceræque ruunt a culmine Musæ.

At, si forte manus raptoris fugerit uncas,

Sæpius in casses Curlei decidit autor

Esuriens, prelique jugum subiturus iniqui

Scalarum

The total ornament of woven thrift.
The lofty Poet, balanc'd thus between
Earth and the ftars, ideal wealth explores,
Urges the tafk, from beetled brain extracts
Intrinfic matter, and with viewlefs thread
Weaves his Pierian ftuff, whom yet intent
Forth from his camp and interrupted toils
An impious harpy tui bulent hath hal'd,
And headlong hurry'd into brutal den
The rhiming wight, artificer divine,
And mock'd the fage refponfes of his God.
Inverted lies his ink-horn: in the birth
His battles dye: the titled pages light,
As tofs'd beneath Cumæan cave the leaves
Of fybil flutter'd with tempeftuous whirl,
Wide through the manfion void fly vagabond
The fport of winds, and with devoted quills
The tatter'd Mufes from their fummit rufh.

    But oft the Bard of ftomach keen, if he
Hath haply 'fcap'd the fhoulder-hooker's claws,
Deluded falls into the toils of Curl,
And, doom'd to drudge beneath the Preffic yoke,

B\

Scalarum afcenfu fuperat faftigia tecti,

Sydereas arces, loca cunctis pervia ventis

Nimborumque minis, crebrifque horrenda ruinis,

Scalarum afcenfu, dominus quas rite vocavit

Ipfe GRADUS-AD-PARNASSUM, Phœboque dicavit.

Hic, ubi promiffis corvos allexit hiantes,

Nocturnifque togis ac tritis veftibus agmen

Pierium ornavit, duplicique accendit amore

Æternæ pariter famæ, victufque diurni,

Expandit niveæ feptena volumina chartæ;

Heu, quantum macris perarandum vatibus æquor!

Nec non et latices infundit cornibus atros,

Tartareos latices, et plumea tela canorum

In bellum exacuit. Novies æftatibus heros

Jam denis (fi vera fides annalibus ævi)

Aruit in caftris, totidemque Decembribus alfit;

Ternaque

By ſcaling ladder mounts his tall domain,
Sydereal turrets, pervious to the blaſts
Of ſundry winds and menaces of ſtorms,
And hideous rent with diſcontinuous chaſms,
He mounts by ſcaling ladder, which its lord
Yclep'd with due propriety the " ſteps
" Of high promotion to the Muſes' hill,"
And conſecrated to the God of day.

    HERE when with windy promiſes he fed
The gaping crows allur'd, and aptly deck'd
With night-gowns and caſt coats the chiming band;
And fir'd their boſoms with the double love
Of fame eternal and diurnal food,
The ſoft ſeducer opens to their view
Rheams upon rheams of ſnowy paper pure;
O what a tract of ocean to be plow'd
By meager Bards! then into copious horns
Inſtills a ſtream of bitter ichor black,
Tartarean tincture, and provoking whets
His grey-gooſe weapons for harmonic war.
Full ninety ſummers (if we credit give
To natal annals) has the letter'd chief
In warfare wither'd, and Decembers froze

Ternaque jam senior variorum sæcula vatum,

Quos aluit, cinxitque togis, tercenta laborum,

In lucem quos ipse tulit, coriisque revinxit,

Viderat.   Ossa cutis tenet unica: nec minus ille

Impiger, et cœptis felix audacibus ignem

Pæonium instigat, prelique refuscitat artes,

Excussi per tanta sagi revolumina raptus,

Per tot aquæ casus, per tot discrimina fustis

Nodosasque minas, ac tali voce profatur.

Conscripti vates, quibus, indignantibus arctam

Tellurem, immensum liceat percurrere cœlum

Mente vaga, et latos amplecti versibus orbes,

Sublimes animæ, placido quas lumine Phœbus

Nascentes olim vidit, vulgoque profano

Secrevit, laurusque suæ solius avaras

Militiæ addixit nostræ, meque auspice dudum

Dexter in has toties Raptorum assultibus arces

Misit

As many told; and now the fage had feen
Three ages laps'd of Poets, whom he fed,
And girt with night-gowns, thrice an hundred lives
Of all their labours, which with plaftic hand
He midwiv'd into light, and bound with hides;
And now he ftalks a fpectre, fkin and bones,
A living fkeleton! yet, not the lefs
The champion keen, and profperous in feats
Of bold emprize, excites poetic fire,
And glad revives his Typographic arts,
Through revolutions of the blanket tofs'd
Aloft fo frequent, through fo many pools
Baptiz'd, and unregenerate by dint
Of fyllogiftic oak and knotty threats,
Preambles thus: Ye confcript Bards, to whom,
Indignant of this narrow globe, is given
With wingy mind to travel through the fkies
Immenfe, and in your verfes comprehend
Broad, ambient orbs; exalted fouls refin'd,
Whom Phœbus at your birth with placid eye
Beheld, and cloyfter'd from the crowd profane,
Whom, only ftudious of his bays, he rais'd
My black recruits, nor inaufpicious led
Beneath my conduct into thefe abodes,

Forts

Mifit inacceffas, et inexpugnabile vallum ;

Et vos, eloquii ftudium quibus alma prioris

Signa fequi et palmam fcriptis ambire folutis ;

Vos, quibus obfcuræ fordefcunt munia vitæ

Degenerefque artes, qui non didiciftis in arva

Immundum jactare fimum, dextrifque ligones

Exercere graves, putrefque invertere glebas,

Quin, teneiis matrum precibus, quin, fortiter iris

Inftantumque minis genitorum et carcere fpretis,

Excoluiftis opes animi campofque Minervæ,

Dignum opus ingenuis ! aures advertite dictis,

O pueri! quos alta vocant præconia laudis,

Et, Curleius honos, generandi carminis ardor,

Dum partes dux cuique fuas ex ordine findo.

Tu, felix operis, conclufo fine libelli,

Ancipiti qui mente novum formare patronum

Jamdudum arfifti Mufæ fcriptifque tuendis,

Quemlibet

Forts inacceſſible to griping foes
Aſſailant, and impregnable defence;
And ye, who ſtudy to purſue the tracks
Of antient eloquence, and court the palm
Of toils proſaic; ye, to whom as baſe
The ſervile offices of life obſcure
And manual arts appear, who never learnt
To caſt on furrows filthy dung, and ply
Unwieldy ſpades to turn the putrid glebe,
But, in contempt of ſoft maternal pray'rs,
In brave defiance of paternal ire,
Revenge denounc'd, and priſon in the rear,
Improv'd the riches of your mind, and fields
Of Pallas, labour of ingenuous hearts;
Attend, O ſtripplings, whom the lofty trump
Of fame delights, who kindle with an itch,
The ſacred luſt of propagating verſe,
Curleian honour! while your leader I
Divide to each his delegated taſk.

   You, who, ſuccefsful in your finiſh'd work,
With doubtful mind have panted long to frame
A new Mecænas, to protect your Muſe,
Chuſe from the Synagogue, or motley heap

                                        Of

Quemlibet Iſachidum, aut nobilitatis acervo

Sorte trahas docili; quoniam ſors omnia verſat,

Jam nunc fortunæ genetrix, et ſortibus uſus

Delius, et dictæ quondam per carmina ſortes.

Hunc aperi librum, et primi lege marginis oram;

Sic acri ratione manum meliora ſequantur

Cæcam fata ducem: videam, cui laurea ceſſit.

Euge, Poeta! patet, centeno fœnore dives,

Lausus, et urbe potens; nec Phœbo gratior ulla eſt,

Quam ſibi quæ Lauſi præſcripſit pagina nomen.

Hunc cape, grande decus, primoque in limine ſiſte

Creſcentis pugilem famæ, plectroque memento

Et fidibus mulcere ſacris: hunc floribus orna,

Undique carpendis, fuſiſque per avia vatum,

Et, quibus ipſe caret, dotalibus obline donis.

Tuqui, atra qui bile tumes, acrique veneno,

Stridentes experte tubas, et bella theatri

Sibila

Of noblemen, whomever chance prefents
Decifive drawn, fince chance, the mother now
Of fmiling fortune, over-rules the world,
And Phœbus whilom from the Delphic ftool
Divin'd by chances what the Sybil fung :
This volume ope, and con the word in front;
So better fate attend that ready hand,
Thy blind conductor ———— Let me fee your man:
Hail, happy Poet! Laufus comes to light,
Plumb-potent Laufus, fam'd for cent per cent,
And leading ftroke at Common-council-board ;
Nor fhines a page more grateful to the God
Than that, which on its bofom bears infcrib'd
The name of Laufus.   Him thy pompous pride
Elect, and in the porch of rifing fame
Thy champion fix : him with devoted ftrains
Be fure, you tickle : him array with flow'rs,
From all fides to be pluck'd, and interfus'd
Among the haunts of antiquated Bards,
And dubbing dawb with talents unendow'd.

AND thou, who, fwell'd with melancholy fpleen,
And rankled venom, haft withftood the fhocks
Of fqualing cat-calls, and theatric wars,

Sibila jam toties, ingratos exue foccos,

Et mecum, ornatos hedera, perpende Poetas,

Sterne decus, furtique reos arceffe labores,

Et pictas veneres crocitantes exue corvos,

Propugnator atrox veterum, Cenforque minorum.

Tu molles elegos, Paphiafque effinge fagittas,

Quæ juvenum inftimulent furibundo corda tumultu,

Extinctafque fenum revocent in pectora flammas,

Quas bona mater emat, curæ lenimen herilis,

Triftitiæque fugam; folo quas nata cubili

Cafta legat, portetque facro pro codice in ædas

Divinas errore pio, rubeatque repertis.

Tu, qui nobilium retinendas leniter aures,

Plaufurafque manus iterumque iterumque theatro

Solicitare velis, mimos modulare canoros,

E:

Loud, frequent, hiffing, ftrip the comic Mufe
Of fock ungrateful, and with critic eye
Reviewing, weigh thofe mighty Poets, crown'd
With partial praife, expofe their artful thefts
And bare the boafters of their borrow'd plumes:
Here fit high Chancellor, of authors old
Afferter keen, and Cenfor of the new.

THINE be the care foft elegies to whine,
And lufcious novels, Paphian arrows point,
To fting the bofoms of unbridled youth
With raging rapture, and recall the flames
Of love extinguifh'd to the veins of age,
Which the good matron decently may buy
The mere amufement of domeftic care
And falve for forrow, which the daughter chafte
In bedded chamber lonely may perufe,
Through pious error carry into church
For godly book, and blufh to be furpriz'd.

You, who would court at crowded opera
The fix'd attention of ingenuous ears,
And choral claps of honourable hands,
To foft Sol-fa melodious trifles tune,

VOL. I.   H h   Unmeaning

Et fine mente fonos, et Hetrufcis apta Cinædis
Carmina, nec vultum pigeat pofuiffe virilem
Nec formis ululare lupi, torvique leonis
Infremere, aut caudam aligeri finuare draconis,
Ardentefque jubas, et fquamea volvere colla.

Tu vero, cui fanguis hebet, quem plumbeus ortu
Cognatum afpexit pigro Saturnus ab axe,
Et fenfus tardante gelu conftrinxit inertes,
Grammaticam laturus opem, fi præmia pofcis,
Si te digna manent genialis pocula zythi,
Amiffis pedibufque fequax, numerifque, Maronem
Et, verbum verbo, curabis reddere Flaccum,
Quos, linguæ Latialis inops, ille ore fecundo
Ruminet, et patrio concoctos carmine donet.

Tu, qui Walpoleum folitus profcindere chartis,
Pro patria antiqua, pro libertate Britanna,
Implefti clamore vias et compita crebro,

Da

Unmeaning founds, and meafures to be trill'd
By Latian eunuchs, nor difdain to lay
The man afide, nor in the forms of wolf
Hideous to howl, and lion grim to roar,
Or wag the tail of wingy dragon, rear
The flaming creft, and roll the fcaly neck.

But you, whofe blood coagulated creeps,
Whom leaden Saturn at the natal hour
Beheld congenial from his laggard orb,
And bound your deadly faculties with ice,
Afford your aid grammatic, if you feek
A due reward, if thee the flowing pot
Of genial ale awaits, purfuing clofe,
Quick, independent of poetic feet,
And numbers apt, majeftic Maro's mufe,
And copious Horace render, word for word,
Which he, quite alien to the Roman tongue,
May ruminate with fecondary mouth,
And deck, digefted into Britifh rhime.

You, who were wont in party-pamphlets keen
To libel Walpole, for old England's fake,
For Britifh freedom, and heroic fill'd

The

Da ventis jam vela retro melioribus aulæ;
Carpe fugam, dictifque tuis tua dicta refelle.

Ipse ego quin, medio pofitus, variafque recenfens
Tantorum feries operum, decus ómnibus addam
Extremum, venerefque manu de more refingam
Incomptas, portas aufus recludere famæ.
At libet interea vatum depromere vitas,
Et ftudia, et mores, et teftamenta fub auras,
Antiquifque novas frontes aptare libellis.

Dixit, et ora macer, longæque fimillimus umbræ,
Albentes oculos, inverfo lumine, torfit,
Lætitiaque cava deduxit flebile rictus,
Fauce fepulchrales, et hiulcis dentibus atros,
Afpectuque tenax famulorum, evanuit hofpes,
Et, claufis furtim foribus, gradibufque remotis,
Inferiora domus petiit.   Sitis excitat illos

Æmula

The ſtreets and high-roads with inceſſant roar,
Now ſhift your ſails, to fairer gales from court
Now tack about, precipitate your flight,
And, changing ſides, your very ſelf confute.

But I moreover, in the circle thron'd,
And recognizing with judicious ken
The various progreſs of theſe wondrous works,
Shall add to all the maſter-ſtrokes of art,
The poliſh'd grace to beauties unadorn'd,
And with this hand unbar the gates of fame.
Mean-while it is our pleaſure to reveal
The ſtudies, morals, nay, the very wills
And teſtaments of Bards defunct, to drag
Their inmoſt ſecrets into light, and fit
New title-pages for old-printed books.

He ſaid, and rueful with a ghaſtly length
Of meagre viſage, ſtalking like a ghoſt,
Roll'd the pale orbs of dim inverted ſight,
With hollow mirth his mournful jaws diſplay'd,
Sepulchral jaws, and black with gappy teeth,
And from their eyes, tenacious of his ſlaves,
He vaniſh'd, ſlily ſhut the door, remov'd
The ladder, and beſought his lower cell.

T

Æmula fcribendi, et calami labor occupat ater.

INCUMBUNT operi, ftudiifque ardentibus inftant,
Ut Birminghamei tectis nigrantibus olim
Certatim artifices, hic follibus, ille caminis,
Infudant. Hinc cultra parant, pars inde bidentes
Confpicant. Alii procudunt ductile ferrum
Paulatim in gladios, quos lævigat alter, at alter
Vaginis habiles, capulifque nitentibus aptat.
Stridet opus, pulfifque gemunt incudibus antra.

Hic tamen Ætneum, pofitis fabrilibus, agmen
Laffatis parcunt manibus, gaudentque ferenum
Refpiraie Jovem, ac, torvos ferrugine, vultus
Lætitiam abluere in placidam. Tum corpora cultu
Splendidiore tegunt; luces tum denique feftas
Aut patriis celebrant ludis, aut ruiis aperti
Dona petunt, hilarefque animis paribufque puellis

Lenæum

THE rival thirſt of ſcribbling them excites,
And labour of the ſable pen employs :
Prone to their jobs of journey-woik they bend,
And eager preſs.   As in their murky cells
The Birmingham artificers inur'd,
At bellows this, that over flaming coals,
Incumbent ſweat.   Theſe knives embroaden, thoſe
Point prongy forks.   Some hammer by degrees
The ductile metal into taper ſwords,
To which another gives the poliſh'd edge ;
Another marries to the ſheath, and fits
The temper'd miſchief with reſplendent hilts;
Laborious diſcord through the forges dins,
And deep the vaults with beaten anvils groan.

YET, here the dun Ætnean band forſake
Their forming implements, refieſh their hands,
Fatigu'd with heavy toil, and joy to breathe
The purer æther, and, inlaid with ruſt,
To waſh their faces into gentle mirth :
With gayer garments elegantly then
They trim themſelves, then ſolemnize the days
Of tutelary ſaints with native games,
Or court the pleaſures of the rural plain,

                                      And,

Igneum libant genetrice sub arbore nectar.

At CURLEIA cohors, antiquis horrida pannis,

Perpetua statione manet, dominique sub armis

Militat, et lento studiorum in marte senescit.

Dii superi! prohibete luem, prohibete nefandum

Vatibus hospitium tenerisque ergastula Musis.

Nos equidem, esurie famæque cupidine dŭcti,

In scelus irruimus vetitum, petimusque cacumen

Stultitia: facilis scalarum ascensus in arcem:

Sed revocare gradus, imasque evadere ad auras

Hoc opus, hic labor est. Oculos quocunque volantes

Tendis, et effugium celso meditaris ab Orco,

Egressum sors dura negat. Tabulata tremiscunt

Jam jam summa domus, altoque horrore feneftræ

Caligant, nec fas capto suspendere funem;

Qualis enim feralis avis, devota Minervæ,

Muribus

And, glad at heart, and pair'd with equal maids,
Quaff apple-wine beneath the parent tree.

　　BUT Curl's recruits, rough-rigg'd with ragged frize,
On guard high-poſted, through the long campaign
Wage war with reaſon, and grow grey in rhime.
Avert, ye Gods, the peſtilence, avert
Such loathſome lodgings from the tuneful ſwains,
And taſky Bridewells from the Theſpian maids.

　　WE, led by hunger and the luſt of fame,
Ruſh through forbidden wickedneſs, and ſeek
The ſummit, fooliſh ! eaſy is th' aſcent
By ladder long; but down to re-deſcend,
And 'ſcape to nether air, this is the pinch,
And this the rub : to whatſoever ſide
You dart your flying eyes, and meditate
Redreſs of woes, and flight from upper-hell,
Hard ſate denies emiſſion.　Hark the roof
Aerial trembles, and the windows dim
Your ſight diminutive with horror ſteep,
Nor dare you thence ſuſpend a ſlender rope ;
For, as the bird of deathful dirge, devote
To prudent Pallas, on the lurch for mice,

Muribus invigilans, juxta flaventia pernox
Farra fedet, latebrafque fagax explorat et antra,
Cœruleos oculos obliquo lumine volvens :
Stat Curleus humi, et partes fpeculator in omnes
Limen obit, fervatque fores, et clauftra tuetur,
Officiique monet vates, atque increpat afper
Oblitos operum, triftique indicit hiatu
Inteftina cavis, fera bella frementibus alvis.

Tu rabie fervente tumes, turpique minatus
Solvere colla jugo, greffumque efferre fub auras,
Ad vultus tamen iratos, et murmura regis
Imperiofa tremis, penfumque orditus eandem
Æterno teris orbe rotam : ceu quem magus olim
Carmine luftravit Stygio, tetegitque potenti
Jam radio, ac tenui gyrum fignavit arena,
Infernas audit voces, tumulifque remiffos
Pallentes cernit manes, trepidufque tumultu

Infolito

Sits nightly watchful by a rick of corn,
And ſage explores their avenues and caves,
Obliquely rolling her cerulean eyes;
Curl ſtands beneath, and, eyeful on all parts,
Eternal centinel, the threſhold weaıs,
And blocks the portals, and the paſſes guards:
Oft of their duty he reminds the ſcribes,
And oft, forgetful of appointed toils,
Severely rates, and, with a diſmal yawn
Preſaging faſt, proclaims inteſtine war,
Lent war againſt their hollow-growling guts.

You ſwelling kindle with indignant rage,
And threaten to releaſe your captive neck
From ſervile yoke, and into day revolt,
Yet, at the tyrant's angry look and tone
Imperious damp'd, you tremble, and renew
Your fuſtian labour in eternal round.
As he, whom whilom with enchanting ſpell
A necromancer hath enthrall'd, and touch'd
With potent rod, and on the ſhallow ſand
Inſcrib'd a circle, hears infernal ſcreams,
Sees ghaſtly ſpectres from their dreary tombs

Up-conjur'd,

Infolito horrefcit, ciicoque immobilis hæret.

 Quo vero accingar Faulkneri dicere laudes

Pro meritis? quibus ille modis, quove ore fonandus,

Mufarum antiftes, divinæ Palladis hofpes,

Et comes, et cultor, dubiæ per lubrica Cirrhæ,

Et cæcos opeium cafus; qui, femper avaras

Indignatus opes animis, et fordida preli

Munera, jampridem Phœbeæ præfidet ædi,

Cuftoditque fores, et, verfo cardine, vates

Sufcipit ingenuos, famæ fator almus honeftæ ?

 Luc ous obfcuris eiroribus effluit ordo

Illius ad tactus : manibus Cadmeia doctis

Signa movet, diverfa locis, et femina paffim

Verborum in fylva, variaque ambage typorum

Vocales explorat opes, me.nbrifque coactis

Hinc atque inde chao plumbi, folidumque per æquor

Oppofitis

Up-conjur'd, fhudders with unufual fright,
And fticks, as bound, within the magic ring.

BUT how fhall I with dignity proclaim
Fair FAULKNER's praifes ? in what ftrains is he,
And by what Poet, to be faid or fung,
High Pontiff of the Nine, Minerva's hoft,
Faft friend and client, through the flipp'ry paths
Of Cirrha doubtful, and the blind events
Of books imprefs'd; who, with fuperior foul,
Of greedy riches, and the fordid gains
Of prefs difdainful, hath prefided long
Chafte o'er Apollo's temple, and ftill guards
The gates, and, turning oft the hinge, admits
Born Bards, and bounteous propagates their fame ?

PERSPICUOUS order from confufion dark
Springs at his touch : with learned hand he moves
Cadmeian elements from narrow cells
Detach'd, and, through the wilder'd wood of words,
And various maze of fcatter'd types, explores
His vocal wealth: with members aptly join'd
From fide to fide of leaden chaos denfe,
And, through the furface of the folid field

Oppofitis jam nunc fpatiis, et frontibus æquis,

Æthereos animæ fenfus mentemque fugacem

Alligat, inque diem fpeciofa volumina profert:

Nec tantum preli fatagit, nec mutus Athenas

Sufpicit antiquas, alieni vinitor horti:

Ille etiam egregiæ jamdudum exarfit amore

Laudis, et ingenua luctari fæpe palæftra

Eft aufus, pulchroque tulit certamine victor

Vivaces hederas ingenti non fine plaufu.

Morborum incertis, dubiifque falutis, amica

Jam præcepta canit medicis, ægrifque medelas

Præfentes miferis, opiferque haud præmia pofcit.

Jam monet agricolas, armis quibus acriter ufi,

Tellurem incipiant curvo profcindere ferro;

Quo

In lines, at equal intervals arrang'd,
And front to front, he binds the pure, fublime
Senfations of the foul and flitting mind,
And into day with cloathing beauty brings
The legible creation.   Nor the prefs
Alone employs his dædal hands, nor he
With filent rapture ftudies the remains
Of Athens, pruner of another's vines :
He too, tranfported with the love of praife
Egregious, long hath glow'd, undaunted ftood
A champion often in the letter'd lift,
And, often victor in the comely ftrife,
Reap'd ripe applaufe and ever-blooming bays.

Now, he reveals to doctors, in the dark
Groping to find fome new diftempers out,
And much mifdoubtful of their promis'd aid,
And wife prefcriptions, aphoriftic rules,
And to the pining patients prefent cures,
Nor fpares his labour, nor demands a fee.

AND now the fwains prognoftical he warns,
What arms exerting, they fhould ftrait begin
To turn their acres with the crooked fhare,

Beneath

Quo fruges mandare folo fub fydere culto,

Et gravibus raftris concretas frangere glebas ;

Quantum operæ pretium nudis meſſoribus adſit

Solibus in mediis rubicundam fternere meſſem,

At, matutinis glifcentes roribus, herbas.

Nec non edocuit, metuentes fraudis, avaros

Ancipitefque fenes, certis ponere nummos

Nominibus liceat fine litibus, unde quotannis

Sint reditus, et res occulto fœnore crefcat.

Nec procul hinc, opibus, corraſis undique pridem,

Jam lapſis, patrios ubi tandem juftior hæres

Vendat agros, armenta, greges, meritoria, villas:

Tecta repente cadunt corvorum antiqua bipenni

Per, denfas ornis, et opacas ilice, fylvas.

Parte alia exponit (digitoque fub indice fignat

Sæpe locum) generator equus quibus impiger herbis

Fervet,

Beneath what fign to truft maternal grain
To mellow-labour'd furrows, and robuft
With heavy harrows break the clotted glebe ;
What full returns of induftry refult
To naked reapers in meridian rays
To ftrow the fields with yellow crops, but mow
The glift'ning meads, with early dews impearl'd.

He too hath taught old Hunkfes in a maze,
Fearful of fraud, where fafely to depofe
Their darling coin, illiable to fuit
Litigious, whence an annual ftock may rife
Excrefcent, and enhance the mother-fum ;
Then advertifes, where the jufter heir,
Faft having flung that guilty wealth away,
Scrap'd from all quarters by the fordid fire,
To fale expofes all his lands, his herds,
His flocks, his mortgages and country-feats :
Prone fall the nefted tenements of rooks
By fudden fteel through venerable groves,
With afh embattel'd, and embrown'd with oak.

Full in another paragraph he fhews,
(And points the paffage with a finger oft)
High-mettled on what foil the ftallion glows,

Vol. I.   K k   Tracing

Fervet, Idumæam referens longo ordine gentem,
Et decus ipfe fuum, palmafque fubinde nepotum.

Mox ubi tecta vacent viduæ mœrentis, et horti
Spectandi, fundufque ferax, ftabulifque fuperbis
Stant nitidæ, domitæque fremant ad fræna quadrigæ.

ILLE feris etiam latronibus atque malignis
Furibus infeftus, dubiæque impenfius urbi
Providus, incautas prima fub nocte puellas
Sæpius admonuit junctas firmare feneftras
Tranfverfo ligno, tum clavibus oftia verfis,
Perplexifque feris, et nexo denique ferro,
Et, quamvis teneris arrectas cantibus aures
Noctivagi alliciant juvenes, votifque minifque
Solicitent, durafque vocent, et limina crebro
Calce terant, Faulknerus ait, cafta ora tenete,

Et

Tracing from Paleſtine his antient blood,
His own atchievements, and his race's palms.

He then ſubjoins, where, beautifully gay,
A mourning widow's houſe is to be let,
Her pleaſure gardens and her fruitful farm
By bidders may be view'd, and where at ſtalls
Her dapple mares in ſtately ſtables ſnort,
Tam'd to the laſh, and foaming on the bit.

He likewiſe, foe to robbers and to thieves
Burglarious, and ſolicitous of mind
To guard the city, providential warns
Incautious maidens at the cloſe of day
Their windows to ſecure with wooden bars
A-thwart the ſhutters, and defend their doors
With keys inverſive, with locks intricate
Of wards, and laſtly, with connected chains,
And though with ſoft, enchanting, ſerenade
Night-wandring youths allure their ears erect,
And importune with promiſes and threats,
Hard-hearted call them, and with frequent heel
Aſſault the threſhold, Faulkner cries, retain

Et claufam fervate fidem. Subfternite rarum
Volcanum cineri, fparfafque extinguite prunas,
Semianimefque faces, tremulafque in lampade flammas ;
Nam, velut atra lues, contacto corpore furtim,
Paulatim irrepfit venis, jam jamque medullas
Perfurit, et fubito tetros depafcitur artus,
Fumantes olim perituro lumine tædæ,
Murorum infixæ rimis, nova robora carpunt :
Ardefcunt tabulæ, rapidis aulæa ruinis,
Bellorum exuviis, heroibus intertexta,
Jam refoluta crepant, donec per tecta repente
Ignis edax prælambit iter, totafque videbis
Ex imo involvi flammis bacchantibus ædes.

Nec tantum cives præceptis firmat amicis
Faulknerus, quin fæpe, joco rifuque foluto,
Multiplici mentes rerum dulcedine pafcit,
Irritat, mulcet, magicis horroribus implet,
Bella manu pacemque gerens, variafque per oras

Terrarum

Chaſte ſilence, and preſerve your bolted faith:
Few living coals beneath your aſhes lull,
Extinguiſh all the ſcatter'd embers, brands
Half-dead, and in their ſockets gaſping lights;
For, as a foul infection unperceiv'd,
The body touch'd, hath crept into the veins,
Reſiſtleſs rages through the tainted bones,
And ſudden ravens on the livid limbs;
So tapers, fumy with departing rays,
Stuck in the chinks of antient walls, acquire
Reviving force: the hangings, rich-inwrought
With warlike trophies and heroic knights,
Crackle, with rapid ruin into duſt
Diſſolv'd, 'till ſudden through the roof aloft
The lambent bane depopulates its way,
And from the bottom you behold the dome
Outrageous wrapt in univerſal flame.

Nor leſs good Faulkner with kind precepts arms
Alone the city, but with weekly wit
And jocund mirth his readers entertains,
Provokes, aſſuages, fills with magic pangs,
In hand alternate bearing war, or peace,
And over various regions of the globe

Them

Terrarum novitate rapit.   Ceu penniger olim

Divorum interpres, citharæque repertor, amictus

Nube cava, portenta refert, vacuasque per aures

Rumores serit ambiguos vocesque bilingues,

Perque virum levis ora volat, stridentior undis,

Ocior et Borea, Famamque reliquit anhelam.

JAM canit Hispanos, jam, rupto fœdere, Gallos

Arma movere animis, sociosque arcessere Suevos;

Quid sibi nempe struant cœptis? cur mænia dudum

Marlburia subversa manu, ingeminata resurgunt,

Liligeræque minæ? cur campos milite complent?

Cur medias impune audent errare per undas,

Aut quassas reparare rates, aut condere classem?

TUM vero in Persas lunatis agmina signis

Turcarum instigat, terrasque reposcere, raptas

Vi,

Them on the wings of novelty tranſports :
As erſt the plum'd interpreter of Gods,
And ſweet inventor of the charming lyre,
Clad with an hollow cloud, portentous deeds
Romantic he relates, through vacant ears
Ambiguous rumours, doubtful ſpeeches ſows,
Flies through the mouths of gaping mortals light,
Than ocean louder, fleeter than a ſtorm,
And out of breath leaves poſting fame behind.

AND now th' Iberians, now the Gauls, he ſings,
Of leagues perfidious, meditating war,
In act to kindle, and invite the Swedes
To ſocial arms ; for what would they project
By ſuch attempts ? why re-ariſe thoſe walls
Sublimer, lately level'd to the duſt
By Marlbro's hand ? and why thoſe lily-threats ?
Why fill they fields with tented legions ? why
Unpuniſh'd dare they ramble through the main,
Repair their ſhatter'd ſhips, or build a fleet ?

AGAINST the Perſians then he ſpurs the Turks,
Emblaz'd with beamy creſcents, and impels
To vindicate their antient bounds uſurp'd :

But,

Vi, monet. At, fubito converfo cardine belli,

Ardentem ftudio fpoliorum, in prælia Kannum,

Spirantemque faces et ferrea mollibus Indis

Fata, ciet; fimul ipfe virum depingit, et infit:

O, qualis, quantufque ruit Koulæus in hoftes!

Olli Pellæus, concedat Julius olli,

Marte fatus. Qui frontis honos! quæ fulgura vultu!

Quique fupercilio terror! Jovis armiger horret,

Ecce, finu, dextraque gravis furit hafta minaci!

Mox autem indomitas immenfis viribus urbes

Cingit atrox, pofcitque aditus, clademque minatus

Fulminat in folidos flammarum turbine muros,

Concuffafque arces et ferri grandine turres

Dejicit ingentes. Jam, fractis impete, portis

Diluviem

But, fhifting fuddenly the fcene of war,
He rouzes into rage the dreadful Kan,
Incens'd with love of fpoils, fell-breathing flames
And rigid ruin to the fofter fons
Of golden Ganges: he mean-while depaints
The chief in warlike attitude, and adds:
O, with what life and fpirit on his foes
Fam'd Kouly pours! let Alexander great
To him his greater, let the Julian fon
Of Mars to him refign the boafted bays.
Thron'd on his front, what majefty appears?
What lightning in his eyes, and on his brow
What terror! lo, the thunder-bearing bird
Of Jove horrific perches on his breaft!
His baleful halbert maddens in his hand!

ANON with mighty forces he invefts
Unconquer'd towns, and fierce demands ingrefs,
Denouncing flaughter with tempeftuous flames,
He thunders deep againft the folid walls,
And batter'd citadels, and baftions huge
Dafh'd overthrows with iron hail, and now
Thick through the rifted gates impetuous rolls

Diluviem infundit belli : ruit igneus enfis.

Hinc trepida cum voce preces, projectaque vota

Victorum ante pedes : hinc torva turbidus ira

Vultus, et ultrices, ferro pendente, furores,

Nec tandem refides repetito vulnere : cœlum

Cædentum horrefcit fremitu, gemituque cadentum.

Terra cruore rubet fufo, perque ardua regum

Atria perque facras ædes Mars impius ardet.

Tum pofitis litui, raucique canoribus æris,

Armorumque minis, trutinam tenet arbiter æquam

Europæ atque Afiæ : fugit irrevocabile Fiat

Et Faulknera fides.   Coeunt in vota tyranni

Adverfi, placidumque nitet pax miffa per orbem.

Tum fulcis redit alma Ceres : tum littora fidis

Albefcunt velis, refplendent oppida gazis,

Et, fœcunda viris, operofo murmure ftrident.

Tum

A warlike deluge : rages uncontroul'd
The flamy fword.   Promifcuous hence are heard
With trembling accent fupplicating yells,
And proftrate vows before the victors' feet :
Hence frowns the human countenance effac'd
With clouded anger, and with fteel uplift
Wrath unrelenting at repeated wounds:
The fky convulfive murmurs to the fhouts
Of flaying chiefs, and groans of dying men:
The pavements blufh with gory tides effus'd,
And, through the lofty palaces of kings
And facred fanes, Mars impious madly burns.

Then hufh'd the fife, the brazen fongs of war,
And threats of arms, in equal fcales he weighs
Europe and Afia.   Sudden flies abroad
The fix'd decree ; for Faulkner fpoke the word.
Contending monarchs into concord run,
And peace fmiles, wafted through the gentle world.
Then fruitful Ceres to the fields returns;
Then whiten fhores with focial canvas, towns
With wealth barbaric fhine, and rich in men
With humming induftry promifcuous buzz.

Then

Tum demum, aeria fufpendens lintea turri,

Præconum ingenti teftatur voce per urbem

Lætitiam, et pulchra fub libertate quietem.

Nec non et multa luftrari luce feneftras,

Igne jubet trivias, flammifque comantibus auras

Stellarum in morem, votifque accendit Olympum

Ipfe prior, primofque meri tibi, Cæfar, honores

Libat ovans; tibi fceptra diu non fordidus aufpex

Imperiumque vovet, ferifque nepotibus optat.

Nic minus heroum, campo qui nuper atroci

Pro patria infracti fteterint, aut, vulnere crebro

Sublapfi, niveam decorarint funere vitam,

Gefta recognofcit, jam jam ventura fub auras

Mufarum æternas, Phœbique recolligit agmen.

Ipse, Deo plenus, primifque imbutus ab annis,

Arbitrium

THEN he, fufpending from a lofty tow'r
The feftal flag, through Devila's domains
By herald hawkers loud proclaims his joy,
Repofe reftor'd, and liberty fecur'd.
With nightly lights he bids the windows blaze,
The ftreets with bon-fires, and the fkies with flames
Meteorous, and earlieft in zeal
Inflames Olympus with his loyal vows :
To thee, great George, exulting he devotes
The prime libations of his cafk ; to thee
A lafting fcepter and aufpicious reign,
No vulgar augur, he portends, and prays
Long to defcend to thy remoteft line.

Nor lefs thofe heroes, who have lately ftood
With patriot fpirit for the public weal,
Unbroken in the field of bloody Mars,
Or, nobly falling by repeated wounds,
Their fpotlefs lives with glorious death adorn'd,
He recognizes, and records their deeds,
Ordain'd to travel into fpeedy light
Immortal, and recalls the rhiming band.
He, big with Phœbus, and from early yeais
Imbu'd, imparts his fentiments unafk'd

To

Arbitrium impertit fcriptori candidus ultro
Cuique laboranti, nec jam fub margine libri
Defignare piget maculas nigrantibus aftris,
Et medicas adhibere manus, et fingere crudos
Matuiam in fpeciem fœtus, formamque premendo,
Quo nitidi tandem coriis, et pumice læves,
Ætherium afpiciant folem, volitentque per orbem.
Haud fecus, et perhibent, quondam Saturnius ulnis
Flagranti prolem Semele fufcepit abortam,
Semideumque Deus lumbi fub vulnere fovit,
Donec, nafcendi completo temporis orbe,
Perfectum effudit, lætafque remifit in auras.

Haud tamen interea dulces Faulknerus alumnos
Servitio premit ingrato, clauditve canorum
Curleio de more gregem, ftabulifve coercet
Præfcriptis, quin dives opum, lautæque tyrannus,
Splendidus ipfe domus, aulam jubet effe patentem
Hofpitio, et vates multo compellat honore

Ante

To pregnant authors in their teeming throes,
Benignly candid, nor difdains to point
The lapfes relative beneath each page
With inky ftars, apply his healing hand,
And lick the crude conceptions into form,
Mature imprefs'd, that, elegantly bound
In oxen-hide, and polifh'd, they may view
The radiant Sun, and flutter through the world.
So Poets tell, Saturnian Jove receiv'd
Bacchus abortive from the flagrant womb
Of Semele, and in his wounded thigh
The nurfing God fuftain'd the Demi-god,
'Till in the full revolving tide of birth
He pour'd him forth, and gave to fecond day.

YET not with bafe ungrateful yoke mean-while
Good Faulkner galls his Heliconian guefts,
Nor after mode Curleian vilely pens
His tuneful cattle, or confines to cribs
Prefcrib'd, but, flowing with abundant wealth,
And fplendid monarch of a ftately dome,
Commands his court in hofpitable wife
Be wide difplay'd, and with profound refpect
Poets accofts, and with accomplifh'd hand

Conducts

Ante fores, cultaque manu in penetralia ducit
Aurea, ſtructa toris.　Pedibus Byzantia lautis
Stragula ſublucent, oſtroque inſignia, multa
Arte laboratos, referunt heroas, et arma,
Tincta cruore recens.　Italo ſtant marmore poſtes
Exciſi ante lares, lauruque hederaque virentes
Majores vatum dextra, lævaque minores,
Jamdudum extincti, redeunt in lumen, et atra
Tela vibrant manibus, pictoque in pariete ſpirant.

Jamque adeo, ſeptus vivis authoribus, hoſpes
Diverſas operum fruges metitur, et inde
Hunc procul, hunc propius, merito locat ordine cunctos.
Nec veteri Baccho, dapibus nec parcit opimis,
Quin, genii mentiſque capax melioris, edules
In medium effundit gazas, comiteſque laceſſit
Ancipites, donis Divum præſentibus uti,
Carnivoros agitare dies, et ſolvere vitæ
Dura mero ſceptriſque graves comittere curas.

At

Conducts officious into golden rooms,
With couches furnish'd.   Turkey carpets flame
Beneath his feet, and, bright with purple, shew
Heroes, embroider'd with surprising art,
And martial arms, imbru'd with streaming blood.
Pure marble pillars of Italian vein
Adorn his hearth, and, green with circling bays
And ivy, Bards, the greater on his right,
On his left hand the lesser, long extinct,
Returning into light their weapons wield,
And breathe, and scribble on the pictur'd wall.

AND now the host, with living authors hem'd,
The various products of their sundry toils
Measures, and this he farther places, that
Self-nearer, all in merit's due degree,
Nor spares his mellow wine, nor dishes rare,
But, big of genius, and capacious heart,
He pours his treasures eatable on board,
And boon provokes his modest mates to pluck
The present favours of the bounteous Gods,
To celebrate glad carnivals, dissolve
The frozen obstacles of anxious life,
And heavy cares commit to sceptred heads.

At focios inter calices et libera menfæ

Gaudia fœcundæ paulatim pectora vatum

Prifcorum exemplis reficit, memoratque labores

Ingeniique fales, decus indelebile preli.

Mox animi dubios, tardofque in carmina laurus

Certatim fperare pares hortatur, et offert

Ipfe manu, jam nunc feri præfagus honoris,

Atque operas, Lucina, tuas, ac præmia fabris

Spondet Apollineis, meritorum haud immemor unquam.

Nec tantum famulos donis oneravit honeftis,

Officio functos, retulitque in luminis oras,

Æternæque potens devinxit opufcula famæ,

Quinetiam occlufos tenebris et carcere vates

Edidit in lucem, Phœboque reduxit aperto.

Ferte duci pia thura, chori, date lilia nymphæ

Hibernæ, pedibufque rofæ fubfternite flores,

Et

But, in the midft of heart–uniting cups,
And free fruition of the joyous board,
He feeds their fancies with examples fair,
Of antient Poets, and recounts their works
And wit, immortal honour of the prefs.
He then exhorts them, timorous of mind,
And flow to venture on the tafk, to hope
For equal bays, with rival rapture ftung,
And tenders with his own impartial hand,
Already confcious of their future claim,
Nor barely promifes Lucina's part,
But ample wages to his diftich–wrights,
Unmindful never of their high deferts.
Nor hath he loaded only his approv'd,
His faithful flaves with honourable hire,
Their infant Mufes ufher'd into light,
And bound their labours to eternal fame,
But alfo Poets, long confign'd to night,
And coop'd in prifon (editor divine!)
Republifh'd and reftor'd to face of Sun.

Ye grateful choirs, your pious tribute bring,
Hibernian nymphs, untainted lillies bear;
Strow rofy blooms beneath his fragrant feet,

And

Et ciines hederis, et baccare cingite frontem.

Salve gentis honos, Pindi facer incola, preli

Lux, et prima falus operum, et fpes ultima vatum,

Sis felix, crefcatque tuis annona tabernis

Libiorum, tectoque foras abeuntibus illis,

Succedant alii, neu defit copia menfæ

Cultorum, at paribus turgefcant horrea fcriptis.

Sint fine labe dies læti tibi, Neftoris anni,

Cumque fuprema dies maturum carpferit orbi,

Parte tui meliore recens, per fæcula vivas.

Tum patrii celebrent numerofo carmine vates

Ductorem, Phœboque ferant propioribus aftris,

Et, quoniam, ante omnes numeros miratus Homeri,

Omnia magna loqui didicit prius ore rotundo,

Marmore ftet Pario fculptus, tumuloque fuperftes

῎Ανϑ☙

And bind his locks with mantling ivy-wreaths,
And facred brows with circling lady-glove.
Hail, thou the nation's rifing ornament,
Divine inhabitant of Pindus, hail !
Light of the prefs, the prime preferver thou
Of poems, and the laft refort of Bards,
Be profperous, and may an annual ftock
Of books increafe to fructify thy fhops,
And, as thefe vended from thy manfion flit,
May new fucceed, nor let a crop of Bards,
Be wanting to thy board, but may thy defks,
The granaries of wit, with copies teem.
Gay days be thine, without a blot, thy years
Neftorean, fage, and when the final day
Shall pluck thee mellow from the weeping world,
Frefh in thy better part may'ft thou furvive.

LET Druids then in fweet Milefian lays
Extol their leader, and advance to ftars
Irradiate, nearer to his parent Sun,
And, fince, enamour'd with Mæonian ftrains,
Above all numbers, he had learn'd to roll
All matters grand with lofty tone rotund,
In Parian marble let him ftand erect,
High on his tomb, and dignify'd with Greek,

The

Ἀνθὸς ἐπιχθονίων, ὕμνων ἄγος οὐρανίωνων,

Θαῦμα Τυπογραφέων, βυλιφόρος ἄρχος ἐκήλυ

Εἰρίνης, ταμίης τὲ πολυφθόγγυ πολεμοῖο,

Θεῖος Ἀθηναίης θεράπων, μεγαθύμος ἀοιδῶν

Ξεινοδόχος, Μυσῶν τὲ φάος, Φοίβοιο τὲ κήρυξ.

FINIS LIBRI TERTII.

SPECULI

The flow'r of mortals, prince of song sublime ;

Mirror of Printers, arbiter of peace

Compos'd, and mouth of loud-tongu'd war profound,

Minerva's minion, godlike host of Bards,

Lamp of the Nine, and herald of their God.

The END of the THIRD BOOK.

THE

SPECULI POETICI

LIBER QUARTUS.

HACTENUS egregias dotes Herois, et artés
Ingenuas, capitifque vagos manuumque triumphos
Inque unum congefta virum tot munera Divom
Expofuiffe juvat.   Noftri metat ille laboris
Jam fegetes, laudifque fuæ præconia vendat.
Eloquii lucrique Deus, Pater annuat illi,

Et

THE

POETICAL MIRROR.

BOOK IV.

THUS far the Mufe with rapture hath reveal'd
　　The hero's excellence, ingenuous arts,
The flying triumphs of his head and hands,
And fuch a groupe of ornaments divine,
Heap'd on one mortal.　May he reap anon
The golden harveft of my toils, and be
The gainful herald of his own applaufe !
On him the God of eloquence and wealth

Et gemina furgens Parnaffus fronte virefcat

Hinc lauris, rubeat lætis hinc difcolor uvis,

Et (quantum imbelles audent fperare Camœnæ)

Sic vigeant Latio Graioque in carmine vires,

Et fubeant meritis, et alant per fæcula famam ;

Ut bonus ipfe lares comitum, ftabula alta Minervæ,

Dignatus toties opibus vultuque tueri,

Mollibus et paleis et puro ftramine lectos

Compofuit, Phœbique gregi pia pabula fudit.

At nos turba fumus, quos non cœnacula nudos

Mille tenent, nec mille queunt fatiare culinæ,

Quamvis quæque bovem macrorum in prandia pinguem,

Immolet, et cellæ veteres menfæque rotundæ

Turgefcant Cerere et Baccho, dominumque potentem

Faulknerum agnofcant ; quamvis captanda catervis

Æra pluat Sydneia manus, cunctique refurgant

Dorfetii,

Affenting fmile paternal, and for him
The facred hill, with double front elate,
Here bloom engreen'd with ever-living bays,
There blufh, impurpl'd with nectareous grapes,
And may the fpirit of his faithful Bard,
(High as my weak abilities afpire
Ambitious) kindle in proportion'd ftrains
Roman and Grecian, bear his weighty worth,
And feed through ages his unfated fame:
As he with wealth and countenance benign
Deign'd to defend the manfions of his train,
The lofty ftalls of Pallas, and compos'd
Their beds with gentle chaff, and cleanly ftraw,
And fother'd well Apollo's hungry herd.

   But we, the clan of authors, are a crowd,
Whom not a thoufand garrets can contain
Unclad, nor yet a thoufand kitchens cram,
Though each fhould facrifice a fatted ox,
To feed the meagre Vandals at a meal,
And antient cellars and Arthurian boards
Teem big with Bacchus and the jolly God,
And own a FAULKNER for the fplendid hoft:
Though Sydney's hand fhould rain upon the rout

Dorfetii, et patrio recalefcant pectora Phœbo;

Innumeri generantur enim prelumque fatigant

Pæonii paffim fabri, qui nocte dieque

Cantandi fervent ftudio, pronique recoctas

Rythmorum verfant maffas, et carmina cudunt.

Ast alii, mufa gravidi, partumque fub ægrum

Nummorum fteriles, et inanes vifcera victu,

Hinc atque inde ruunt excelfis arcibus oras

In liquidas cœli, furnofque et balnea crebri

Pervolitant: adeunt equites plebemque tributim;

Evolvunt, laudant, recitant fine fine labores

Injuffi, prenfifque manu cervicibus hærent,

Et latera obtundunt cubitis, plaufumque laceffunt,

Nunc his, nunc illis cunctantibus extorquentes.

Sin quem verficulis miferis rebufque beatis

Infanum arripiant, caput aggrediuntur opimum,

E:

Revolving treafure, and the total race
Of Dorfets rife, and all their bofoms glow,
Re-animated by their native God.
For numberlefs artificers of rhime
Byfshean fpring, and overload the prefs:
They night and day on batter'd anvils beat
The Runic mafs, and hammer verfes out.

    BUT others, pregnant with the Mufe, and bald
Of current cafh, and belly-timber void,
Juft in the nick of fickly-teeming time,
From lofty turrets into bare-fac'd light
Rufh diverfe, and itinerant through ftews
And baths fly flocking. Knights and commons they
By tribes accoft, their bulky works unfold,
Extol, unbidden without end repeat,
Cling to the collars of their hearers faft
With hands Harpeian, pound their paffive fides
With punching elbows, and provoke applaufe,
And now from thefe, and now from thofe extort.

    BUT if they feize a Bedlamite, poffefs'd
With wretched metre and a blefs'd eftate,
They keen attack the precious butt, foment

                             The

Et monſtrum vocale fovent, et carmine palpant,
Inque vicem illius tollunt ſuper æthera nugas :
Ingenii mirantur opes, mirantur acumen
Mentis, et in meritos generoſi pectoris æſtus.
Ille, quidem Aoniis jam captum retibus, auro
Se redimit, proditque Maro manumiſſus in ævum.

Quod ſi præcautum ventoſis laudibus inflent,
Fraternoque ideo poſcant poſito quaſi jure
Pio charis-captis fiat modo ſponſor amicis,
Aut (levius quod ſit) numerandum accomodet aurum
Aſſem deeſſe refert loculis, ac jure —— (ſiniſtre)
— Jurando diriſque ſacris et fœdere ſancto
Conſtrictum, ne ſe ſponſorem tradat habendum,
Quatenus ad nummos alienos attinet, ulli.
Caſtalii ſin fontis opes in rem fore credant,
Innumeros jam ſe numeros præſtare paratum.
Sic ait, atque ſuo gladio transfigit inermes.
Illi autem invicti dubio certamine perſtant

Acrius

The mufeful monfter, madrigal with rhime,
Then waft his tiifles to the very ftars,
Admire the riches of his eafy vein,
His tafte refin'd, and bounty-ftreaming heait
To merit.   Captive in Aonian toils,
He feals his ranfom with a golden fee,
And marches off, a Maro dubb'd for life.

But fhould they puff a poet-fcenting fox,
And by the right of brotherhood, as fix'd,
Demand, that he would kindly but become
Bail for his dear-arrefted friends, or launch
With greater eafe the money to be paid ————
He cries, he has not in his purfe a foufe,
Is bound befides unluckily by oath,
And imprecations, and a folemn vow,
In money matters never to be bail
For moital debtor.   But if they conceive
Coin from the mint of Phœbus can fuppoit
Their finking credit, he is ready now
To tell them numbers without number down.
He fays, and ftabs them naked with their own
Retorted weapons.   But unvanquifh'd they
In dubious conflict perfevere, and charge

(Since

Acrius (imperio quoniam vicina miniftrat
Verba ferox ac tela fames) obftantibus inftant
Cominus, et cunctos pro chartis rite quotannis
Edendis jam nunc —— jamdudum —— denique —— femper,
Seu vectigales, obfeffos dedere nummos
Solicitant, orant, impellunt, impete cogunt.

Nec mora curriculo linguæ, nec carminis ufquam
Auriculis requies: refonat chorus alter, et alter,
More gruum, vatefque premunt longo agmine vates.
Quam multæ noctu pendent laquearibus altis
Mufcarum foboles, foliifque virentibus hærent
Jam fub vere novo, quam multa examina ludunt
Solibus æftivis, et circum cymbia lactis
Plena alis ftrident, aut rauco murmure mellis
Obvolitant urnæ, roftrifque bibacibus ora
Contingunt: gentes fuccedunt gentibus atris
Aeriæ, prædamque petunt, pulfæque revertunt
Nectareum ad ftagnum: cantu domus intima muffat.

SED

(Since bold neceſſity, to might ally'd,
Supplies her ſons with eloquence and arms)
Oppoſing crowds with recollected heat,
Addreſs, implore, beleaguer, batter, ſtorm
All to ſurrender their invaded caſh,
As taxes duly levy'd by the year,
For old-new volumes —— to be publiſh'd now ——
Anon —— long ſince —— and finally —— for ay.

Nor pauſe to rapid vehicle of tongue,
Nor truce from poetry to glutted ears
Enſues: but chorus after chorus clangs,
Like vagrant cranes, deſcending from the clouds,
And Bards on Bards in long ſucceſſion preſs.
Thus numerous nocturnal flies depend
From vaulted roofs, and cling to verdant leaves
In orient ſpring; thus numerous the ſwarms
Sport in the Summer-ſun, and round the pails
Of foamy milk with ceaſeleſs pennons flap,
Or with hoarſe murmur hover o'er a crock
Of hoarded honey, and with tippling beaks
The ſurface kiſs : aerial tribes to tribes
Sable ſucceed, and ſeek the clammy ſpoils,
And, chac'd, return to ſip the candy'd ſweets:
The dairy deep rebuzzes to their hum.

Sed si laudis amor mentisque potentior aura

Æthereas foveant flammas, atque integer ipse

Frontis adhuc vates fugiat malegrata potentum

Tecta procul, Clariumque Deum testetur, et unum

Arte colat, Cyrrhæque Deas, et numen anhelet,

Horridus exuviis pannorum, in carmine magnos

Induit arma duces, ostroque insignit et auro,

Et vacuo Cererem, et sicco canit ore Lyæum.

Vos adeo, quos Phœbus amat, quibus ire per urbem

Forte datur, vescique libet, depromite vires

Ingentes animi; dubius pudor absit egenis,

Ingenuusque rubor, tremulæque infantia linguæ:

Quidlibet audendi præscripto jure poetis

Fas erat antiquis, maneatque nepotibus æquum.

Ast operi servate modum finesque Camœnis,

Stringite

But if lov'd praife and impulfe of the mind
Predominant fhould feed etherial flames;
If yet the Poet, chafte of front, fhould fly
The faucy manfions of the fordid great,
Confefs the God of infpiration, him
Alone invoke, and from his raptur'd breaft
The nymphs of Cirrha and their magic breathe,
He, rude in tatter'd regimentals, decks
Poetic heroes with refulgent arms,
Flufhes with purple, daubs with gold, and fings
Ceres with empty, Bacchus with dry mouth.

Ye therefore, whom Apollo loves, to whom
Perhaps is granted to pervade the town,
And feed free-booting, fummon to your aid
Affurance brazen; far from needy Bards
Be backward fhame, and diffidential blufh
Of merit, and the paufe of infant tongue.
Your antient Poets by prefcriptive right
Dar'd any thing, and let that privilege
In full fee-fimple to their heirs remain.

Yet fet fome meafure to your journey-work,
And limits to your lucubrations deep,

Nor

Stringite neu madido digitorum forcipe tædas,
Scriptando laffi jam nocte fub intempefta,
Qua volucres pecudefque tacent, et fœnora Drufo
Captitat in fomnis, ærifque obftertit acervo :
Nam capiti repetita nocent commercia Phœbi,
Pieriufque labor, feras productus in umbras,
Mortales hebetat vifus, oculifque ferenam
Sæpius obducit nubem, fenfumque fagacem
Raptorum, æterna tenebrarum nocte recondit.

Sin ftudiis oculi nimiis cultuque frequenti
Mufarum ægrefcant, minimum fi, cuncta tuentis
Æthereum per inane, jubar modo folis inertem
Perftringat miferis aciem, dubiaque revifat
Luce gravem, retinete globos cum fanguine faltem,
Et fævas vitate manus TAYLORIS et artes ;
Quippe ferox, lucique facræ Phœboque parenti
Jamdudum infeftus, lufcis mortalibus almum,
Sæpe diem eripuit, loculifque recondidit aurum,
Mercedem fceleris, curruque effugit ovanti.

Ast

Nor trim your lights with finger-fnuffers moift,
Fatigu'd with fcribbling in the dead of night,
When birds and beafts enjoy ferene repofe,
And Drufo catches in his greedy dreams
At cent per cent, and o'er his brazen bags
Unrefting flumbers; for the tuneful craft
And labour, lengthen'd into mid-night fhades,
Obftruct the vifual edge, o'er poring eyes
Induce a cloud tranfparent, and involve
The vivid fenfe, fagacious to difcern
The face of Catchpole, in eternal night.

  But if your eyes with over-care and pains
Inceffant ficken, if the fmalleft glimpfe
Of Sol, all-feeing through the liquid void,
Should touch your blunted organs, and with light
Dubious revifit, yet preferve from blood
The fightlefs balls, and fhun the cruel hands
Of couching TAYLOR and his cauftic arts;
For he, relentlefs and habitual foe
To facred light and her etherial fire,
From dim-ey'd mortals often hath purloin'd
The lovely day, and in his fob inclos'd
The golden fee, reward of guilty deed,
And fled fafe off on his triumphant car.

BUT

Ast illum tandem denſa inter nubila preſſit

Pœna ſequax, captumque dolis agitavit acutis :

Ipſe ſuis aris cecidit, propriaſque per artes

Juſtitiam agnovit feram, ſenſitque retortos

Felorum horrores et fumi vindicis iras.

Ventum erat ad ſedes almæ genetricis et arces

Muſarum antiquas, æternum pignus amoris

Virginei caſtique decus venerabile ſceptri.

Hic Taylor vatem, jamdudum lumina lippum,

Arripuit, fumoque acri ſubjecit, et orbes

Vertit, et invertit, crebris laniatibus actos,

Et ſalſis lachrymis mixtoque cruore fluentes

Punxit acu, et multo flagrantes lavit aceto

Sæpius incaſſum, prædaque potitus abivit.

At magis atque magis crudo creſcente dolore,

Et viſu, vates, et deficiente crumena,

                                                      Dira

But him at length, with murky clouds enwrapt,
Purſuing vengeance overtook, and ſtung
With agonizing ſtratagems : he fell
On his own altar, through his practis'd arts
Late juſtice he confeſs'd, and felt the rage
Of his own weapons, and the muſty wrath
Of tearful ſmoak, retorted on himſelf.

He fortun'd once to ſaunter through the ſhades
Of Alma-mater, and thoſe antient tow'rs
Rear'd to the Muſes, everlaſting pledge
Of virgin love, and venerable pride
Of chaſte Eliza's ſcepter-wielding hand :
Here boaſtful TAYLOR ſeiz'd a blear-ey'd Bard,
Afflicted long, and undertook to cure:
His tender orbs he fumigated, turn'd,
Inverted, butcher'd, prick'd with pointed ſteel :
Salt ſtreaming, ſanguine, flaming them he bath'd
With pungent vinegar, infus'd full oft
In vain, and 'ſcap'd ſucceſsful with his prey.

But now the malady, raw-red, encreas'd
Still more and more, while ſight and caſh decreas'd :
The Poet mutters execrations, brays

The

Dira fremit ; terram tundit pede, pectora pugnis

Pulfat, inops animi, furiifque ardefcit acerbis,

Et fefe ultorem ftatuit : molitur honeftas

Infidias, medicoque fidem mentitur amicam,

Indicitque diem fubeundi callidus artes

Tabificas memoratque horam notumque cubile.

Jamque dies feralis adeft, Taylorque tepenti

Elapfus lecto, textum membra induit aurum,

Illufas virgis veftes, humerifque fuperbis

Injecit vivo fulgentem murice lænam,

Et capiti, argento cinctum radiante, galerum

Turrigero impofuit : nutant in vertice plumæ.

Nec vero inftantis latuerunt omina fati;

Nam (quod et ipfe videt) fumorum confcia cornix

Importuna domum fupra volat, atque caminum

Sæpe cavum roftro raptim petit, et ferit alis,

Atra

The floor with foot, his bosom beats with fists,
And raging, mad in bitterness of eyes,
With fury glows, and purposes revenge:
Plots not dishonest he contrives, and feigns
A blind dependance on the Doctor's aid,
Then, crafty, fixes on a certain day
Of undergoing scarifying arts,
And hour appoints, and anatomic room.

AND now the day, the dismal day had dawn'd,
And TAYLOR, flipping from his tepid couch,
Array'd his limbs in woven gold, with sprigs
Embroider'd robes, and o'er his shoulders proud
His costly cloak, with living purple bright,
Umbrageous cast, and on his tow'ring head
Don'd the cock'd hat, with radiant silver brac'd,
Broad-circling: nods the plumage on his crown.

Nor did the signals of approaching fate
Not then appear; for (what his eyes behold)
Conscious of smoak the warning raven flies
Oft o'er his house, his hollow chimney pecks
With eager beak, and flaps with angry wings,
Croaking vaticinal the black portents

Jam ftridet, mœftique canes in limine latrant,

Et fimul ipfe duas tranfverfas cernit avenas

Præ foribus, triviifque cadit ter lapfus et alte

Virgatas auro furas et ferica tingit,

Immundo ter crura luto, vifuque recepto

Quas illi fe tefte dedit vetus hofpes Eous

Regales equidem nugas, leve pignus amoris

Ter gemmas radiis varias liquidaque corufcas,

Luce, decus digiti, fœde inquinat ——

ILLE, tamen capitifque fui fraudifque togatæ

Immemor, at Proteus variæ non immemor artis,

Seu lupus impaftus barbatam currit ad efcam,

Urget iter, vatifque gradus ad limina tendit.

Cuncta

Of Gods incens'd: moreover, in his hall
Cats mewing fcream, and on his threfhold dogs
Bark, mournful howling, and before his door,
The very Doctor fees two crooked ftraws
Acrofs, and thrice he ftumbles, in the ftreets,
And falling thrice with fœtid ooze bewrays
His clocks, high-fprig'd with interwoven gold,
And filken hofen, and his ray-ey gems
Reflecting liquid light, his finger's pride,
Thofe very brilliants, which forfooth his good
Old Indian friend, the great Mogul, reftor'd
To fight, prefented, —— royal toys indeed, ——
Mere baubles —— trifling tokens of his love,
He blurrs defac'd ————————

YET he, forgetful of his precious head
And academic fraud, but, Proteus-like,
Forgetful never of his wily fhifts,
Keen as a pike, to catch the barbed bait,
Swift-gliding darts, precipitates his courfe,
And fteers directly to the Bard's abode.

P p 2

ALL

CUNCTA favent cœptis immitibus : oſtia belli

Cæci dura patent ; nitido circum ordine menſam

Stant tripodes, niveoque Ceres modo ſtructa caniſtro,

Quin et ahena, focis jam jam ferventia, et alma

Fictilium ſeries et Eoæ munera frondis

Arida concreto cannæ cum nectare lætum

Augurium oſtendunt ventri, pacemque per ædes.

ILLA, animi fidens, Taylor ſibi ſacra parari,

Jamque locum ingreſſus vacuum peragravit, et altos

Compoſuit vultus, pictaſque in pariete nymphas

Luſtravit, luſtrando gravem ſi falleret horam.

Nunc admiranti ſimilis, ſimiliſque ſcienti,

Arcanos volvit libros ; nunc ambulat anceps,

Vulnificaſque manus crudelibus improbus auſis

Accingit, mentemque lucri ſpe paſcit inani.

PROTINUS appenſo tacita dulcedine vultus

Objectat

ALL objects favour his inhuman fchemes ;
The rigid gates of blind fulphureous war
Expand their folds, and round the table ftand
Soft-feated ftools in elegant array,
And recent cates, in fnowy bafkets pil'd,
The bubble-boiling kettle on the hearth,
The China cups, and wither'd leafy birth
Of Indian fhrub, with reedy fweet, refin'd
And petrid, fpeak glad omens to his maw
Of matin meal, and through the manfion peace.

HE deem'd thofe rites devoted to himfelf,
And entring, travers'd through the vacant room,
Then grave compos'd a philofophic face,
And con'd with curious eye the painted nymphs,
That grac'd the wall, if conning he might cheat
The tedious time.   Now fedulous he turns
Myfterious volumes with important brow,
As much admiring, and not knowing lefs ;
And now he walks from fide to fide, and tucks
For bloody deeds his laniating hands,
And feeds his fancy with evanid gain.

ANON with fecret pleafure he confronts
The glafs appendent, faithful mirror clear,

And

Objectat speculo, veneresque recolligit oris,
Et stupet, alta tuens, et, se miratus in illo,
Stultum subridet, stultum subridet imago.

Cum subito juvenes, pulsi seu turbine venti,
Hinc inde irruere, et certatim cominus hostem
Fumigeri prensare trucem: pars brachia stringit,
Parsque pedes prendit; pars colla tumantia torquet,
Intenditque caput terrae, quam saepius ipse
Sanguine foedarat: qualis pollutus adulter
Caede Agamemnonia, merito correptus ibidem
Supplicia expendit: sic jura poetica poscunt.
" Obstupuit steteruntque comae, et vox faucibus haesit."
Haud secus, intentus, praedae, inter farris acervos
Ore trahit Cererem per limina tartareus mus,
Quem vigil incautum felis si forte per umbras,
Seu conspexit avis, sapienti sacra Minervae,
Latroni exiguo raptim involat ungue tenaci,
Luctanti incassum, et trepidanti mortis in ore.

JAM

And recollects the beauties of his face:
Amaz'd he gazes, and, adoring felf,
Fond ideot fmiles, fond ideot fmiles the fhade.

WHEN fudden rufh'd the fumigating band
With whirlwind rapture from their ambufcade,
And hand to hand with rival fury grafp'd
The baleful foe : fome bind his arms, and fome
Invade his feet; fome twift his tumid neck,
And bend his head averted to the ground,
The ground, which often he defil'd with gore,
Like bafe Ægyfthus, ftain'd with royal blood,
Seiz'd on the fpot of perpetrated guilt,
He fuffers penal, local vengeance due ;
For juftice, this poetic juftice claims.
Amazement ftruck him; upright ftood his hair;
His voice was tongue ty'd.   Thus, intent on prey,
With felon-fangs the fubterraneous moufe
Drags through his den the yellow-bearded grain,
Whom if Grimalkin, or the plodding bird
Of fage Minerva through the fhade hath 'fpy'd,
Swift on the puny pilferer it fprings
With clutching claw: the captive wretch in vain
Refifts, and trembles in the jaws of death.

Thr

JAM manibus pedibufque fimul funambulus hofti
Obluctatur atrox, finuatque volubile corpus
Huc, illuc; frendent dentes; cava lumina flammas
Subvolvunt; fpumis incandent ora coactis.

Tum vero ingentes fremebundus pectore ab imo
Effundit gemitus: refonant clamore feneftræ
Perculfæ, reboat paries, laquearia plangunt.
Sed quanto magis ille vias explorat et artes,
Illum fumigeri tanto magis acrius urgent,
Horrendifque premunt amplexibus, atque catenis
Quadrupedem in diverfa trahunt, jamque oribus horrent
Eumenidum, Stygioque choro tetra orgia ducunt.

Est vas confectum folido de pondere plumbi,
Crecavum et patulum vaftoque immane barathro,
Illuc immergi quod circum quernea veftis:
Quodque mathematici nequicquam fingere certant,

Undique

THE Doctor, train'd to brave the doubtful rope,
With hands and feet reluctant to the foe,
From fide to fide his pliant body writhes :
Fell gnafh his teeth ; his livid eye-balls flame ;
His jaws fierce whiten with envenom'd foam.

THEN heavy groans from hollow bofom deep,
With hoarfer murmurs intermix'd, he pours :
The rattling windows echo to the yell,
The walls rebellow, and the roofs rebound :
But ftill the more evafive arts he tries,
Him more and more the fumigators urge,
With horrible embraces clofe-comprefs,
And, tugging diverfe, drag by neck and heels
Indiffolubly bound ; and now they ftare
With fury-faces, and in Stygian choir
Their orgies lead, abominable rites.

A VASE there is, compact of folid lead,
Wide-yawning, broad, and vaft with hideous gulph :
An oaken cheft quadrangular, with brafs
Adorn'd, invefts the huge circumference,
And (what in vain philofophers contend
To hammer out) from every fide exact

Undique respondet centro, quadratque rotundum.
Hoc Superi (ut quondam cecinit divinus Homerus)
Qui neque frugiferæ vescuntur munere terræ,
Nec latices tibi, Bacche, sacros perque ora rubentes
Prælibant, nullo signarunt nomine ; at acri
Alvorum fremitu durisque laboribus acti,
Mortales Lasanum dixere, Ereboque sacrarunt.

Huc quicquid vates prædæ melioris adepti
Sunt noctu, læti Baccho, geniisque benigni,
Mercedes operum solidas mensæque ruinas
Mane ferunt, Ditique vovent, et rite refundunt.

Tertia jam plenos reparavit Cynthia vultus
Candida, dum frater radiis libamen opimum
Decoxit, levibusque dedit diffundere ventis,
Ambrosia dites, et odoros nectare, fumos.

Jamque duo juvenes immensis viribus ægre
Attollunt Lasanum, vasta sub mole gementes :

Alter

Respects the center, and the circle squares.
For this the Gods, who neither eat the fruits
Of earth, nor tipple face-inflaming wine,
(As Homer sings) no title have devis'd :
But mortals, tortur'd with embowel'd pangs
And knotty toils, a Close-stool have 'yclep'd,
And black devoted to the Stygian gloom.

WHATEVER dainty provender the Bards
By night have inlaid, gay with Bacchus boon
And pamper'd genius, hither by return
Of morn they bring, full wages of their toils,
Seraphic songs, and ruins of the board
They vow to Dis, and lowly bent refund.

Now silver Cynthia thrice had fill'd her orb
Repair'd, and Phœbus with concocting rays
Matur'd the rich libation, and inspir'd
The gentle Zephyrs to diffuse the fumes,
That breath'd Ambrosia, and with Nectar flow'd.

AND now two youths of mighty vigour scarce
Upheave the close-stool, groaning with the weight
Unwieldy, vast : another, whirling round

A masly

Alter anhelantem contorquens igne verucam

Humori immergit, ſtagnumque volatile volvit:

Fervet opus, ſtridet ferrum perque atria flamen

Fumiferam glomerat graveolenti turbine noctem.

Tum vero Taylor, monſtris exterritus atris,

Horruit, et, plenus fumi propioris odore,

Reddidit iratam proprio de gurgite Lympham:

Mox alvi collegit opes, et, murmure rupto

Clauſtrorum, intonuit, croceaque ruente procella

Bella canit, ſtimuliſque furens ultricibus ardet

Flamina flaminibus, fumumque repellere fumo.

Illi autem, indomiti crudo certamine Martis,

Et palmæ accenſi ſtudio prædulcis, hianti

Immergunt Laſano ſacrum caput, atque revolſum

Fumanti obtendunt auræ, ſtagnoque recocto

Perfundunt

A maſſy poker, ſtreaming liquid fire,
Deep plunges red into the darkſome lake,
And rolls the ſtagnate volatile abyſs ;
The work warm waxes, hiſſes loud the ſteel,
And, through the dome condenſing, ſpreads about
A glut of eſſence and a night of ſmoak.

The Doctor, frighted at theſe black portents,
Horrific ſhudder'd, and, replete with whiff
Of nearer odour, from his conduit-pipe
A cataract of angry water ooz'd,
Then quick collected his intrinſic force,
And with eruption from poſterior gate
Loud thunder'd ; ſudden as the ſaffron ſtorm
Tumultuous ruſhes, open war he ſings,
And, breathing vengeance, kindles to diſcharge
Blaſt againſt blaſt, and fume with fume repel.

But they perſiſting in the conteſt crude
Of Mars, and ardent for the glorious prize,
Incentive ſweet, his votive head immerge
With rapid impulſe into myſtic mouth
Of gaping ſtool, and thence retracted hold
Incumbent o'er the ſmoaky breeze exhal'd,

Perfundunt nares, et inungunt lumina nardo.

Et jam cultra tenent, et acuto fpicula ferro

Dira vibrant, trepidumque metus ferit acrior illum.

Ter conatus erat perrumpere vincula, terque

Concidit, ac tales effundit pectore voces,

Ingeminans tremulas nafo crifpante querelas.

" Heu ! quoniam de me fceleratas fumere pœnas

" Stat vobis, fixaque fedet fententia mente,

" Nec lachrymæ profunt quidquam, nec vota jacenti,

" Per genium obteftor, per caftæ Palladis arces,

" Et Phœbi choreas et fpem furgentis Iernes,

" Ne laurus, ne (quæfo) manus maculate cruore

" Plebeio ingenuas : procul abfit luridus Alma

" Matre furor, mœftifque reis patefiat Afylum

" Mufarum, et placidis requiefcant fedibus offa,

" Exagitata malis. Extremas deprecor iras :

Sin

With hoary tribute, twice concocted, they
Perfume his nofe, and eyes anoint with nard.

AND now they grafp deftructive knives, and wield
Fell bodkins, pointed with terrific fteel.
Him panting, trembling, keener horror fmites:
Thrice he effay'd to burft his chains, and thrice
He fell, and pour'd thefe accents from his breaft,
In doleful dirges through his curling nofe.

" Alas! fince cruel you decree my doom,
" My pains the purpofe of your fettled mind,
" Nor tears, nor vows your fupplicant avail,
" I low conjure you by your genial God,
" By chafte Minerva's venerable tow'rs,
" The train of Phœbus and the rifing hope
" Of old Ierne, never ftain your bays,
" Oh! never, never your ingenuous hands
" With blood plebeian: far be favage rage
" From Alma Mater: let the Mufes grant
" An open refuge to the fons of woe,
" And let thefe ill intreated bones obtain
" Repofe in gentle fhades.   I deprecate
" Your utmoft wrath.   But if I have deferv'd

Severer

" Sin merui graviora, fago ferar ales in aftra

" Raptus ab excuffo ; jactu date membra cloacam

" In mediam ; puteo fubmergite nuda rigenti,

" Exantlate minas, capitique infundite pœnas :

" At pueri, ne, grande nefas ! ne, flebile vifu !

" (Horrefco referens !) partes abolete viriles,

" Quæ mihi turgefcunt venturæ femine famæ

" Nunc olim, et nondum genitis Tayloribus ardent.

" Deliquere manus : manibus celerate furores,

" Et faltem innocuæ crudeles parcite vefti.

" Sed quid fata parant? quid torres ? tela quid ifta?

" Ardentes cohibete faces, avertite ferrum.

" Jam furiis accenfus agor, jam Tartara fpiro,

" Sit mifero fpatium, puræ modo fpiritus auræ.

Dixerat, inque atros abierunt verba vapores :

Vindice flammarum Enceladus fic fornice fumum

Nubigenam evomuit tetramque bitumine noctem,

Ingemuitque

" Severer vengeance, lofty let me fly
" From well-tofs'd blanket; headlong into jakes
" Infernal caft me ; naked into pond
" Congealing plunge me; all your threats exhauft,
" And difembogue your tortures on this head
" But do not, youths —— (inhuman to be done!)
" O! do not —— (lamentable to be feen!
" I dread to tell ——) my privities unman,
" That fwell with feeds of future-blooming fame,
" And pregnant glow with Taylors unbegot.
" My hands have finn'd: againft my guilty hands
" Your fury wing, and fpare my fpotlefs garb ——
" But what prepare the deftinies ? what mean
" Thofe baleful brands? thofe weapons what ? with-hold
" Your flaming links: avert the deadly fteel.
" The fiends, foul fiends now carbonade me; now
" I fuck Avernus : give me, wretched me,
" An ell, an inch-room —— but a breath of air".

He faid, and flitted into fmoak his words.
Thus huge Enceladus from lab'ring womb
Of red volcano's belch'd fulphureous globes
Of cloudy vapours, and a pitchy night;
While, high incumbent on the fon of earth,

Vol. I.   R r   Deep

Ingemuitque imis radicibus infuper Ætna.
I nunc, et demens vanos effare triumphos :
Ex fumo effulge; tibi te geftire licebit
Omnibus et lippis notum ac tonforibus effe.

Tuque adeo Juvenis, cujus fortiffima dextra
Luminibus patriis monftrum exitiale fubegit
Tu novus Alcides (fi quid mea carmina poffunt)
Immortalis eris, mixtufque heroibus heros.

Interea miferis jampridem vatibus hofpes
Vitam agis in patriis, haud unquam degener arvis,
Mercurio Phœboque potens ; tibi ridet in aula
Bacchus et æqua Ceres, Phœbique impune forores
Carmine folicitas, viridique recumbis in umbra.

At nos, ingenii confifi viribus ægris,
Plorandum induimur foccum ; rifumve cothurno
Moturi tragico ; blanda fpe divitis auræ
In fcenam irruimus rapti, cæfofque tyrannos

Cædimus :

Deep from her bafe Trinacrian Ætna groan'd.
Go, frantic, now, and publifh in gazettes
Thine empty triumphs, brighter out of fmoak
Arife exulting ; boaft acquaintance free
With blear-ey'd coblers and with barbers-boys.
And thou, O youth, whofe daring hand fubdu'd
The monfter, fatal to Milefian eyes,
Thou (if thefe verfes aught avail) fhalt fhine
A new Alcides in the page of fame,
And hero mix'd with heroes eterniz'd.

MEAN-WHILE, old hoft, and ftill the trufty friend
Of needy Poets, on paternal fields
Thou liveft, undegenerately frank,
Not lefs by Hermes than Apollo blefs'd :
On thee bright Bacchus in the focial hall,
And Ceres, faithful to thy merit, fmile :
You court the Nine in meafures unreftrain'd,
And reft, reclin'd beneath the verdant fhade.

BUT we, relying on the fickly force
Of genius, wear the comic fock full fad,
Or ftrut in bufkins tragically gay ;
We rufh with rapture on the ftage, depofe

Tyrants

Cædimus: ætherio juvat infanire theatro,

Et fuperos agitare Deos, et tollere manes:

Tigna, fono difiupta, tonant, trepidantque ruinis.

Splendida fin mufam paupertas fallat hiantem,

Ceu tenues umbræ, circumvolitamus odores

Ambrofios animis, et lauto carmine cœnas

Pingimus aerias, cantufque ciemus inanes.

Nos adeo fatuus Parnaffi decipit ignis:

Te fequimur, Fortuna, leves; te prendimus, acres

In fomnis: at tu, tardis mortalibus alma,

Serpis humi, et fuperas fugis indignata Camœnas.

Quin tandem, tu Diva, tui (nam te quoque vates

Agnofcunt, dominamque colunt) miferere clientis;

Fulgentes huc flecte oculos; huc tende feraces

Grata manus, et nos aurato numine cinge.

Ponam aras, caftaque manu tibi rite Sacerdos,

Dona

Tyrants depos'd, and bravely flay the flain;
In airy theatre we ranting rave,
Pull down the Gods, and conjure up the fiends:
The burfted rafters of the garret roar
With vocal thunder, and with ruin quake.

But fhould fome fplendid interval of want
Deceive the gaping Mufe, like fubtil fhades,
In thought we flutter round ambrofial fteams,
In dainty verfes elegantly drefs
Unreal feafts, and empty fongs excite.
Thus we, mifled by wild poetic fire,
Thee, Fortune, light purfue, thee greedy grafp
In dreams: but thou, to tardy mortals kind,
Low-crawling fpurneft at the Nine aloft.

Yet thou, O Goddefs! (for the Poets thee
Confefs, and hail their arbitrary queen)
At length thine eyes bright-beaming hither turn,
Indulgent hither ftretch thy fruitful hands,
And with thy golden deity defend
Thy poor petitioner.   To thee fhall I
Erect an altar, and thy ritual prieft,
Frefh incenfe bearing with officious hand,

Shall

Dona ferens, puri primos Heliconis honores
Libabo: specie cedet Cytherea, triformis
Diva pudicitiæ dono florente, Minerva
Artibus, ingenio Pœan, tibi robore Mavors.

Tum vastos terræ tractus cœlique rotundos
Complectere polos animo, tibi tempora lætæ
Serpentes lambent hederæ, æternumque virebit,
Et Fortuna mei prostabit fronte libelli.
Aut si Castalia fervet prurigine pectus,
Quicquid composui vestri, Dea, protinus esto.

Nunquam audis ingrata preces? ergo irrita ventis
Vota cadunt? pereunt calami? membrana per annos
Invigilata jacent, blattis epulanda malignis,
Dum nos atra fames premit intra limen iniquum?
Ante diem letho comittam scripta? parentis

Sin

Shall dedicate the due libation prime
Of pure Pierian : Cytherea then
To thee shall yield in elegance of mien,
·Sequester'd Dian in the rosy gift
Of continence, the spinster-queen in arts,
In genius Pæan, and in valour Mars.

THEN shalt thou measure with Newtonian wand
The vast circumference of pendent earth,
Deep in thy mind the starry pole sublime :
Fond ivy, creeping in ambitious wreaths,
Shall kiss thy temples, and, for ever green
In science, Fortune shall adorn my book,
And in the front fair patroness appear:
Or if thy bosom with Castalian itch
Should, goddess, glow, whatever verses I
Have manufactur'd instantly be thine.

WHAT ? hear'st thou not ungrateful ? must my vows
Fly vagrant with the winds, my pens be lost ?
My written rheams, the watchful work of years,
Neglected lye, to feast malignant moths,
While hunger goads me, coop'd in narrow cell ?
Shall I commit my labours to grim death,

Before

Sin magis ipfe, pii partes defendere præfens,

Ingenuos cerebri curarim tollere fœtus?

Ac tandem ediderem lætas in luminis oras,

O! quale hofpitium mifero mihi denique reftat?

Quæ vos fata manent, noftri pars charior, œftro

Tot concepta facro, ferventes carmina furnos

Atque fepulchrales raptim vifura cloacas?

Hei mihi! væ vobis! heu, longum per mare ductæ

Aoniæ merces, duroque in littore fractæ

Spes vatum, et nulli procerum quæfita fupellex!

Sic nos infanis queremonia fundimus auftris;

Sic foliti tranfire dies.   At nox ubi denfa

Telluris gremium fufcis amplectitur alis,

Mortalefque monet dulci Jovis ira Lyæo

Triftitiam eluere, et crepitanti fulgure ligni

Solvere frigus iners, mœftaque fugare tenebras,

Defertum exilis dubio nec lumine tæda,

Nec

Before their deſtin'd day ? but if, reſolv'd
To play the pious, tender parent's part,
I ſhould ſupport the children of my brain,
And bring the brood Grubbean into light,
O! what reception ſhall I meet abroad,
Unhappy pilgrim ? what diſaſtrous ends
Await you, verſes, dearer part of me,
So many verſes delicate, conceiv'd
In higheſt rapture, doom'd to viſit quick
Hot, ſingeing ovens and ſepulchral jakes ?
Ah, wretched ſcribe! ill fated lines! alas,
Aonian venture, through tempeſtuous ſeas
Far-fetch'd, and wreck'd upon the rocky ſhore!
The hopes of Bards irrevocably daſh'd,
And not one bidder for the broken wares!

Thus to the winds we vent our plaintive cries :
So paſs my days.   But when nocturnal ſhades
This world invelope, and th' inclement air
Perſuades men to diſſolve benumbing cold
With pleaſant wines, with crackling blaze of wood
To cheer the melancholy-brooding gloom,
Me, lonely ſitting, nor the glimering light
Of make-weight candle, nor the joyous talk

Nec lepido fermone levat jucundus amicus
Me tacitum! innixus cubito, folufque fub umbris
Sufpiro horrendis, per mentem plurima volvens:
Seu carmen, renuente Deo, lachrymabile condo,
Umbriferofque cano lucos et myrtea tecta,
Aut ftrepitantis aquæ malefanam in margine nympham,
Aut dependentem ramo Damona faligno,
Et nodo fidi devinctum vindice amoris.

Interea vero fitis infatiata laceffit
Nequicquam ardentem, Divofque in vota vocantem:
Non etenim ficcis folamen faucibus affert
Quis Deus, aut dulci declinat lumina fomno:
Quinctiam fi forte graves fopor irriget artus,
Mens turbata, vigil, ftudio ftimulata bibendi,
Aerios calices, volitantia pocula Zythi
Caftalii captat: linguam tactura fubinde
Ludit imago avidam, et rictus fruftratur hiantes.
Continuo fomni vinclis excuffus amœni,
Ufque furente fiti, flammis accendor eifdem,
Incufoque Deos, umbram execratus inanem.

Vivitur

Of loving friend delights; diſtreſs'd, forlorn,
Amidſt the horrors of the tedious night
Darkling I ſigh, with heavy head reclin'd
On elbow-prop, and feed with diſmal thoughts
Mine anxious mind, or ſome times mournful verſe
Indite, and ſing of groves and myrtle ſhades,
Or deſperate lady, near a purling ſtream,
Or ſhepherd, pendulous from willow-tree
In vengeful nooſe, the faithful lover's knot.

MEAN-WHILE I labour with eternal drought,
Burning in vain, and hoarſe for liquid aid
The Gods invoking; for no God affords
Drop to my lips, or to mine eyes repoſe:
But if a ſlumber haply ſhould invade
My weary limbs, my reſtleſs fancy ſtill
Awake, diſtracted, ſtung with luſt of drink,
Tipples imaginary pots of ale,
Caſtalian viſion, that, in act to touch
My fervent tongue, deluſive bobs about,
And tantalizing mocks my gaping jaws.
Releas'd from chains of placid ſleep, anon,
With raging flame I find the ſettled thirſt
Still gnawing, and the ſapleſs phantom curſe.

S ſ 2

Thus

Vivitur hoc pacto grato sine munere vitæ,
Nec quos maturis decoxit solibus æstas,
Degustare mihi fructus licet, haud melimela,
Haud vestita genas lanugine persica molli
Poma, nec hirsuto juglandes tegmine scabras,
Nec regum vos digna, Deum vos mespila mensis,
Ambrosias epulas, dulcesque putredine succos!

Hæc mala magna quidem, verum et graviora sequuntur:
Immites hyemis pluvias gelidasque pruinas
Et ventos perpessa diu, femoralia tandem
(Quid non vincet edax ætas) ætate peresa,
Rupta pelle, patent: hiat immedicabile vulnus.
Deplorandum, ingens, vastaque immane ruina!
Qua data porta, feri rauco cum murmure venti
Una Eurusque Notusque ruunt, Boreæque tumultus,
Qui cronios nectit glaciali compede fluctus,
Ingruit: incursant maletutis clunibus agmen
Acre procellarum et spirantia frigora febres.
Mercibus haud aliter variis onerata carina
Barbaricoque auro pontum domitrix Ægeum
Ioniumque diu secuit, Lylibeia donec

Littora

Thus do I live from pleasure quite debarr'd,
Nor taste the fruits, which summer-sunny rays
Mature, John-apple, nor the downy peach,
Nor walnut, in rough furrow'd coat secure,
Nor medlar-fruit, for monarchs a desert,
For Gods a feast, delicious in decay.

Afflictions great! yet greater still remain:
My galligaskins, that have long withstood
The winter's fury, penetrative rains,
A-slant impell'd, and keen encroaching frosts,
By time subdu'd (what will not time subdue ?)
The lining rent, immedicable wound,
An horrid chasm disclose, with orifice
Wide, discontinuous; gates, at which the winds
Eurus and Auster, and the dreadful breath
Of Boreas, that congeals the Cronian waves,
Tumultuous enter, and my buttocks bare
Assault, loud, mutinous, with chilling blasts
Portending agues. Thus a ship full-fraught
With wares choice, various, and Barbaric gold,
Long sail'd secure, or through th' Ægean deep,
Or mad Ionian wide; 'till cruising near
The Lilybean shore, with hideous crash

On

Littora fubradens, freta pervolet, inque Charybdin
Horrendam fremitu, rapidaque voragine Scyllam
Irruat intortam, fcopulifque illifa refultet :
Nec tanti fufferre valet certaminis ictum,
Quin coctis ilex inimicum amfracta cavatis
Imbibit humorem : ventis agitata tumefcunt
Æquora fævifonis : nautas ferit uvidus horror ;
Defixis torpent oculis ; mors infidet ori :
Torrentem eliciunt, malorum robora cædunt,
Vela trahunt, diras effundunt, numina, votis
Adverfata, vocant. Undæ volvuntur in undas
Præcipites : fletur, gemitur, difcurritur, actum eft !
Alta fremunt, cœlum ruit, ingeminante procella :
Puppis, aqua revoluta, jacet fub gurgite vafto.

Haud terris leviora manent difcrimina vates
Jactatos, merfofque malis, clauftrifque gementes
Tectorum anguftis. Animo fine fructibus acri
Carpferunt flores : claris nihil artibus illis
Impendiffe diem, aut noctem invigilaffe Camœnis
Profuit : at rebus propriifque penatibus orbi,
Faftidiofa terunt nequicquam limina regum

Exclufi,

On vaſt Chaṙibdıs, horrid with hoarſe roar,
Or Scylla, rapid with voracious whirl,
She ſtrikes rebounding, whence the ſhatter'd oak,
So fierce a ſhock unable to ſuſtain,
Admits the brine in at the gaping ſides :
The crowding waves, guſh, with impetuous rage,
Reſiſtleſs, overwhelming ; horṙors damp
The mariners, death in their eyes appears :
They ſtaṙe, they lave, they pump, they ſwear, they pray,
(Vain efforts ¹) waves, high-rolling over waves,
Ruſh headlong in, implacable amidſt
Laments, confuſion, anguiſh and deſpair.
The deeps rebellow with redoubled wrath,
The tempeſt howls, 'till, delug'd by the foams,
The ſhip ſinks, foundṙing in the vaſt abyſs.

    Not lighter perils Bards attend, on land
Toſs'd overwhelm'd, and groaning with a tide
Of evils in the ſtreights of airy cells.
They with ambitious appetite have pluck'd
Unfruitful flourets to have toil'd the day
In gentle aṙts, and watch'd the muſeful night
Them ṅought avaıls ; with fortune unendow'd,
Unhous'd, they wear the threſholds of the gṙeat

Exclufi, retroque pedes per devia tendunt

Rura fenes· duris illufi carmina paffim

Rupibus et furdis effundunt vota procellis.

O Patria! O, quondam Druidum domus inclyta divis,

At fævis jam fracta malis, oppreffa minorum

Jamdudum imperiis dominorum, et fordida luxu,

Hofpitio nec læta facro, nec amica Camœnis

Dulcibus! ecqua graves abrumpet meta labores ?

    Hæc ubi mufea nuper modulabar in arce,

Gratior occubuit laffo mihi fomnus, et, ecce !

Vifus adeeffe puer, fragrantes rore, capillos

Concuffit, cytheraque humerum fufpenfus eburna,

Divinum explicuit frontem, et fic ora refolvit.

" Parce piis lachrymis, et inanes pelle querelas ;

" Nuncius ipfe Deum et Genius telluris avitæ

" Advenio, nec te pigeat fubiiffe laborem

" Vocalem ; at pudeat cœcæ venalia Divæ

" Caftra fequi, curruque rapi fulgente, virumque

                    " Frontibus

In vain, excluded, and in life's decline
Wander through pathlefs wilds, there figh their ftrains
To rigid rocks, and vows to heedlefs winds.
O native foil ! O whilom the domain
Of Druids, fam'd for venerable faints,
But broken now with cruel evils, crufh'd
By petty tyrants, fordidly profufe,
Nor gaily prone to hofpitable rites,
Nor to the tuneful fifterhood benign !
Alas! what goal fhall terminate our toils ?

WHEN lately thus in meditative fort
I chanted, fleep with fweet oppreffion lax'd
My wearied limbs, and lo! methought, a youth,
Approaching fhook his azure locks, that breath'd
Ambrofial dew, while on his fhoulder hung
An iv'ry harp : his countenance divine
He full difplay'd, and in thefe accents fpake :
" Reftrain thy pious tears, thy vain complaints
" Hence banifh ; I, the meffenger of Gods,
" And guardian genius of this antient ifle,
" Arrive ; nor thou renounce the tuneful toil ;
" But blufh to follow fortune's venal camp,
" Rapt by the fplendor of her gaudy car,

" Frontibus indignis viridantem obtendere laurum,

" Et fontem inceſtare ſacrum, et ſcelerare Thaliam."

Tuque adeo cœlo gens acceptiſſima puro,

Et regum Divumque parens uberrima pridem,

Filia cœruleæ divinitus Amphitrites,

Orbis opes complexa ſinu, pulcherrima magnæ

Tu ſoror Albionis, genus aſſere: jam tibi priſca

Maddeniam tendente manum pietate reſurgis:

Nos etiam auſpiciis melioribus, ecce! videmur

Per lucos errare pios, valleſque, ſerenis

Fontibus irriguos, puroſque recentibus auris.

Qui novus attonitas mentes ferit impetus? unde

Lætus ubique chorus? revireſcit laurea Phœbi;

Jamque tot annorum video clareſcere nubem

Luctificam, et rerum jam panditur aureus ordo.

O clarii ſpes alta Dei, lux advena tandem

Gentis Ierneæ, decus ingens Angligenarum!

In terras iterum deducens æthere Divam

Aſtræam,

" To dedicate thy never-fading bays
" To worthlefs heads of mortals, and pollute
" The facred fpring, and defecrate the Mufe."

AND thou, chafte nation, deareft to the fkies,
In elder days, of kings and demi-gods
The fruitful mother, daughter of the main
Broad-circling, nurfing in thy gentle breaft
The world's wide opulence, twin-fifter thou
Of great Britannia, faireft of the fair,
Affert thy race: thou re-arifeft, borne
To priftine piety by MADDEN's hand:
With better omens now we feem to ftray
Through pious groves, and verdant vallies, bath'd
With lucid ftreams, and pure with fanning gales.
What fudden rapture ftrikes our ravifh'd minds?
Whence all around the glad-confenting fong?
Apollo's bays with greener pride revive;
And now I fee the gloomy cloud of years
Brightning a-pace, a golden age reveal'd.

O THOU ! the Poets rifing hope, at length
Hibernia's borrow'd light, Britannia's boaft,
Conducting bright Aftræa from her orb

Aſtræam, non aſper ades : cape debita dextræ

Fræna diu, meritiſque datos maturus honores

Aggredere, O, lætæ cuſtos fidiſſime gentis !

HAUD mora, Pierides in honeſtæ prælia laudis,

Te propiore, pias audebunt edere voces

Altius indigenæ. Quamvis hinc inde tyranni

Arma fremant horrenda, faces et funera paſſim,

Lenibus imperiis et amœna pace fruemur

Dumque faves, caſtiſque choris Helicona recludis,

Certatim ediſcent claris majoribus orti

Exhaurire ſacros latices: divinior illos

Ardor aget, patriæque novo ſtimulabit amore.

QUINETIAM tellus, jampridem ignota colono,

Exuet ipſa feros habitus, cultuque nitebit

Dum Cererem culmo mirabitur incola læto

Turgentem,

To vifit earth, propitious hither come,
Affume the reins of delegated fway,
Long fitted for thine hand, and ripe approach
Thofe princely honours, on thy merits high
Conferr'd, moft faithful guardian of our ifle.

HER tuneful train beneath thy prefence, fir'd
With rival thirft of honeft fame, fhall dare
To raife their pious notes, nor brook delay.
Though lawlefs tyrants fierce on ev'ry fide
Threat hideous arms, wide-wafting flames and death
Promifcuous, we ferenely fhall enjoy
Thy mild commands, and pleafurable peace.
And, while thou fmileft, and unlockeft pure
Thy native Helicon to veftal choirs,
The noble youth, with emulation fmit,
Shall quaff the facred ftream ; diviner heat
Shall rouze, and fting them with a patriot flame.

THE barren glebe, long ftranger to the plough,
Shall caft her favage garb, and cultur'd fmile;
While, flufh'd with joy, the peafant fhall admire
Glad Ceres, fwelling in the milky ftalk,

And

Turgentem, et conjux, telas meditata futuras,

Linigeram afpiciet fegetem viridemque Minervam.

Inter telorum ftrepitus bellique procellas

Ipfe potens animi dabis aurea munera genti,

Jura fidemque viris et honorem, labe carentem.

Haud aliter Mofes, divino numine quondam

Præmonitus, terræ potiores duxit alumnos

Per ferri fylvam et rutilantes ignibus enfes,

Conftituitque gradum fola fub rupe viator;

Lumina tum cœlo affixit, virgaque rigentem

Percuffit filicem: fons effluit; ægra falutem

Gens ftupefacta bibit. Foliis arbufta virefcunt

Arida; vere novo fcopulofa cacumina rident.

Forsan et affurgens aliquis felicibus aufis

Te canct, et rerum dictis æquabit honorem

Crefcentem

And his gay confort, weaving in her mind
The future web, unfated fhall furvey
The linten harveft and Minerva green.

AMIDST the din of arms and ftorms of war,
Of fpirit mighty to the nation thou
Shalt golden gifts impart, and to her fons
Juft laws, firm faith, and honour void of ftain.
Thus erft, admonifh'd by the voice divine,
The prophet led the chofen feed through woods
Of horrent fpears, and flame-reflecting fwords,
And ftopp'd his pace, a fojourner, beneath
The dreary rock; then up to heav'n he caft
His ardent eyes, and fmote the rigid flint
With potent rod: a fountain gufhes forth;
The fickly pilgrims with amazement drink
Refrefhing health; the wither'd brambles bloom;
With fudden fpring the craggy defart fmiles.

AND haply thee fome Bard, with bolder flight
Soaring, fhall fing, with everlafting lays
Shall match the growing glories of his theme,

And

Crefcentem æternis, gratique per oppida cives
Veridicas recinent laudes, STANHOPEAQUE regna.

Tum vero, egregiis præpollens artibus, alma,
Te, Mater, FREDERICE canet, teque aufpice fundet
Mentis opes, decorifque tui monumenta per orbem,
Et magnum agnofcet generofa in prole parentem,
Regificumque jubar. Nec te, GULIELME, tacebit,
Quem Galli tremuere truces, quem marte tonantem
Jam nunc, et belli volventem pectore molem
Immanem impubi, verfis infignibus, hoftes,
Bis perjura cohors ! patriis in montibus horrent.

Rupibus atque dolis nequicquam imbellibus illi
Confifi, rabida arma gerant, fictique tyranni
Nomen inane crepent. Coeant in fœdera Galli
Fœdifragi; fervile jugum minitentur Iberi.

Te

And grateful tribes through joyful towns repeat
Unfabled praises, and a STANHOPE's reign.

THEN loyal Alma, fraught with arts refin'd,
Thee too shall found, O FREDERIC, and, cheer'd
Beneath thy sanction pour her mental wealth,
Wide through the world diffuse thy rising fame,
And in the son beneficent confess
The godlike father, and the royal beam.
Nor shall she not egregious WILLIAM hail,
At whose high name the Gallic legions fierce
Have trembled, whom, loud thund'ring through the field,
And deep revolving in his youthful mind
Th' unwieldy weight of war, the rebel band,
Twice perjur'd race, with recreant ensigns now
Far-flying dread upon their parent hills.

ON rocky dens and coward wiles in vain
Relying, let them brandish blades, and boast
Their idol, mock of majesty rever'd :
Let Gallia, faithless to religious leagues,
Be leagu'd with them in conspiration foul,
And proud Iberia threaten servile chains :

Te celfi genitoris honos, te libera virtus,

Freta Deo, patriæque falus per tela, per ignes,

Et, nivibus canos, et acerbos frigore, campos

Immifere ducem. Prifcorum interrite fanguis

Heroum, et regum genus inviolabile! faufto

I pede, frange minas, animos extingue rebelles :

Has tandem inferias umbræ refer ultor avitæ,

Cæfareumque decus geftis ingentibus auge.

Jam liceat prævifa loqui, jam carpere honores

Lauricomos, numerifque facris ornare triumphos,

Degenerem ut pariter moniti dedifcere morem

Terrarum procul hinc cives pia figna fequantur ;

Eque tuo gentes aveant haurire falutem

Fonte fuam, ferroque focos arafque tueri,

Aut fractas inter leges patriæque ruinas

Morte

Thee, princely chief, thy father's high renown,
Thee virtue free, dependent upon God,
Nor lefs thy country's fafety have allur'd
Through darts, through flames, and territories hoar
With wafteful fnows, and edg'd with bitter ice.
Undaunted blood of heroes and the feed
Of righteous kings, inviolable, go,
Propitious go, their threatful fury break,
The rebel-fpirits diffipating quench ;
Thefe victims offer with avenging hand,
As juft atonements to the grand-fire fhade
Of injur'd majefty, and aggrandize
Thine houfe paternal with illuftrious deeds.

Now let the Mufe what fhe forefees declare,
Now pluck victorious laurels, and adorn
Thy rifing triumphs with devoted lays,
That, warn'd to fhake unmanly bondage off,
Far diftant hence the citizens of earth
May catch the bright example, and attend
Fair freedom's banners, and ambitious thirft
To draw their fafety from thy fpring, with arms
Affert their civil and religious rights,

U u 2   Or

Morte frui, neu forte velunt fuperefle pudori.

Te mox, haud fractum furibundo turbine Martis,

Lætus Hyperboreis reducem pater almus ab oiis

Victorem accipiet: perfolvet debita frater

Vota Deo, caftaque choros cum conjuge fanctos

Templorum inftituet.　Greffum quafcunque per urbes

Tendis, inexpleto refonabunt compita plafu,

Plebefque procerefque regent veftigia fignis,

Haud incerta tuis.　Pelopæa per oppida qualem,

Monftrorum horrentem exuviis, fpoliifque fuperbum,

Magnum agnovérunt ultorem Thefea Graii

Hinc, inde innumeri: tacitis virtutibus ille

Incaluit, patrioque puer procul enfe refulfit.

Hos inter Britonum plaufus nec cedit amori

Gens Hiberna pio.　Fera prælia marmore vivo

Ardebunt,

Or in their country's ruin with her laws
Enjoy deſtruction, nor ſurvive their ſhame.

THEE ſoon, unbroken by the raging ſtorm
Of madding Mars, from Caledonian coaſts
Return'd with conqueſt ſhall thy ſceptred ſire
Gladly receive ; thy royal brother waft
His vows repeated to the King of Kings,
And gratulating with his conſort chaſte,
Bid loud hoſannas through the temples ring,
Devoutly joyful.   Through well-peopled towns
In long proceſſion as you paſs, the ſtreets
With mix'd applauſe inſatiate ſhall reſound
And denizens and potentates direct
Their faithful ſteps by thine.   As from all parts
The ſons of Greece innumerable flock'd
To ſee young Theſeus, rough with horrid hides
Of ſlaughter'd monſters, and elate with ſpoils,
And hail'd their great avenger, as he mov'd.
He conſcious glow'd with ſilent worth, and ſhone
The ſon, atteſted by the father's ſword.

NOR, while Britannia loud acclaims thy deeds,
Shall juſt Hibernia not approve her faith,

Ardebunt, alterque fremet Gulielmus in ære ;

Concordes animis dum te veneramur ovantes,

O Pater ! O Princeps, populos qui legibus æquis

Et pietate regis, pace auges, marte tueris !

Qui premis, immani gaudentes clade, tyrannos,

Imperii sine fine avidos, miserasque refulcis

Præsidio gentes ; qui bello vindice terras

Concutis infidas, pacemque per arma secutus

Consulis Europæ, et pelagi moderaris habenas.

Impavidos, spirante Deo, patriaque jubente

Hinc vocat aura duces, peregrinis fœta triumphis.

Hinc mercator, opes regum indignatus inertes,

Audet adire polos per inhospita syrtibus arva

Sulcat iter, gaudetque undis, fruiturque procellis.

Hinc

As truly loyal, and her love as warm.
In living marble fhall thy battles burn ;
In threatning brafs anothei William breathe.
While thee with joint affection we revere,
O Sire, O Monarch, who with equal laws
And piety doft rule, with peace enlarge,
With war defend the freely-fubject realms;
Who crufheft lawlefs tyrants, that rejoice
In favage flaughter, lufting for mifrule
Illimitable; but with guardian aid
Upheaveft nations from the depths of woe;
Who thund'ring fhakeft with avengeful war
Perfidious kingdoms, and, purfuing peace
Through rightful arms, confulteft the repofe
Of Europe, guiding with a dext'rous hand
The naval reins, that curb the wat'ry world.

WITH foreign triumphs pregnant, hence the breeze,
Jehovah's breath, and Britain's martial voice
Invoke the dauntlefs admirals to fea.
Of regal wealth's uncirculating ruft
Indignant hence, the merchant braves the poles,
Through fucking fands his doubtful journey plows,
Exults on furges, and enjoys the ftorm.

                                        Hence

Hinc artes crevere tuis.   Hinc India fluxit

In Thamesin, serisque recens Augusta triumphis

Jam splendet, lateque movens insignia regnat,

Heroum nutrix, regum domus, et caput orbis.

F   I   N   I   S.

ΦΑΥΛΚΝΟΓΟΝΙΑ.

Hence arts have flourifh'd ; for thy people hence
Hath India flow'd into the breaft of Thames,
Refplendent hence, with lofty trophies crown'd,
Augufta rifes, and difplays a-far
Her ftreaming glories, nurfe of martial fouls,
Domain of kings, and emprefs of the globe.

T H E   E N D.

ΦΑΥΛΚΝΗΡΟΓΟΝΙΑ,

προς τον το πανυ πρεσβυν

Σαμυηλην Μαδδηνον

ΜΟΥΣΑΩΝ Ελικωνιαδων θεραποντα Θεαων
Δεξιον, οτρηρον βαθεων δρηστηρα κυπελλων,
Τον ποτε ποιπνευοντα φιλοις ιερην περι κρηνην,

Και

FAULKNER'S NATIVITY.

I SING the vocal harbinger of wit,
And faithful flave of Heliconian dames,
Officious bearer of Caftalian cups
Capacious, miniftring with ready hand
To circling clients from the facred fpring
Delicious draughts, nor quaffing not fometimes
The cryftal, pure, enthufiaftic ftream
With lips as pure, infpiring, and infpir'd,

Apollo's

ORIGO FAULKNERIANA,

Ad reverendum admodum virum

SAMUELEN MADDENUM.

MUSARUM veterem famulum, fidumque clientem,
 Plena miniſtrantem ſociis, pariterque bibentem
Pocula, et ætherio fœcundas caimine lymphas,
                                        Fatidicum

FAULKNER'S NATIVITY.

I SING the minion of Aonian maids,
 Divinely warbling through the muſeful ſhades,
Egregious minion, with ſurpriſing art
Dextrous to play the buſy butler's part,
Diſpenſing bumpers to the ſocial ring
Of ſuppliant ſuitois from the ſacred ſpring,
And ſometimes tipling, ſuch the critic's claim,
A cryſtal portion of the magic ſtream,

X x 2

Apollo's

Και ποτε πινοντα κρυσαλλινον ενθεον υδωρ,

Δεινον Απολλωνος γηρυκα, περιδρομον ομφην,

Οιος εγερσιβοητος αδει δια νυκτος Αλεκτωρ,

Εγγυθεν ερχομενην δροσεραν ροδοδακτυλον Ηω,

Τοιον σαλπιγκτην εκαλητελελαομεν, αινων

Αξιον αεναων στοματων απο χαλκεοφωνων,

            Και

FAULKNER'S NATIVITY.

Apollo's awful oracle, exprefs
Itinerant, prædictive of the God
Approaching, as the crefted cock, enwrapt
In nightly fhades, proclaims the dewy dawn
Of rofy-finger'd morn, precentor meet
Of glowing rapture, worthy to be hymn'd
In brazen accents from according peal
Of tributary tongues, the champion bold
Of letter'd youths, effaying fong, whom thou,

        O Madden,

Fatidicum Phœbi comitem, Phœbumque canentem

Venturum, qualis gallus criſtatus in umbris

Præcinit Auroram rauca jam voce propinquam,

Dignum Cyrrhæo præconem numine, dignum

Laudibus æternis, et ahena voce ſonandum,

Magnanimumque

FAULKNER'S NATIVITY.

Apollo's herald awful, as his nod,
And loud præcurſor of the coming God,
Loud as the cock, whoſe monitory cry
Proclaims Aurora roſy-finger'd nigh,
Worthy præaudience, worthy choral praiſe
From clarion-tongues in ever flowing lays,
Undaunted champion of Athenian wards,
Imbibing arts, and budding into Bards,

Whom

Και προμαχον, Μαδδηνε, νεων μεγαθυμον ενισπω

Κεκροπιδων, ες αυτ⊙ αγων πολυδωρ⊙ Αθηνης,

Πατριδ⊙ ηδε πατηρ, πανδημι⊙, ηδε θεορτ⊙

Της αγαθης Εριδ⊙ χινητηρ κ̄ χορυφαι⊙

Εθρεψας, τιμητε ςεφεις, επ' αμεινονα θηγων

Γει 'χιαν καλην-τε φυην, Φαυλκνηρον αριςον

Φορμιζω· Συ δε Καλλιοπη τεκ⊙ ερανιων⊙

Μνημοσυνης,

FAULKNER'S NATIVITY.

O MADDEN, leader of ingenuous arts
Munificent, thy country's common fire
And vital genius, zealous to foment
The ftrife of glory, haft regal'd with food,
And crown'd with honours, whetting their innate
And foaring fancies to fublime attempts :
Faulkner I fing : and thou, feraphic Mufe,
Daughter of gay Mnemofyne divine,
Calliope, to whom thy father gave
To trace all nature, and in hymns extol

Gods,

Magnanimumque cano pugilem, fabrumque fagacem,
Crefcentem in vates, juvenum, quos ipfe per annos
Cecropii tutela Laris, generofa Minervæ
Progenies, patriæque pater communis, et aufpex
Te ftimulante Deo, pulchri certaminis auctor
Muneribus, MADDENE, foves, et honoribus ornas,
Quo magis ingenium, raptum ad meliora, refingas.
Faulknerum refero, tuque, O regina fororum,
Calliope, mihi lenis ades, placidiffima proles
Mnemofynes, cui cuncta Pater cognofcere pridem,

Et

FAULKNER'S NATIVITY.

Whom thou, O MADDEN, Alma Mater's pride,
Thy country's parent, and propitious guide,
Rous'd by celeftial energy to raife
A glorious conteft and a luft for praife,
With gifts haft gladden'd, and with honours grac'd,
To whet their genius, and refine their tafte.
Faulkner I fing : and thou, divinely fprung,
From bright Mnemofyne, for ever young,
Calliope, to whom thy facred fire
Gave to pervade all nature with thy fire,

And

Μνημοσυνης, η παντα Πατηρ, κατενευσε νοησαι,

Τυς-τε Θευς παιδας-τε Θεων υμνησιν αειρειν,

Τυ ἱενεην γονεας-τε, Θεα, κατα μοιραν αειδε·

Περιηθεν, αγυσα χορυς, αιεγειρε παλαιαν

Μοι κιθαριν, ψυχην-τε προχει θειαν δια μολπης

Ημετερας, τνειυσα μεν☉ βαθυδινον Ομηρυ,

Οιον

FAULKNER'S NATIVITY.

Gods, and the fons of Gods, explore his birth
And parents high with not inferior flight.
Defcending choral from Pierian hill
Awake thy fhell, and through my lays infufe
Unwonted vigour, breathing irreftrain'd
Ætherial heat, the torrent epic tide
Of deep-ton'd Homer: fuch, as on the fhore

The

Et fidibus celebrare Deos, puerofque Deorum,

Annuerat, fublime genus clarofque parentes

Rite viri memorare velim: tu, Diva, choreas

Huc age Pierias, citharamque ciere vetuftam

In numeros ne parce novos, quin verfibus affla

Indigenis ignefque facros, vatique furorem

Phœbeum altifoni, rapideque ruentis Homeri,

Ceu

FAULKNER'S NATIVITY.

And high extol in tributary lays
The Gods and heroes with peculiar praife,
In claffic juftice to thy client's name,
His myftic birth and parentage proclaim,
And, foft conducting the Pierian quire,
Revive the magic of thine antient lyre;
Infufe, O Goddefs of the tuneful throng!
Celeftial fpirit through my native fong,
The foul of Homer, burfting into found,
Sublimely folemn, rapidly profound,

Οιον εν αιγιαλω πολυ μαινεθαι ευρει ποντυ
Ιχαριοιο Θεν☾ τ' ανεμοτρεφες, η Κρονιοιο,
Τοις-τε κυλινδομενοις εθι κυμασι κυματα βαλλει,
Δεινον αρει, δεινον δε πεσον κατεραξεν ολυμπον.

Τον δε, κασιγνητη Τιτανων οβριμοεργων,
Μυνογονον γαιης υπο κευθεσι γεινατο Φημη,
Πλεξιππων η κεντρον αγων, κỳ οπηδ☾ αεθλων,

Ουκ

FAULKNER'S NATIVITY.

The vaſt Ionian, or the Cronian main,
Vex'd by the winds, tumultuous rages wide
With loud miſrule, billows on billows rolls
Precipitant, and, dreadful as they riſe,
And dreadful fall, the diſtant welkin rends.

HIM Fame, the lateſt of gigantic race
Titanian-born, within the dark receſs
Of vaulted earth her only ſon produc'd.
She, whilom gauntlet of heroic knights
Errant, and light attendant on their feats
In tilted tournament, had inly felt

Nor

Ceu quondam Icarii, aut Cronii, furit æquoris æftus
Concitus, et rabie ventorum ad littora volvit
Undarum montes : tellus tremit, icta fragore,
Et cœlum horrefcit, fractifque remurmurat iris.

   Illum Fama, foror tumidorum extrema Gigantum,
Unigenam peperit cæco telluris in antro :
Ipfa comes, ftimulufque ducum, per dura ruentum,
                            Indomito

FAULKNER'S NATIVITY.

In awful pomp, as, when with warring waves
The wild Icarian, or the Cronian raves,
The mountain billows with tumultuous roar
Swell into rage, and thunder on the fhore:
Dire as they rife, and dire defcending clafh,
The diftant poles rebellow to the crafh.

   Loud Fame, fair fifter of the Titans fell,
Produc'd beneath a fubterranean cell
Her darling Faulkner: fhe, who ftinging feeds
The fouls of heroes, and attends their deeds,

Ουκ ηδει κραδιησι βιην κỳ δεσμα Θεοιο

Τȣ τυφλȣ, μαλακον δε καταφρονεȣσα μαχητην,

Φοιϐω απορρητȣς ασεϐης ανεφαινεν ερωτας

Ανδροφονιο Θεȣ κỳ Κυπριδ☉ ιμεροεσσης,

　　　　　　　　　　　　　　　　　　Αιεν

FAULKNER'S NATIVITY.

Nor yet the prowefs, nor tenacious chain

Of fightlefs Cupid, but indignant ey'd

The foft affailant, and profane betray'd

To folar ken the God of battle, mix'd

In fecret dalliance with the Cyprian queen.

　　　　　　　　　　　　　　　　　　Ever

Indomito nondum perfenfit pectore vires,

Idalii nec vincla Dei, quem, numine fpreto,

Imbellem irrifit : folita quin cæde madentis

Gradivi Paphiæque Deæ rimofa profanam

In lucem, arcanos jamdudum, traxit amores,

Garrulitate

FAULLNER'S NATIVITY.

As yet a novice to the pleafing bane
Of downy Cupid, and the filken chain,
His darts derided, and expos'd the charms
Of Venus, blended with the God of arms;
To peeping Phœbus, glancing from above,
Reveal'd the mazes of myfterious love.

EVIR

Αιεν αμετροεπης. Νυν δ' οξεα κεκληγυια

Επlατο ενθα κỳ ενθα διοτρεφεων δια βυλων,

Ηδε καταθνητων αγορων. Τη πλειςον εαυτης

Γαιε-τε σωφροσυνη, κỳ αναιδεα πολλ' αγορευε,

Κυπριδα μυρομενη, κỳ δακρυα θερμα χευσα.

Τη

FAULKNER'S NATIVITY.

EVER of tongue incontinent, but now
Loquacious, loud, and turbulent, fhe hies
Through jovial fynods, and affembled tribes
Of mortals: much fhe glories in the gem
Of virgin honour, and as much defcants
On Cytherea's gallantries, bewails
Her late mifhap, and mollifies the gall
Of keen reproaches with a tepid flood
Of tender tears.   The laughter-loving queen

Of

Garrulitate frequens: at jam ftridentior hofpes

Hinc atque inde Deum cœtus hominumque coronas

Pervolitat, permulta, fuo lætata pudore,

Præfatur, Venerique gemens opprobia nectit.

His

FAULKNER'S NATIVITY.

EVER profufe of tattle-bearing tongue,
But now for treble defamation ftrung,
Wide through the fynods of ambrofial fkies,
And mortal crowds itinerant fhe flies,
Much of that honour, which fhe never loft,
Harangues, and much at Cytherea's coft,
Then fighs, and, fquinting with malicious leer,
As through compaffion, drops a tender tear.

At

Τη ρα χολωσαμενη περικαλλης δια Θεαων,
Δηθα κακ8ς Φρονε8σα δολ8ς, νυν υςερον αυτης
Αγριον, αρ[αλεον, βροτον ιμερον εμβαλε Θυμω.

Ου δ' ετι των προ]ερων Φημη μεμνημενη αινων,
Ου μεν Αθηναιης κ] Ενυ8ς ερ[α μεμηλε,
Ουτε, βελεσσι δαμεισα κεαρ χρυσης Αφροδιτης,
Της Αρετης μιν εθηκε [ερας Θεα Φωσιν αγαυοις.

'Η δ' ευτ'

FAULKNER'S NATIVIY.

Of peerlefs beauty, meditating long
Baleful revenge, deftructive wiles, incens'd
Her icy bofom with the glowing guft
Of brutal appetence, outrageous, wild.

No longer Fame, unconfcious of herfelf,
And former triumphs, trumpetefs attends
Minerva's, or Bellona's arduous toils,
Nor, deep transfix'd by Cytherea's darts,
Prefents herfelf the plauditory prize
Of patriot-zeal, creative wit, or worth
Pre-eminent. The giddy goddefs, like

A fudden

His commota, diu pulcherrima Cœlicolarum
Ultrices regina dolos triſteſque revolvit
Inſidias, animamque Deæ mortalibus ægram
Succendit ſtudiis, avidiſque furoribus urget.

Non jam Fama, ſui laudumque oblita priorum,
Palladis, aut felix Bellonæ reſpicit artes,
Nec, telis percuſſa tuis, Cytheræa, medullas,
Se pretium egregiis ponit virtutibus æquum.

Jamque

FAULKNER'S NATIVITY.

At her incens'd, the queen of beauty bleſt,
Long harbour'd vengeance in her brooding breaſt,
Revolving deep deceits ; at length ſhe fires
Her ſoul with ſavage, mortal, groſs deſires.

No longer Fame her former glories heeds,
Minerva's labours, or Bellona's deeds,
Nor, deeply ſmitten by the ſofter dart
Of golden Venus, preying on her heart,
Devotes herſelf the memorable prize
Of worth illuſtrious to the brave, or wiſe,

Η δ' ευτ' εκ νεφεων αφνω βορεαο θυελλα

Ορνυμενη, δεινοιο ποθυ βυπληγι μανεισα,

Ηριπεν υρανοθεν ταχ' επι χθονα πυλυβοτειραι.

Η Μητηρ μεγαλη-τε Θεων Ανδρων-τε πεσυσαν

Αψ αυτην κολπυις υποδεξατο λιμεσσιν.

Η δ᷎

FAULKNER'S NATIVITY.

A fudden tempeft, burfting from the clouds,

Impetuous, raging with the baneful fting

Of gadding Cupid, from empyreal height

Shot prone, incumbent on all-feeding earth:

The mighty mother of immortal Gods

And mortal men her panting at her fall

Receiv'd, and with foft fragrant bofom footh'd.

DIVESTED

Jamque, velut Boreæ delapfa repente procella

Nubibus, infani correpta Cupidinis œftro,

Volvitur in præceps: aft illam mollibus herbis

Ingens Terra parens hominumque Deumque cadentem

Sufcepit, blandoque finu recreavit anhelam.

DEPOSUIT

FAULKNER'S NATIVITY.

But raging, goaded with a luftful fting,

Like Boreas rufhing with tempeftuous wing,

Shoots from on high: the fragrant lap of all ----

Suftaining earth receiv'd her headlong fall.

Z z 2   UNGODDESS'D

Η δ' αποδυσα Θεαν, κỳ κυρη βυκολευση
Ειδομενη Ͽνητω Ͽαλερων Φοινικα παρειων,
Καλλιροον-τε κομεϊν περι διρην μαρμαροεσσαν,
Οσσε-τε κυανεησιν υπ' οφρυσιν αὑ φαεινω,
Αλσεῷ εν βησσης πολυβενθεσιν ειαρινοισι,
Νυμφαων Ͽαλαμοισιν, επεκραιαινεν εελδωρ.
Εν δ' εμιγη Φιλοτητι Διακτορω Αργειφοντη,
Ου λιπαραις Φθονευσα Θεαις, καθυπερθεν ευσαις.

Ανδρῷ

FAULKNER'S NATIVITY.

Divested of divinity, ſhe ſeem'd
A ſhepherdeſs with purple-bluſhing bloom
Of cheeks untutor'd, lovely-flowing locks
Around her marble neck, and eyes beneath
Her jetty brows, that darted humid rays
Attractive; and, invelop'd in the ſhades
Of interwoven arbours, vernal haunt
Of nymphs, enjoy'd her amorous intent.

In love licentious there ſhe mingled lay
With Maia's youthful ſon, herald of Jove:

For

Deposuit pudibunda Deam, similisque puellæ
Ruricolæ roseasque genas, et lactea circum
Colla comas, hinc inde vagas, oculosque sub atris
Dulce superciliis fluitanti luce coruscos,
Mercurio commixta Dea est; et, amore soluta,
Indulsit genio, satiris lustrata, per antra,
Frondiferasque domos nympharum, in saltibus imis
Strata, nec invidit cœlestia tecta Deabus.

Quippe

FAULKNER'S NATIVITY.

Ungoddess'd she, with innocence array'd,
Assumes the figure of a rural maid:
Loose with the gales her wanton tresses flow,
Her dimpled cheeks with living purple glow,
And, sweet, beneath her brows, to mortal sight,
Her star-fed eyes reflect their liquid light.
Deep in a gloomy cave, the vernal seat
Of nymphs and satires, a secure retreat,
With Maia's boy she lay dissolv'd in love,
Nor envy'd all the radiant dames above:

For

Αιδρῷ γαρ στιβαρᾳς-τε ποδας κỳ ευρεας ωμᾳς

Ψευστο Θεῷ πυκτων δε φανη Φαυλκνηρῷ αγητηρ

Βριθυ δεμας, μεγαλην-τε φυην κỳ χειρας ααπ]ᾳς

Πορφυρεᾳ θεραπων Θανατᾳ Μοιρας-τε μελαινης

Ος

FAULKNER'S NATIVITY.

For lo! the God had fraudulently feign'd

The legs Herculean and the fhoulders broad

Of man effential: Faulkner full he feem'd,

In crude encounter brave, athletic chief

Huge, Atlantean, arm'd with maffy fifts,

Horrific minifter of gory death

And rueful deftiny, renown'd for hofts

Of

Quippe Deus firmofque pedes humerofque valentes

Induerat fefe furtim : per prælia crudis

Præftantem pugnis, Faulknerum corpore refert

Immani, tum mole gravi dirifque lacertis,

Purpurei famulum lethi, fatique cruenti,

Mille

FAULKNER'S NATIVITY.

For lo! the God, to perpetrate his fraud,
Adopts the legs robuft and fhoulders broad
Of man material : he difplays the mien
Of full-fed Faulkner, dreadful to be feen,
The foremoft champion in athletic lifts,
Of bulk enormous, with Milonian fifts,
Refiftlefs hero, minifter elate
Of purple death and unrelenting fate,

Fell

Ος μεν ρα βριαρας αιδι προιαψε Φαλαγγας

Ταυρκων, ραβδω δε Φρενας κỳ θυμον εθελγε,

Αλκης αμβροσιησι Θεας ενι κυδιανειρας

Βακχευων· χειλεσσι γεγηθε δε μειλιχιοισι,

Ευναων Λυφιαο μελισδομεναο παρ οχθας

Νησω

FAULKNER'S NATIVITY.

Of oxen overthrown : with magic wand

He charm'd the quick æthereal fenfe, and footh'd

Her beating breaft with gentle ravifhment,

Within the circle of her waxen arms

Ambrofial, feafting on the goddefs bright

Of men illuftrious, by the pleafant banks

Of Liffey, gliding with melodious lapfe

Irriguous,

Mille boum infignem fufis, virgaque potente

Æthereum fenfum, divinam numinis auram,

Et ftupefacta modis permulfit pectora miris;

Ipfe fed, ambrofiis Divæ bacchatus in ulnis,

Nectareum interea labiorum lætus amorem

Libavit Lifii prope ripas, lene fluentis,

Felici

FAULKNER'S NATIVITY.

Fell foe to beeves, beneath whofe fury fell

A thoufand victims to the fhades of Hell.

He gently waves his magic wand, and charms

Her fancy: ·lock'd within her filken arms,

The felon riots, and with rapture fips

The balmy nectar of her dewy lips

Faft by the banks, wheie filver Liffey flows

With lulling murmurs to their foft repofe,

Νησω εν ηγαθεη, πλειςοι ποθεν εξεγενοντο

Ηρωες κρατεροι κ̩ αμυμονες αρητηρες.

Την γε Θεοι μακαρες ποτ᾽ εραννην εξονομηνοι

Ωγυγιην, ιερων πυλυανθεα κηπον Αοιδων,

Λοιγαιων οφεων παντοιων αμμοραν αιαν·

Νυν δε βροτοι καλεϋσιν Ιϐερνιαν αφραδεοντες

Μητερα

FAULKNER'S NATIVITY.

Irriguous, in that hofpitable ifle
Of arts and arms, whence populous arofe
Undaunted heroes and unblemifh'd priefts.
The blifsful Gods in antient days yclep'd
The glebe Ogygia, Flora's bloomy pride,
And Paradife of pious Bards, exempt
From all the brood of fnaky pefts: but now
Mortals, unblefs'd with elegance, or wit,
Profane the facred foil, and rudely ftile
Hibernia mother of Bœotian oafs,

Barbarian

Felici tellure, fatæ funt unde priorum

Heroum ingentes animæ, cœlique capaces,

Innumeri fine labe viri.   Dixere beati

Hanc olim Ogygiam Superi cognomine gentem,

Floriferum, et caftis vocalem vatibus, hortum,

Immunemque feris ferpentibus undique glebam:

At nunc mortales miferi, minimeque periti,

Bœotum appellant genetricem, dura fonantum,

Confociata

FAULKNER'S NATIVITY.

In that fair ifle, rever'd, through length of years,

For dauntlefs heroes, and unfpotted feers.

The blifsful Gods in antient days proclaim'd

The foil delicious, and Ogygia nam'd,

The bloomy garden of Apollo's train,

And free from reptiles of pernicious bane:

But now the race of mortals rude revile

The genial climate, and Hibernia ftile

A a a 2

The

Μητερα μωραων κ̣ τιτθιδα βαρβαραφωνων,

Συν Βρετονων γαιη καιπερ φιλοτητα ταμ̄σαν,

Της γε κασι͡γνητην, ηδ' αρχης, ηδ' ερατεινης

Γρκ☉ Ελυθεριας, θειον γεν☉ Ωκεανοιο.

Αυθ υποκυσσαμενη πολυηχης εννεα μηνων

Φθινοντων, εν γας͡ρι φερ̄σ' ολ͡κωδει, φορτον

Νυμφη ζωον εκρυψε, γοον δ' ελ͡σφυδνον επασχε,

Εισοκεν

FAULKNER'S NATIVITY.

Barbarian nurſe of jabberers untun'd,
Though bound to Britain by the ſacred ties
Of amity ſororal, though ſhe ſtand
The prince's bulwark unappall'd, and foul
Of lovely liberty, the daughter pure
Of hoary ocean, Panopæa fair.

 THE noiſy nymph here pregnant had conceal'd
Her pilfer'd joys, nine tedious months elaps'd,
Feebly ſuſtaining in her turgid womb
The living load, and deadly dole ſhe felt,

Till

Confociata licet communi jure Britannæ

Telluri, Germana foror, mavortia jactet

Pectora, tam fceptri, quam libertatis amœnæ

Munimentum ingens, pelagi divina propago.

  Hic turgente, novem completis menfibus, alvo

Conceptum geftabat onus, vivumque tegebat

Nympha, potens linguæ, luctumque iterabat amarum ;

                                   Lucinæ

FAULKNER'S NATIVITY.

The dam of ideots and the nurfe of Teagues,
Though link'd to Britain by religious leagues,
Her loyal fifter, rival in renown,
Brave to defend the grandeur of the crown,
Nor lefs the people's precious rights maintain,
Divine, free daughter of the circling main.

  The noify nymph, here fixing her abode,
Big in her womb fuftain'd a living load :
Nine months had roll'd, nine tedious months in vain,
She figh'd in fecret, and enhanc'd her pain;

                                   Till

Εισοκεν Ερμειας παρα γυνασιν Ειλειθυιας

Πολλα πεσων ηρατο Διος μεγαλοιο Θυγατρα

Χερσι Φιλης κρατερον-τε πονον κ πευθος αμυναι

Θυμοβορον. Καταβη δε Θεα γενηετειρα καρηνων

Μακρων Ουλυμπυ πολυδειραδος αιξασα,

Γρηι φυην εικυια μογοςοκω, αμφιπολαων

Πρεςβυταλη πιςων Κυθερειη κ Διονυσω,

Αιδοιη Λυχαδι, κλειτην πολιν η κατ᾽ εναιε

Εβλανην,

FAULKNER'S NATIVITY.

Till Hermes, proſtrate at Lucina's feet,

Implor'd the daughter of imperial Jove

With hands officious timely to diſpel

The bitter pangs, and agonizing throes,

That pierc'd his love.   The birth-compelling pow'r

Deſcended, ruſhing from the ſphery tops

Of ſteep Olympus, in the midwife guiſe

Of Mother *(a)* Lucas, venerable dame,

(a) A celebrated Midwife in Dublin, in the Year 1705.

Sageſt

Lucinæ ante pedes donec folertior Hermes
Multa Jovis magni fupplex oravit alumnam,
Luctanti quo ferret opem, manibufque levaret
Suppofitis uterique graves animæque dolores.
Illa autem, officii non immemor, ætheris alti
Lapfa jugis, raptim ftiidenti turbine fertur,
Et fpeciem genitalis anus fit, maxima natu
Servarum, Veneri et læto fidiffima Baccho,
Cana Lucas, late claram quæ fedula quondam

          Eblanam

FAULKNER'S NATIVITY.

Till Hermes, proftrate at the feet ador'd
Of kind Lucina, much her aid implor'd,
With lenient hand to mitigate her woes,
And free his love from foul-confuming throes.
Swift from the fummit of Olympus-tow'r
Defcending rufh'd the birth-compelling pow'r;
The midwife-majefty compos'd appears
With front of fapience, authoriz'd by years,
And bufy buftles in the borrow'd mien
Of Lucas, menial to the Cyprian queen,

          And

Ι6λαιχν, αγαθη-τε πρααν πορε παιδοτοκοισι

Χειρα κοραις, αγονοις-τε γονυ ποθον ηδυν ενωρσε,

Σφοδρα-τε καρποφορυς αυτας εδιδαξε γινεθαι,

Και δεπας αμφιετυσα μεγα πλεον αμφικυπελλον

Νεκταρεοιο τοτυ κυκλον-δε κελευε νεεθαι.

Νυν δε Θεαν ελεαιρε Θεα, ςυγερ' αλγε' εχυσαν,

Την ταχεως ελιχανε, θυρας ανεωξε γενεθλης,

Μητερα ρεια πονων απελυσε, σαωσε-τε παιδα. Αλλ

FAULKNER'S NATIVITY.

Sageſt of clients in the truſty train
Of ſmiling Venus and Lyæus boon,
Who dignify'd Eblana's pomp, the town
Her mazy manſion, to the teeming fair
Diffus'd her dextrous aid, potent of ſpell
Inflam'd the frozen with intenſe deſire
Of genial joys, inform'd exhauſted nymphs
To thrive, exuberant with annual fruit,
And miniſtring the goodly goſſip's cup,
Big with nectareous juices, bade it flow
In circling eddies potable, at ebb
Duly repleniſh'd.   But the goddeſs now
Condol'd a ſiſter goddeſs in exceſs
Of writhing anguiſh: her anon ſhe found,
Unbarr'd the gates of birth, releas'd from pain
The lab'ring mother, and preſerv'd the boy. BUT,

Eblanam incoluit, gravidis operata puellis
Mite puerperium, ftudiifque inflavit opimis
Jamdudum fteriles, docuitque tumefcere fœtu:
Quinetiam ingentem pateram de more miniftra
Implevitque mero, bibulumque coegit in orbem.
At miferata Deam Dea, fævis cafibus actam,
Continuo quæfivit eam, fubitoque reperta,
Nafcendi patefecit iter, tumidoque dolore
Exfolvit matrem, et puerum manumifit in auras.   UT

FAULKNER'S NATIVITY.

And Bacchus, flowing with facetious vein,
The fageft matron of their trufty train,
Who dwelt in Dublin, with officious care
Relax'd the burdens of the pregnant fair,
With rich receipts the barren tutor'd well
To pant for pleafures, and prolific fwell,
And, filling high the goffip's cup profound
With tides nectareous, bade it reel around.
But now the goddefs, handy to redrefs,
Condol'd a fifter goddefs in diftrefs:
Her foon fhe found, with fellow-feeling joy
Reliev'd the mother, and preferv'd the boy.

Αλλ' οτε υιον εον τα πρωτα ποδηνεμ℺ Ερμης

Νηπιον εν λεχεεσσι λιζυ κλαιοντ' ενοησε,

Εκ δ' εζελασσε, καρη καταρεζας χειρι, κỳ ειπε.

Χαιρε συ, τεκνον εμον, γλυκιων πολυ φιλτατε παιδων,

Χαιρε καταθνητ℺ περ εων, μονοτυν-τε λελοζλως

Ωκυμορον-τε

FAULKNER'S NATIVITY.

BUT, when the swift interpreter of Gods
Perceiv'd his infant in the cradle first
Squalling harmonious, with effusive glee
He smil'd the father, strok'd his pate, and said:
" Hail thou, the dearest of delicious babes,
Hail, son, though mortal, and ordain'd to trudge
Through busy life with mutilated limb!
Short is thy period: but immortal hands
On thee shall shed, beneficently fond,

Perpetual

UT vero infantem primum Pater audiit ales

Altius in cunis plorantem, et acuta querentem,

Subrisit, tenerumque caput palpavit, et infit.

" Salve, noster honos; proles dulciffima, falve:

Quamvis fata brevi deducant ftamine vitam

Mortalem, et membro dederint traxiffe minorem,

Immortale decus, tibi fplendida munera fundent

Dii

FAULKNER'S NATIVITY.

But, when the rapid legate of the fkies
Firft heard his infant's iterated cries,
A cradle-concert, he ferenely fmil'd,
Soft-ftrok'd his noddle, and addrefs'd the child:
Hail, beft belov'd of lovely bantlings, hail!
In limbs though feeble, and in figure frail,
Ordain'd to hop one-footed through the race
Of life precarious, and a fpan thy fpace,
The deathlefs Gods munificent fhall fhed
Their fplendid honours on that hopeful head.

B b b 2

Thee

Ωκυμορον-τε βιοιο δρομον. Σοι γαρ, Φιλοτιμω

Αμβροτον ηδε κλεⓖ κỳ φαιδιμα δωρα Θελοντες

Αθαιατοι δωσυσι. Σε Θρεψει Παλλας Αθινη,

Σοι πληκτρω χαριεντι βαλει Φορμιϳγα λιϳειαν

Λαμπρⓖ αναξ Ελικωνⓖ· αμειβομεναι μελεεσσι

Δεινα λιϳοφθυϳγοις δια πληθεⓖ, υατ' αλοντⓖ,

Μυσαι δ' εν τριοδοισι καθ' ημεραν υμνησυσι

Κυραων παιδων-τε γλυκυ-ϛενοεντας ερωτας,   Ους

FAULKNER'S NATIVITY.

Perpetual glories, and peculiar gifts

Refplendent.   Thee fhall fage Minerva rear;

The radiant king of Helicon for thee

With magic touch awake the melting lute,

And, loud-refponfive with alternate voice,

The trivial Mufes through the wavy prefs

Of ear-arrefted multitudes refound

In venal fongs the fweetly mournful vows

Of nymphs and fwains, whom, void of nuptial rites

                                                      And

Dii fuperi. Te culta finu nutrice fovebit
Pallas, et Æoliam citharam tibi luminis auctor
Multifonam molli pulfabit pectine Phœbus :
Nec non in triviis alterna voce canoræ
Per turbam auritam, rauca dulcedine captam,
Pierides alte refonabunt fæpius ignes,
Nequicquam fidos, et amores, flebile dulces,
Nympharum ac juvenum, premeret quos dura parentum

Cura

FAULKNER'S NATIVITY.

Thee fhall the queen of polifh'd arts profefs'd
Rear with her hand, and cherifh in her breaft :
For thee the radiant Heliconian king
Shall gently touch the fweet Æolian ftring,
And trivial Mufes, through the glad-ear'd throng,
With voice refponfive to the lofty fong,
Harmonious warble in diurnal ftrains
The doleful flames of dying nymphs and fwains,
Whom cruel parents would confine at home,
Beneath the fplendors of a ftately dome,

And

Ους οιδς αγαμδς-τε γονεις θρεψειαν αεικες

Εν μεγαροισιν εοισιν, αει κατα θυμον εδοντας·

Αυτοι δ' αλληλων απολαυεμεν εν Φιλοτητι

Κρυπ]αδίη (τδς γαρ μαλα Σειρι☉ ωρσεν ερατων

Ατρον) επεσσευοντο, ἡ ασβετον ποθεεσκον,

Πεινατοντες αμα τυγυρα πολυ μαλλον εν αυλη.

Αλλα

FAULKNER'S NATIVITY.

And lonely pining, tenderly ſevere,

Parents would feaſt in edifices proud:

But they (by Sirius over-ruling ſtar

Of lovers led) precipitately ruſh'd,

And glow'd with inextinguiſhable flame

To melt in folds of intermingled ſweets

Felonious, and enjoy the dearer choice

Of wedded want beneath an humble cell.

But

Cura domi folos, aleretque fub ædibus altis,

Connubii expertes, et lenta tabe perefos :

Aft illi (quos uffit atrox, heu! fydus amantum

Sirius) alternis ardebant cedere flammis,

Furtivifque frui votis, humilique taberna

Jejunos agitare dies, noctefque jugales.

AT

FAULKNER'S NATIVITY.

And feed indulgent, but condemn to moan

Unwedded long, and pine whole nights alone.

But they (for Sirius with impulfive fires,

The ftar of lovers kindled their defires)

Rufh'd headlong, fmitten with alternate charms,

To melt by ftealth in one another's arms,

Preferring true-love with an empty maw,

The dirty cottage, and the bed of ftraw.

BUT

Αλλα τεον ποτι δωμα γελων Υμεναι⊙ ακοιτιν,

Αμφοτερον κερδ⊙-τε ποσιι κ̢ χαρμα φερυσαν,

Πομπευσει θαλεραν, πολυολβον, θαυμα γυναικων

Θηλυτερων, χαριτων-τε χαριν, κ̢ σπερμα Διωνης.

Οιην Πανδωρην, εναλιγκιον Αθανατησι

Στηθεα λειριοεντα κ̢ ομματα λαμπετοωντα,

Ασκραι⊙ ποτ' αειδε πατηρ, οιηδε μεν Ηβη

Αμβροσιην πνειυσα χαριν νεοθηλε⊙ ωπ⊙,

Μαρμαιρει,

FAULKNER'S NATIVITY.

But to thy dome fhall Hymen gay conduct

A confort florid, opulent, and fair,

The gentle wonder of her fofter fex,

And, grace of graces, from Dione fprung :

Such, as of old the fage Afcrean Bard

Pandora, rival of celeftial maids,

With lily-bedded breafts, and planet-eyes

In rapture imag'd; fuch, as Hebe, flufh'd

With rofy bloom, breathing ambrofial charms,

Majeftic

AT tibi lautus Hymen, votis haud mollibus impar,
Solennes inter pompas ad limina ducet
Matronam florentem annis, opibufque beatam,
Aucturam gemino felices lumine tædas,
Nympharum primam tenerarum, ortamque Dione;
Afcræus qualem cecinit pater inclytus olim
Pandoram, niveo referentem pectore Divas,
Sydereifque oculis: qualis divinitus Hebe,
Purpureæ fpirans decus immortale juventæ,

Ora

FAULKNER'S NATIVITY.

BUT to thy dome fhall gladfome Hymen guide
A dainty dame in blooming beauty's pride,
With wealth abundant, and in triumph led,
To fill thy coffers, and adorn thy bed,
The pink of damfels, delicately fine,
And, grace of graces, from Dione's line,
Bright as the nymphs, inhabiting the fkies,
With lily-bofom and refulgent eyes.
Blefs'd like Pandora, fuch, as Hefiod fung,
With Hebe's Cheeks, and Polyhymnia's tongue;

Μαρμαιρει, ραδια-τε ρεει Πολυυμνια φωνη·

Τοιην κοσμησει Κυπρις, Διος· εκγεγαυια,

Και χευσει πολυ καλλος επ' αυτην, ηπερ Αθηνη

Θεσμοφοραν, δεινην, εριδων ακος εννεαπηχυ,

Ηλακατην, ως τοι καλαμον κατενευσε Φορηναι,

Μυσαων λειβοντα μελι, γλυκυφωνον αοιδην.

Τυ

FAULKNER'S NATIVITY.

Majeſtic ſhines, and Polyhymnia flows
With verbal volubility. For thee
The Cyprian queen, daughter of Jove ſupreme,
A conſort ſuch ſhall modulate, and pour
Beauty redundant round the finiſh'd piece,
To whom propitious Pallas hath aſſign'd
The regal diſtaff, legiſlative, long,
Nine-cubit-medicine of inmate-jars
And hot contention, as to thee the quill,
Scepter of Bards, diſtilling honey-ſtrains.

Thf

Ora nitet, liquidaque fluit Polyhymnia voce.

Talem forte tuis amplexibus aurea finget

Diva Cypri, prolefque Deum rectoris, et olli

Cognatas veneres propriofque afflabit honores,

Cui Pallas vibrare colum dedit imperialem,

Legiferam, rixæ novies-cubitale levamen,

Ut tibi figniferum vatumque volatile fceptrum,

Carminibus calamum Phœbeo melle fluentem.

UMBRARUM

FAULKNER'S NATIVITY.

THE tongue, melodious with a vocal tide,
And cheeks, with ever-blufhing purple dy'd :
Such fhall fair Venus for thy nuptials frame,
And lavifh all her beauties on the dame,
To whom Minerva gives to wield for life
The law-difpenfing diftaff, cure of ftrife,
Nine-cubit-cure, as fhe to thee devotes
Her pen, the channel of mellifluous notes.

C c c 2

FOR

Τ8 δημ8 σκιοεντ☾ αναξ υπενερθεν αμαυρ☾,

Σπλαγχνα καταρρηξας βασιλειας ηεροεσσης,

Παγκρατε☾ τοι κηλα Θεας, τυφλης περ ε8σης,

Αργυρεην χρυσην-τε βιην πλ8τοιο καμειται·

Ες δε μελαν πεταλον τυπικον πονον αυτ☾ ελιξει

Μαινομενον Φλεγεθοντα πυρι κρατερα προρεοντι,

Ταρταρεον-τε φυρει πολυν Στυγ☾ υδατι λυγρω.

Τ8Τ●

FAULKNER'S NATIVITY.

The murky monarch of unbody'd ſhades,
Rifling the bowels of his gloomy realms,
Shall fabricate for thee the temper'd arms
Of mole-ey'd fortune, all-ſubduing force
Of minted ſilver bright, and yellow gold ;
To feed thy toils voluminous, and black
He ſhall confound the deep infernal gulph,
Livid with rage, waving with fluid fire,
And blend Tartarean ooze with Stygian ſtum.

This

UMBRARUM interea vindex, Erebique tyrannus,

Interiora fui rimatus vifcera regni,

Obfcuroque inftans operi, victricia cæcæ

Eruet arma Deæ, tibi lumina divitiarum ;

Inque recudendas tabulas, fignifque notandas,

Multiplices foliis, totum Phlegethonta ciebit,

Undantem flammis, tortumque voraginis æftu, .

Tartareumque lutum Stygia mifcebit amurca.

Hoc

FAULKNER'S NATIVITY.

FOR thee the monarch of the fhady train,

Burfting the bowels of his dark domain,

Shall fortune's all-fubduing arms unfold,

Her beamy filver, and her burnifh'd gold;

To ftamp the volumes of thy black-leav'd toil,

His ebon hand fhall Phlegethon embroil

With baleful bubbles, waving flames, and mix

Tartarean ooze with melancholy Styx.

I THIS

Τΰτο μεν εξερεω, το δε κ̀ τετελεσμενον εϛαι,
Τΰτο μαλ' ατρεκεως —— Τις μοι κλονῷ ϟαια τυπῇει
Γϗαϖιϟης; ανδρων δε ροῷ ποθεν ημιν ; εκειϟη
Φρϗρα θαμεια, ποδας γυμϟη, παλαμας-τε μελαιϟα,
Θριξι, πολυσχιϛοισι-τε σχημασι πεφριϟυια,
Φωϟην δ' αρρηϟτῷ, καιϟων ιασχϗσα πελωρα,
Και δεινϗς πολεμϗς, κ̀ δηϊδας αιματοεσσας,
Σε ϛϛεπῇω χρυσω ϛιλβησι-τε πορφυρεησι

Δαιδαλεον

FAULKNER'S NATIVITY.

Thɪs I foretel, nor ſhall it not befal,
This, this unerrant —— But what ſudden din
Aſſaults mine ears ? this inundation whence ?
That bare-foot-band of centinels, who crowd
Thy rubric portal, ſable-handed guards,
Briſtling with horrent bruſh of upright hairs,
And parti-colour'd robes, a-gape with rents
Wide, diſcontinuous, of unbroken voice
Inceſſant, roaring monſter-brooding news,
Rumours, and horrid wars, and battles, dire
With bloody deeds, their monarch ſhall array
Diſtinct with tortile gold and purple pride :

Nay

Hoc tibi vaticinor, quod poftera proferet ætas,
Hoc equidem haud dubium——Sed quis fragor impulit aures?
Turbidus unde virum fluxus? nempe ifta caterva
Nuda pedes, et nigra manus, atque horrida villis,
Multiforifque togis, rubræ cuftodia portæ,
Infracta fed voce canens miracula rerum,
Mavortifque minas, pugnafque cruore rubentes,
Te regem tortoque auro variabit et oftro
Ardenti, tardafque manu rimata cloacas.

Obfcœnis

FAULKNER'S NATIVITY.

I THIS declare, which by divine decree
Shall come to pafs, this prophecy to thee ———
But, lo! what fudden tumult ftrikes aloud
My frighted organs? whence that wavy crowd?
Thofe frequent clients, gate-befieging bands
With naked feet, and black-polluted hands,
With locks horrific, as Medufa's hairs,
And garments, gaping with a thoufand tears,
Of voice unbroken, roaring with full yell
Tremendous wars and bloody battles fell,
Shall thee their king, for typic empire born,
With braided gold and purple pride adorn :

The

Δαιδαλεον κρειοντα ϛελει, Πενιη δε κỳ αυτη,

Ιχνευσασα ρυπϒς, ποιησει πλϒσιον αισχροις

Πορνιδιων ρακεεσι, παλαι μεν αϛαλμασι, νυν δε

Τϒ καλλϒς εναροισιν, απερ κεκαθαρμενα μοχθꙮ

Πλαϛιϰꙮ υδραλετοιο παλινδρομꙮ εις πανυλευκα

Φυλλα μεταλλαξαι ρυθμων εριηϛαν αρϒραν.

Ερϰꙮ

FAULKNER'S NATIVITY.

Nay thee fhall dirt-exploring want enrich

With harlot-rags, the gaudy trappings once

Of orient, but polluted badges now

Of fun-fet beauty, which the kindly moift

Revolving labour of the plaftic mill

Shall grind, expanfive into virgin leaves

Of paper pure, the fnowy field of rhime.

For

Obfcœnis etiam pannis ditabit egeftas,

Te pannis, quondam dominantum infignibus, at jam

Fractarum exuviis Venerum, revolubilis olim

Quas mola contritas luftralibus abluet undis,

Compreffumque chaos foliorum in candida tendet

Corpora, chartaceum generandis verfibus æquor.

PALLADIAS

FAULKNER'S NATIVITY.

The very hand of groveling want explores
The dirt, induftrious to promote thy ftores
With rags, once beauty's ornamental arms,
But now the reliques of abandon'd charms,
Which by degrees the mill's revolving pains
Shall purge irriguous, and reclaim from ftains,
Then plaftic fafhion into purer prime
Of virgin leaves, the fnowy field of rhime.

VOL. I. D d d FOR

Ερχ⊙ Αθηναιης ανδρων-τε μολιβδινα παντα

Οπλα μελιφθογγων σοι τευξεται Αμφιγυηεις,

Οις Φθαμεν⊙ κρυοεντα φθονον προβαλης τε, κ̇ αυτοι

Τον παρεοντα πονων καρπον, κ̇ κυδ⊙ αμεινον

Αφθιτον ανθρωποισι μετ᾿ εσσομενοισιν αρωνται.

Συ δ᾿ ισην οισει-τε δικην, υπαλας-τε Θεμιστας,

Αιμυλιης-τε λογυς, κ̇ εφετμας αιολομητυς

Πηγασ⊙.

FAULKNER'S NATIVITY.

For thee fhall fweaty limping Vulcan forge
The literary, leaden Panoply
Of fweet-mouth'd Bards, by which thou may'ft prevent
The blafting breath of envy pale, and they
May reap the prefent harveft of their toils,
Diurnal nurture, and from after-times
Undying honour. Pegafus fhall bear
Thy well-weigh'd juftice, abfolute decrees,
Thy bland orations, and expreffes, fraught
With fundry counfels. I, the flying poft,

High-mounted

PALLADIAS acies ac dædala Mulciber arma
Muſarum efflabit plumbo, quibus ipſe reſtingas
Horrendam invidiæ rabiem, Pindique coloni
Maturas carpant ſegetes impune laborum
Inſtantum, ſeroſque inter memoranda nepotes
Late ſcripta ferant, nunquam decus interiturum!

JURA, pari librata manu, legeſque ſupremas
Velle tuum, et chartas, hinc blanda voce fluentes
Et grata novitate leves, riſuque ſolutas,
Inde graves fluxu rerum, imperioque minaces,

Pegaſus,

FAULKNER'S NATIVITY.

FOR thee ſhall Vulcan caſt the leaden guards
Of letter'd arts and armament of Bards,
By which their champion may repel the rage
Of gnawing envy from the current page,
His hackneys proſper in their labour'd lays,
And purchaſe preſent bread, and future bays.

THY juſtice, pois'd in ever-equal ſcales,
And ratify'd decrees beyond appeals,
Thy ſpeeches bland, and manifeſtoes rare
With wiſdom checker'd, Pegaſus ſhall bear,

D d d 2

While

Πηλασ⊙· αυταρ εγω ταχυς αγγελ⊙ αυλος εφ' αυλω

Μυκησω κοιλω κερατι σμαραγυντι βοειω.

Σοι δ' επεα πλεροεντα Πατηρ, βροτολοιγ⊙ Ενυω

Σμερδαλεον σαλπιγγα μοθυ, σοι ποτνια Μητηρ

Χαλλειας φωνας, εκατον ςοματ' εγγυαλιζει·

Τ' υνεκα Φαυλκνηρυ λιγυρον κλε⊙ υποτ' ολειται,

Αυταρ,

FAULKNER'S NATIVITY.

High-mounted on his back, myſelf ſhall wind
The hollow-braying, hoarſe-reſounding horn.

  To thee thy father flippant ſhall impart
His wingy words, Bellona, bane of men,
Her battle-breathing trump, thy mother dread
Her brazen voices, and an hundred tongues:
Whence FAULKNER's glory, vagabond, and ſhrill
Shall never die. While, born of baſer earth,

Men,

Pegafus, ecce! feret: fimul ipfe, per oppida raptus,
Per cava raucifono reboabo cornua cantu.

    VERBA fuo de fonte pater, volucrefque loquelas,
Horrifonam Bellona tubam, tibi Mater ahenas
Alma dabit centum voces, centum ora profunda;
Unde nec altus honos, nec amandi rauca tacebit
Gloria FAULKNERI. Seclis labentibus, alte

                                              Fixa,

FAULKNER'S NATIVITY.

While pofting I his airy back adorn,
And wind with braying-blaft the hoarfe-refounding horn.

    To thee thy father glibly fhall beftow
Words on the wing, a never-ebbing flow,
To thee Bellona, breathing death afar,
The dreadful trumpet of tumultuous war,
Thine awful mother furnifh thee with lungs,
Her brazen voices, and an hundred tongues:
Hence FAULKNER's glory, founding, and fublime,
Shall never fink beneath the gulph of time.

                                           The

Αυταρ, επιχθονιων γενεων καταδυσσομεναων

Συν σφετεροις ερɣοισι, φανει πολυμηχανꙮ Ηρως,

Ευκλειας-τ' αλλων σπειρων, ιδιαν-τε θεριζων·

Ουτε σφαλεις εν αɣωσι, μενꙮ πολεεσσιν ομοιꙮ,

Αρχοντων, μεɣαλυς-τε λοɣυς βασιλευτερꙮ, αρξει,

Ηɣεμονας-τε, βοην πολ' αμεινων, ηɣεμονευσει,

'Ειτ'

FAULKNER'S NATIVITY.

Men, and the labour'd monuments of men

Sink into dark oblivion, he ſhall ſhine,

Sowing with artful hand the round applauſe

Of others full, and reaping ripe his own.

Compos'd in conteſt, not unequal he

Single to thouſands, with ſublimeɪ airs

Important, over mighty monarchs grand

Shall ſultanize, and, brac'd with bolder lungs,

Their leaders lead : vindictive whether he

Would

Fixa, ruent monumenta virum : perſtabit at ille

Et ſator, et meſſor famæ, nec viribus ullis

Ceſſurus, late reges, par millibus unus,

Voce reget, ducetque duces ; ſeu fulmine veſtri

Mavortis

FAULKNER'S NATIVITY.

The buſy tribes, who buſtle o'er this ball,

Shall with their labours undiſtinguiſh'd fall :

But he ſhall ſtand, receive what he beſtows,

And reap the harveſt of the praiſe he ſows :

Invincible, ſufficient match alone

For thouſands, he with more majeſtic tone,

(Such is the prowefs of his parts to plead)

To kings ſhall dictate, and their leaders lead ;

Whethei

Ειτ' Αρεῷ, Γυλιελμε, τευ βροντη σμαραγιζοι,

Γαλλαων κρατερας ρηϊνυσκων ιφι φαλαγγας·

Ειτ' αναγινωσκοι Πατρῷ μεγαλητορῷ ιρας

Συνθεσιας, ας τω πυκινας πολυβυλῷ υφαινεν,

Ειρηνην τεμψων ανδρων καλα φυλα βεβαιαν.

Αυτῷ,

FAULKNER'S NATIVITY.

Would thunder, WILLIAM, by thy Mars inspir'd,

With hideous ruin through the wedgy ranks

Of gallant Gauls, or calmly recognize,

And ratify thy godlike father's leagues

Inviolable, which the trusty knight

With loyal heart, and ministerial head

Profoundly plann'd, diffusing through the realms

Concord, and mutual faith, and settled peace.

THAT

Mavortis, Gulielme, fremat, cuneofque frequentes

Gallorum effringat; magni feu fœdera patris

Sancta recognofcat, quæ plurima texuit olli

Mente alta, ftabilemque ftruat per fecula pacem.

FONS

FAULKNER'S NATIVITY.

Whether, ambitious to record his name,

He thunders, WILLIAM, with thy martial flame,

Fierce on thy foes, and through the thick array

Of banded Gauls depopulates his way,

Or recognizes, as affairs require,

The leagues religious of thy godlike fire,

Thofe leagues, full fraught with myfteries of ftate,

Which GEORGE the LITTLE plann'd for GEORGE the GREAT,

To trim the balance, and reftore the peace

Of Europe, fettled on a folid bafe.

VOL. I.   E e e   BUT,

Αυτῷ, των επεων κρυνῷ, κ̓ λαμπας αοιδων,

Τ8ς κροτοφ8ς ιερησι θαλων Δαφνησι θεοιο,

Πανδερκης ος παντα τρεφει, κ̓ κυδει χρυσοι,

Τας-τε κατα πιολεας παναχαιων ευρυαγυιας

Και πεδι᾽, αθαναλοισιν απερ μελεεσσιν εκοσμει,

Ο πλαςθεις, απορῷ, τυφλῷ ποτε γυμνοποδησε.

Αυταρ

FAULKNER'S NATIVITY.

That matchleſs maſter, fountain undefil'd

Of poeſy divine, and lucid lamp

Of lofty Bards, whoſe hoary temples bloom'd

With vernant enſigns of the God, who views

And chears, and clothes this univerſal orb

With golden glory, through the tow'ring towns

Of Greece combin'd, and thoſe ungrateful plains,

Which he had hymn'd in ever-during lays,

Bare-footed, wander'd, indigent, and blind.

But

Fons fandi, vatumque jubar, caput ille revinctus

Festa fronde Dei, solus qui cuncta tuetur,

Et fovet, **atque** parens radianti numine vestit,

Argolicas **nudis** lustravit passibus urbes,

Et, quos æterno decorarat carmine, campos,

Errabundus, inops, divini luminis expers.

Hic

FAULKNER'S NATIVITY.

THAT laurel'd sage, the polar-star sublime

Of Bards, and fountain of heroic rhime,

Fir'd by the God, whose universal eye

Surveys all things beneath the lucid sky,

And gilds with glory, nature's master-piece,

Wide through the towns of many-peopled Greece,

And those opime, inhospitable plains,

Which he had honour'd with immortal strains,

A pilgrim, void of necessaries meet,

And eyeless, wander'd with unshodden feet.

E e 2

But

Αυταρ οʃ᾽ Απολλωνι Φιλ☉, πεταλοισι Σιβυλλης

Ανθησει, καρποις παλαμαων μυσοπολαων,

Βριθομεν☉ βαρει χρυσω χαλκω-τε πυρωπω,

Καν περι μιν δειλοι πολεες πιπʃωσιν αοιδοι

Των Κριτικων πνοιηεσιν επηνεσι μορμυρουντων,

Σηματ᾽ εχων εν χερσι Θευ, κʲ κηλα τινασσων

Αιεν

FAULKNER'S NATIVITY.

But Faulkner, sacred to the Delphic shrine,
Shall flourish with Sibylla's mystic leaves
Luxuriant, loaded with scale-sinking gold
And beamy brass, imbost with royal head,
And harp Hibernian, the mature returns
Mercurial of his Muse-productive hands.
Though meagre Bards innumerable fall
Around him, wither'd by the blast malign
Of snarling Critics, he, sustaining still
Apollo's banners, brandishing aloft

Minerv

Hic vero, Phœboque facer, levibufque Sibyllæ

Fœcundis foliis, auro fplendefcet et ære,

Ingenuæ fructu dextræ, vatumque minorum

Per varios lapfus, criticafque hinc inde procellas

Signa manu Phœbea gerens, ac tela corufcans

Palladis, et clypeo coriorum indutus amico,

Grande

FAULKNER'S NATIVITY.

But Faulkner, breathing through Pierian caves

The God, fhall flourifh with Sibylla's leaves,

Light as they flutter, reaping fhall amafs,

In heavy gold and flame-reflecting brafs,

The daily tribute of his vagrant bands,

And harveft of his Mufe-miniftrant hands.

Though puny Poets by the baneful blaft

Of fnarling Critics fall around him faft

He, calmly waving through the loud alarms

Apollo's enfigns and Minerva's arms,

With

Αιεν Αθηναιης, υπο δερμασιν ομφαλοεσσι

Την ατερ ωτειλης νικην φλοισβοιο φορησει.

Ως το Διος δενδρον κρατερης ριζησι πεφυκος,

Πολλαων μελιων βορεω καταβαλλομεναων,

Υλην εισηκει κατ' αθεσφατον υψικαρηνον,

Τηλεθαον-τε κομας, βαλανοισι βαρυνεται, αυτο

Αλσος

FAULKNER'S NATIVITY.

Minerva's arms, beneath the tough defence
Of polifh'd hides, unwounded fhall attain
The folid trophies of the paper-war.

As Jove's high oak, with deep retentive root
Secure, while heaps of afhen ruins lie
Promifcuous round, by rapid Boreas rent
In fome immeafurable foreft ftood,
And antient now renews its leafy youth
Umbrageous, green, and teems with ruffet maft,

Itfelf

Grande decus, dulcemque gravi fine vulnere palmam

Verbofæ referet pugnæ.   Jovis arbor ut olim

Immenfa in fylva validis radicibus hæfit,

Fraxineas inter ftrages, Boreæque furores,

Fronte minax, ramifque recens, et glandibus uber,

Ipfa

FAULKNER'S NATIVITY.

With helmet-hides invefted, without fcar

Shall boaft the triumphs of the wordy war.

As in fome deep, immeafurable wood,

The roots confirm'd, a ftately oak hath ftood,

And, while by Boreas afhes rent around

With frequent ruin ftrow the parent ground,

Difplays its leaves, the verdant pride of Jove,

And branchy teems with maft, itfelf a grove:

Th.

Αλσ⊙ εον. Τοι⊙ δ' αλφησων εξοχ⊙ εςαι

Αρχετυπ⊙, γραφεων-τε φοως, αινησι κỳ ηδε

Νυν φερεται, σαυτον-τε φερει, δελτοισι-τε μιχθεις

Σοισι, θαλει Δρυοπεζος αει τεκίων παρα πασιν

Ανθρωποις μεροπεσσιν υπ' υρανον αςεροεντα.

Ως

FAULKNER'S NATIVITY.

Itself a grove: such eminent shall stand

The prime of Printers, and the light of Scribes:

Fann'd by the breath of popular acclaim,

Now, now he flies, and self-supported soars:

Exprefs'd at length in capitals his own,

Our oaken-footed Elzevir shall branch

With spreading honours through the dialects

Of Babel-tongues beneath the starry sky.

THUS

Ipfa nemus. Talis, venturo Quercipes ævo

Dædalus, ingenio Phœbi fuperabit alumnos

Hermeolus, dubiifque diem fcriptoribus almum

Infundet: jam jamque virum rumore fecundo

Fertur ovans, et fefe effert, mixtufque libellis

Ipfe fuis prodibit ovans, cunctafque per oras

Axe fub aftrifero viget, æternumque vigebit.

Sic

FAULKNER'S NATIVITY.

The prince of Printers, thus, the light divine
Of authors fair, fhall eminently fhine,
Difplay the praife of others, and his own,
And by his proper characters be known.
Our hero, propt with royal oak, the fame
Shall ftand, and flourifh in eternal fame,
Wide through the various dialects, that roll
From torrent tongues beneath the ftarry pole."

Ὡς εφατ' Ερμειας, Διῶ αγγελῶ αιολοφωνῶ,

Εν—τε καθιζε κλινη. Φημη δ' ετερωθεν ανεςη,

Και, μοι τεκνον, εφη, τρις χαιρε· Γεοργιῶ εςω,

Τ' ὄνομα γαρ σε πρεπει βασιλειον· τον δε τεκ8σα

Τοιον, υπερχαιρω κακιαις, εξ ημετεροιο

Αισχεῶ,

FAULKNER'S NATIVITY.

THUS Hermes Jove's ambassador, attun'd
To various eloquence, harangu'd, and sate.
When FAME, uprising from her cloudy couch,
Swell'd with prophetic exstasy : thrice hail,
Attested son! Æolian GEORGE be thou,
Nor does the name of royalty rever'd
Not well befit thee.   Bless'd in such a plant,
I triumph beyond bounds, if thou but reap

Unspotted

SIC fatus Divum interpres, Cyllenia proles,

Conticuit tandem, lectoque refedit: at, inde

Affurgens, hæc FAMA parens placido addidit ore:

Ter, mihi chare, puer, falve: tu GEORGIUS efto;

Nomen enim regale decet cœleftibus ortam

Progeniem, nec me talem peperiffe pigebit;

Euge canam, quin læta malis, e crimine noftro

Si

FAULKNER'S NATIVITY.

So fpoke the newsful meffenger of Jove,

And fate: when, ftarting from her dark alcove

Thus FAME began: dear object of my vow,

Hail! fon, thrice hail! egregious GEORGE be thou:

The name is regal, and befits my boy:

My late affliction's now become my joy;

And

Αισχεος, αυτος ελων εθλον κλεος αι κε τυχηαι.

Μη δεδιης· α γαρ αρτι Πατηρ μεν υπεσχετο, δωρα

Παντα, φιλος τοι, τις ποτε βυκολος αμφι ρεεθρα

Καλα βαθυσχοινυ λιμνης εριχυδεος Ερνης

Υμνησει· τω γαρ θνητω κ̉ θειος Απολλων,

Φοιβος εκων, η Παν, η μυνω δευτερα Πανι

Η Στανοποιο

FAULKNER'S NATIVITY.

Unspotted glory from my foul disgrace:

Nor dread the sequel; for whatever gifts

Thy father, rapt in vision, hath reveal'd,

A friendly swain along the rushy banks

Of winding ERNE's memorable lake

Shall gladly chant; for to that simple swain

Auspicious Phœbus, or indulgent Pan,

Or

Si modo Faulknerum melior te fama fequatur:

Nec dubites; quæ quippe pater tibi cunque retexit,

Dona Deum, cuftos pecoris, tibi fidus, amœnas

ERNÆ propter aquas (Ernæ quem fama fefellit?)

Arguta quondam refonabit arundine, qualem

Delius ipfe pater, feu Pan, feu, proxima Pani,

Gratia,

FAULKNER'S NATIVITY.

And I fhall triumph in my guilty fhame,

If hence thou gather but a fairer fame.

Nor thou mifdoubt: whatever gifts thy fire

Hath promis'd, raptur'd with prophetic fire,

A friendly fwain the rufhy banks along

Of glorious ERNE fhall record in fong;

For Phœbus, Pan, or, what is next to Pan,

The bright indulgence of a godlike man,

The

ΙΙ Στανοποιο χαρις δωσει συριγγα μελιπνην.

Ες φαΘ ερχομενων, συ δε Κοσκινομαντις Αοιδων

Ταυτα γραφεντα τυποις Φανερωσεις, οψιτελεςα

Χειρι καμων, Μυσων-τε χοροις παντεσσιν αναξεις

Αεριοις πολυσεμνΘ, οταν μεγα δωρον ιδηαι

Καισαρ Θ

FAULKNER'S NATIVITY.

Or STANHOPE, fole fubordinate to Pan,

Unbidden fhall beftow the rural reed

Of dulcet breath.   With type-compofing hand

Thou, fieve-fhear-oracle of airy Bards,

Thick rufhing into day, Lucina's prieft

The fated volume, late to be fulfill'd,

Shalt print, and publifh, and with awful nod

Controul the total rhime-retailing band

Of moon-fed authors, when thou fhalt behold

Hefperian

Gratia, digna Deo, STANHOPI donaverit illi :

Hæc eadem, vatum venientum in luminis oras

Tute fagax, urnamque movens, jam fata per orbem

Edideris, felixque operum dominabere turbæ

Mufarum aeriæ, quum donum videris ingens

             Cæfaris

FAULKNER'S NATIVITY.

The grace of STANHOPE fhall beftow that fwain

The pipe, fweet-breathing, and the rural ftrain.

But thou, the juft difpenfer of rewards,

And fortune-teller of afpiring Bards,

Thefe fage predictions, full in black and white

Impreffing, late fhalt midwive into light,

Diffufe the glories of thy hand, and reign

Aloft fole monarch of the tuneful train ;

             When

Καισαρ☉ Εσπεριοιο, πελωριον ερχ☉ Ιερνης,

Σφων προΓονων προεχοντα πολυκλειτων αρετησι,

Ανδρα, φιλον μοι τεκνον, οταν σκηπΊυχον ιδηαι

ΑρΓαλεοις ακαμαντα πονοις, Θεραποντα Θεμις☉,

Και λαυ φιλοκαλον αΓον, κ͗ ποιμενα πιςην.

Τ Ε Λ Ο Σ.

FAULKNER'S NATIVITY.

Hesperian Cæsar's delegate benign,
Hibernia's rising, ornamental, prop,
Surpassing far his ancestors renown'd
In princely merits: when thou shalt behold
Him sceptred, him in doubtful times approv'd,
The people's faithful guide, and guardian just.

T H E   E N D.

Cæfaris Hefperii, decus et tutamen IERNES,

Quum jam, nate, virum regnantem videris illum,

Qui meritis et honore, patrum non degener hæres,

Egregios præcurret avos, quique audiet æquus

Et populi rector, fidufque per ardua paftor.

F I N I S.

FAULKNER'S NATIVITY.

When thou fhalt fee that princely patron fmile,

By Cæfar fent to blefs Hibernia's ifle,

Him regnant, honour'd, whofe defert exceeds

His gieat piogenitors in pious deeds,

Him high-approv'd, through difficulties try'd,

The people's guardian, and the nation's guide.

THE END.

JUDICIUM HERCULIS.

A O N I I prope fontis aquas lætafque choreas
 Pieridum, et femper viridantem vertice Pindum,
Ire lubens exul videor; dum intacta priorum
Signa fequor vatum longe, perque afpera tendens
Heroum prærupta gradum, explorare receffus
Et celfas aperire vias virtutis in ævum,
Mente agito, caftumque ferens in templa triumphum,
Vera cano per ficta, procul, procul ite profani.

 Vix fatus Alcmena quondam puerilibus annis
Egreffus, primoque genas veftitus honore
Pubertatis adhuc, fefe in fecreta vetuftæ
Tecta tulit fylvæ, fteterat qua plurima quercus
Sacra patri, Dryadumque domus. Tacuere receffus,
Horrentemque nemus meditanti contulit umbram,
Quodnam iter inftituat vitæ per devia certum ;
Se quibus aufpiciis agat, et quo numine mentem

          Crefcentem

Crefcentem accingat; fedes ubi pofcat amœnas,
Palantemque pedem felici limine fiftat.

QUUM geminæ fubito nymphæ, quarum altera Virtus,
Altera (fic olim vates meminere) Voluptas,
Ancipiti occurrunt juveni. Ditiffima dona
Huic Venus ipfa dedit, totamque Cupidinis armis,
Inftruxit. Nutrita vagam prope populus amnem
Qualis vere novo, aut frondenti vertice pinus
Affurgit, tenerafque comas leni explicat auræ:
Talis erat formæ fpecies; ubi fœdere ftricto
Majeftas et amor coeunt, licet igne fluentes
Languefcunt oculi, turgentia pectora cycnis
Candidiora patent, vel qua decuere, latefcunt:
Lactea colla nitent, puro ftant ordine dentes
Oris ebur; rubuere genæ, rubuere labella
Blanda, fupercilium nifi qua via findit utrumque
Nigrefcunt, redoletque Sabæam fpiritus oris
Nectarei, luduntque comæ per colla vagantes:
Atque his aggreditur juvenem placidiffima dictis,
Dulce decus terris, cœli manifefta propago,
Quæ Phœbi florem intonfi, celfaque tonantem
Fronte refers, grata tibi non indebita carpe
Dona manu, memorique animo mea dicta reconde.

TE

Te Venus alma vocat, faciles tibi lilia nymphæ
Cana legunt, nitidasque ardent iterare choreas:
Deliciis lætare datis, risuque secundos
Conde dies, dum membra vigent, et mobilis ætas
Flore rubet, roseusque decor sibi poscit amoris
Molle ministerium, et genialia dona Lyæi.

Ecce Deum cætus, puro qui lumine amicti
Cœli templa tenent, æterni nectaris haustus
Ducunt, et dapibus per limina læta frequentes
Incumbunt late ambrosiis, et gaudia nunquam
Interrupta bibunt; procul absunt cura metusque
Et labor. Aspirant Zephyri fragrantibus alis,
Et ver perpetuum semperque innubilus æther
Ridet, et astrorum circumsonat aureus ordo.

Ipse Deus, quem rauca cient ad castra nefanda
Æra ducem, insidiæque truces et ferrea messis
Bellorum, ac tepido fluitantes sanguine campi
Crudeli pascunt ludo, discordibus armis
Abstinet, et magno demum devinctus amore
Idaliæ petit antra Deæ, quibus ipsa cubile
Molle struo, subeoque animos infusa per artus.

Quin pauci, quibus alma Venus Venerifque propago
Arrifere, vident ferias fine fine, meoque
Cœleftem in terris agitant fub numine vitam.

In mea regna refert fol arduus auricomum ver ;
Luxuriatur ager, vivos induta colores
Prata vigent, fylvæ frondent, volucrumque querelis
Dulce ftrepunt, fomnumque leves ambagibus amnes
Rorantem inducunt, viridi de margine flores
Dum fefe mirantur aquis, pronique fugaces
Certatim lambunt latices atque ofcula libant.
Tum natura jubar, brumalibus excita fomnis,
Ætherium fentit fubito, revocanfque juventam
Virgineam genetrix mihi dædala munera fundit.

Tum noftri pertentat apes divinitus ardor,
Hyblæum exefis prorumpit rupibus agmen
ilicibufque cavis, dependent eminus uvæ
Stridentes, quatiuntque alas, dulcique labori
Arma parant, arbufta petunt pars, thurea fœtu
Candenti, faltufque fuga pars alti comantes :
Aft aliæ campos, et apricis floribus hortum
Spirantem explorant, croceafque impune per herbas
Mellifluos paffim bibulæ prædantur odores.

Tu.

Tum variæ fenfim pecudes, armenta, feræque
Me repetunt, dominamque fovent, latum unde per orbem
Quæque fuos edunt generatim in fæcula fœtus.
Squamea quinetiam liquido fub marmore Ponti
Turba meis recalent flammis, paffimque beatum
Imperium agnofcunt, et lufu muta fatentur.
Aufcultant elementa modis haud mollia blandis;
Clarefcunt nubes, expirant murmura cœli,
Atque fopita vadis immanior unda recumbit.

Dixerat, obftupuit fubito Jovis inclita proles,
Ignibus icta velut cœleftibus : æger anhelat
Spiritus, offa tremunt, fudantia membra rigefcunt,
Itque reditque color fugitiva per ora, perit vox,
Jamque labantem animum et ceffurum cominus hofti
Flammantes produnt oculi, fignantque loquaces ;
Cum virtus fefe ore ferens, geftuque decoro,
At blandis minus apta dolis, in prælia vires
Colligit ipfa fuas ; qualis digreffa Deorum
Concilio, palmamque ferens atque ægide fulgens

Pallas

Pallas in arma viros agitat.   Frons altior olli,

Mente gravis, rerumque fagax, pia dextera fceptrum

Imperiale tenet, feftæque in vertice laurus,

Vernat honos, nutatque decus fælicis olivæ.

CANDIDA quinetiam ex humeris, variata figuris,

Veftimenta fluunt, opus immortale Minervæ,

Virgineumque Deæ donum; per textile cœlum

Undantem vomit orbe diem fol aureus, inde

Germanæ exoritur Lunai obfcura viciffim

Majeftas, per regna faces quam rite minores

Innumeræ afpiciunt, crebroque fatellite ftipant.

Inde Aftrea, viris nondam depulfa, refulfit,

Suftinuitque pares dubio libramine lances.

Inde et fidentes animifque immanibus aufi

Telluris juvenes, regni ftellantis habenas

Extorquere graves, et non violabile fceptrum:

Montibus agglomerant montes, fictafque per auras

Bella movent, vulfafque vibrant radicibus ornos.
Ter pater ipfe dedit vocem; ter vindice raptos
Fulmine, et errantes flammarum turbine fudit.

Tum vero intextas, alia de parte, videres
Terribiles vifu formas, rabidumque Leonem,
Intortamque Hydram, et furibundum dentibus aprum,
Æripidafque feias et anhelas naribus ignes,
Et diras volucrum facies, taboque fluenti
Roftroium horrentes, pedibufque rapacibus uncas
Harpyas. Illinc aptantur Amazones armis,
Virgineoque gerunt animos in corde viriles.
Goigonis hic (credas vixiffe) tricorporis ingens
Terror adeft. Stygiufque canis fremit ore trilingui.
Se quoque contextum proles Tirynthia, monftris
Clavigeramque manum, tergumque agnovit honeftum
Ornatum exuvis. Claro mens omine rerum
Piotinus impulfa, et famæ præfaga futuræ
Ardefcit. dum fic virtus oracula pandit.

NATE Deo, meritifque Deos aditure, beatum

Me duce carpe viam, non te genuere parentes

Degenerem, aut tantis nequicquam viribus auctum.

Ipfe tibi genitor cœlo demifit ab alto

Me vitæ fociam, et confanguinitate propinquam.

Sunt autem geminæ Stygia de gente forores,

Quæ terris agitant furiis hominefque procellis

Funditus, atque Deum fanctiffima munera raptim

Funeftant: Fortuna fugax et blanda Voluptas.

Hinc temerata fides, hinc læfi vulnera juris,

Et patriæ violatus amor: non fanguine nati

Abftinuere patrum, thalamifque jugalibus hofpes

Hofpitis, alternas meditantur, amicus amico,

Infidias, gazifque inhiant raptafque recondunt.

Hos famæ trahit aura leves, hi munia rerum

Primarum, ac titulos inhoneftis artibus optant.

Aft illi, nullis obftricti legibus æqui,

Imbellem in venerem ac luxum folvuntur inertes.

VOL. I. H h h Corporis

Corporis interea decrescit robur, acumen

Mentis hebet, pronoque ruit cum corpore consors.

Tunc inamarescunt epulæ, Venus, ipse Lyæus,

Tunc demum penitus toties exculta clientes

Deserit antiquos, meritorum oblita, Voluptas.

Vitæ summa brevis, miserisque obnoxia curis,

Et certis mens acta malis, incerta futuri.

Heroum vero ex oculis depellere nubem

Mortalem, superumque vias aperire repostas,

Hoc Virtutis opus. Regum indignata furores

Castrorumque minas, alto stans vertice montis,

Ecce! mihi turris nitidum caput intulit astris :

Huc pauci ascendunt, alas quibus ipsa ministro.

At multi, in mediis jam jam conatibus ægri,

Præcipites horrent apices, retroque tuentur,

Inque imas immane ruunt vertigine valles.

Qui montem superare velit, me lumine recto

Aspiciat : tamen obliquo via tramite tendit

Mille

Mille per ambages, tum lurida regna ferarum,

Defertafque fitu latebras, hinc rupibus atque hinc

Horrida praeruptis atque afpera vepribus antra.

Aft, ubi paulatim pedibus victricibus altum

Ventum eft ad culmen, fubito tibi rofcida circum

Prata virent, vivi manant per gramina fontes

Irrigui: gravidis dependent fentibus uvae

Injuffae; florefque eadem cum fructibus arbos

Inducit: ambrofia redolet fpirabilis aura,

Lucus et affiduo volucrum vocalis amore

Confonat: humanas gentes procul inde videbis

Cafibus errantes, vacuifque laboribus actas.

Ut quondam in tenebris tumulique fub aggere turmam

Saltantem educunt lemures, dum fydera teftes

Mirantur, Phœbeque polo pallefcit; at illi

Feftum agitant, lufuque leves pafcuntur inani.

Nec mora, praeteritae laetatus imagine vitae,

Atque iter ingreffus per fanctum limen Olympi,

·Divorum

Divorum accumbes epulis, gratiſſimus hoſpes,

Et conjux Hebes, mixtuſque heroibus heros.

Annuit Alcides : dextra de parte ſerenum

Ter cœlum intonuit, terque inſonueie receſſus,

Arboreuſque ſpecus manifeſta luce iefulſit.

Per nemus umbriferum ſimul ambo paſſibus æquis,

Et manibus junctis, animiſque jugalibus ibant.

THE

THE

JUDGMENT

OF

HERCULES.

Της δ' Αρετης ιδρωτα Θεοι προπαροιθεν εθηκαν.

HESIOD.

——————— *Qui potiores*
Herculis ærumnas credat, fævofque labores,
Et Venere, et cænis, et plumis Sardanapali.

TWO nymphs of old contending ftrove
    To gain the mighty fon of Jove;
Virtue and Pleafure were their names;
Alcïdes ftood between the dames,

            A blooming,

A blooming, but unfettled youth,
Yet willing to be fway'd by truth,

The latter fummons all her charms,
Scarce equall'd by celeftial arms,
The taper waift, the fwelling cheft,
The languifh not to be exprefs'd,
The bloom of either cheek, which fhews
The lilly mingled with the rofe,
The rolling eye, whofe humid fire
Darts fudden, uncontroul'd defire,
The hair, that wanton'd with the wind,
In ringlets o'er her neck reclin'd,
The coral lip, and arch'd brow,
That might engage a Cynick's vow,
The veins, fky-tinctur'd thro' the fkin,
The fmile, that dimpled on her chin,
The robes, that flow'd with carelefs air,
And half the fnowy bofom bare;
When thus the weening nymph began
To captivate the godlike man.

Hail! happy youth, whofe form divine
Befpeaks a Jove in every line,

O! boin

O! born for univerſal ſway,
And boundleſs love without allay,
Aſſert, aſſert thy native right,
In pleaſures matchleſs, as in might.

THE heav'nly beings, who poſſeſs
An endleſs round of happineſs,
Securely lead their Halcyon days
In downy indolence and eaſe;
No care their gentle breaſt annoys,
No labour to malign their joys.

THE happy few, whom Jove hath bleſs'd
With ſenſe, ſuperior to the reſt,
To me their chief fruition owe,
And lead the lives of Gods below.
For me the Sun renews the ſpring,
The ſeaſons ſmile, the warblers ſing,
The ruder winds are huſh'd aſleep,
And azure ocean ſmooths the deep,
The ſcaly people of the main,
Tho' mute, in ſport confeſs my reign.

FOR

For me the fhepherds tend the flow'rs,
And weave the crown, and arch the bow'rs,
For me the fpicy Zephyrs blow,
And ftreams in tuneful murmurs flow;
The fummer-rofe difplays its bloom,
And bloffoms breathe a rich perfume:
For me, purfu'd through every clime,
The lufty autumn in his prime
Unlocks his ftore, delicious feaft,
To gratify fight, fmell, and tafte.

The barren winter too performs
My rites, tho' difcompos'd with ftorms,
And labours to fupport my crown,
Although the face of nature frown.
Lo! then the nymphs and fwains advance
To mingle in the mazy dance,
The lyre awakes the foul to miith,
And gives the fofteft paffions birth;
Whilft love, and youth, and gay delight
Expel the horrors of the night:
No troubles interrupt the fcene,
Or, if a doubt fhould intervene,
Lyæus ftands with fprightly air
To wafh away the dregs of care:

The

The various feafons thus agree,
In one perpetual jubilee,
To propagate my gifts divine,
My gifts, and all thofe gifts be thine,
If thou —— fhe caft fo fweet a look,
That all the growing hero fhook;
Her form, her words his heart unftrung,
While wild confufion chain'd his tongue;
And yet his eager eyes intent
Had utter'd more than half confent.

WHEN Virtue with becoming grace,
But far lefs foft, alluring face,
Prepar'd her fuit, a goodly queen,
With more majeftic look and mien,
A living crown of ivy boughs,
And olive, mantling o'er her brows,
Adorn'd her head; her gentle hand
Suftain'd the fcepter of command;
Her awful front was deeply fage,
Th' effect of thought, and not of age;
Her eyes, that fed no loofe defire,
Keen fparkled with celeftial fire;

Expreffive emblems grac'd her robe:
There might you fee the pendent globe,
The Sun, the Moon, the ftarry pole,
And all the planets, as they roll.
There Heav'n was fill'd with ftrange alarms,
And angry Gods appear'd in arms:
The rebel fons of earth arife
Thrice 'tempting to ufurp the fkies,
And mountains huge on mountains pil'd;
The fire of Gods indignant fmil'd,
And thrice his dreadful thunder hurl'd,
That funk them to the nether world.
There lawlefs Luft was curb'd by reins,
And mad Ambition bit his chains,
While Juftice high-enthron'd prevails
With temper'd fword and equal fcales.

THE fon of Ammon, as he view'd
The figures, undetermin'd ftood:
A dawning ray of thought refin'd
Quick darted thro' his op'ning mind;
He look'd on Virtue o'er and oer,
The more he look'd, fhe charm'd the more;
When thus the Goddefs filence broke,
The hero panting as fhe fpoke.

'Tis

'Tis Pleafure's tafk by fpecious fhows
Of joys to nourifh real woes;
Short are the tranfports, which fhe brings,
Her fweets but ill reward her ftings:
Profufion madly runs before,]
And blindly fcatters all her ftore,
While poverty with racks and wheels
Tormenting preffes on her heels:
Self-love and felf-fufficient pride
With floth are ever by her fide,
Delufion holds her glafs between
The fenfes and her gaudy queen,
And fancy fond her art employs
To grafp at uneffential joys,
But flounders in a vaft abyfs,
Where Gorgons glare and Hydras hifs.

Short and uncertain is the date
Of mortal men, and fix'd their fate;
'Tis mine to add by worthy ways
In glory, what they want in days;
To file the paffions from the ruft
Of fordid floth and brutal luft;
With induftry to purchafe wealth,
With temperance to ftrengthen health;

Inftead

Inſtead of ſelfiſh views confin'd,
To plant the love of human kind,
To point the duties, which extend
To father, brother, kinſman, friend.

Above the reach of human pride
Upon a mountain I reſide,
To which but few from earth aſpire,
Whom Jove hath wing'd with purer fiie;
For millions, who propoſe to climb,
Are frighted at the top ſublime,
And, looking backward as they ſoar,
Fall lower than they were before.

That hero, who would reach the height
Muſt keep me ſteadily in ſight;
Thro' dreary wilds his road he makes,
O'er pointed rocks and thorny brakes;
But, once the difficulty paſt,
A Paradiſe appears at laſt,
From whence he views with high diſdain,
The pilgrims of the nether plain,
And thence, when ſummon'd by his fate,
Paſſes thro' bright Olympus' gate,

With

With joy reviews the paths he trod,
And from a mortal grows a God.

ALCIDES hail'd the voice divine,
And, bowing, faid " my life be thine."
Thus was the fon of Jove refin'd
To chufe the beauties of the mind,
Virtue with pain entail'd to wed,
While Pleafure from his prefence fled:
But, Phillis, had the hero feen
A nymph like thee in mind and mien,
The mien, where in conjunction fweet
The tender loves and graces meet;
The mind, adorn'd with ev'ry art,
That could engage the coldeft heart;
Good-nature, join'd to folid fenfe,
And wit, that never gives offence;
A double conqueft he had won,
Nor in the conqueft hazard run,
Exalted Virtue without ftain,
Tranfporting Pleafure without pain.

HYEMES

HYEMES GLACIALES,

A P U D

HIBERNOS

JAMDUDUM agricolæ vultum potioris Olympi,
  Et fulcos, nimia flaventes meſſe, malignis
Spectabant oculis. Tandem feralis Erynnis
Bis rabiem evomuit Stygiam, bis lapſa per oras
Hibernas, miſeris viduavit civibus urbes,
Et campos late cultoribus. Improba raptim

(Seu

T H E

FROSTY WINTERS

O F

I R E L A N D,

In the YEARS 1739, 1740.

LONG had the swains with envious eyes beheld
  The smiling face of better Heaven, and fields
A-float with golden grain.   At length from Hell
A baneful fury twice effus'd her breath
Malign, twice, gliding o'er Hibernia's coast,
Her cities widow'd of their mournful tribes,
And wide the region of laborious hinds.

(Seu cafu fatoque gravi, feu vindice coelo

Heu! fcelerum, ac toties violati numinis ira)

Ecce! repente lues ventorum devolat alis,

Perniciem ftragemque ferens: fremit arduus Æthei,

Iracunda polorum armamentaria pandens;

Perque orbem natura, vices oblita priores,

Horrefcit. Talis labefactam perculit horror;

Cum genetrix hominum, Satanæ primæva nefandis

Victa dolis, vitæ media inter munera fructus

Avulfit vetitos, mortem depafta futuram.

Confeftim prono vaga lapfu flumina, tanquam

Divinam ad vocem torpentia, circumfiftunt,

Perque lacus tractufque maris jam campus aquarum

Infolitum miratur onus, jumenta liquentes

Perfultare vias, hominumque impune catervas

Allabi, rapidifque rotis volitare quadrigas.

Interea

A FELL infection, (whether through the ftroke
Of chance, or fate, or vengeful Heaven, (how due
To crimes repeated!) and the treafur'd wrath
Of God offended,) on the rufhing wings
Of winds defcended, harbinger of death,
And defolation.   Bellowing aloft
The fky gave fignal: burft the magazines
Of elemental war from pole to pole;
While nature, fick'ning through the frighted globe,
Forgetful of her ufual tenour fhrunk,
As into chaos: fuch a fhock fhe felt,
As when, deluded by the tempter's wiles,
The mother of mankind, amid the gifts
Of life immortal, difobedient pluck'd
Forbidden fruit, and tafted future death.

THE vagrant rivers, in their prone career
Congealed, arrefted, at the voice divine
Horrific ftood, and through the liquid lakes
And arms of ocean watry fields admire
Unwonted burthens. Fiery foaming fteeds
Bound o'er the polifh'd plain, and human crowds
Securely glide, and glowing chariots fly
With rapid wheels. Beneath the glaffy gulph

Interea tardi concreto in gurgite pifces,

Et pigræ conftant duro fub carcere phocæ.

Quin borealis Hyems, annique effœta feneêtus

Altius aftringit gremium telluris inertem

Omniparæ.   Pecudes occumbunt agmine crebro,

Cumque fuis alimenta feris ; non fuccus in herbis,

Graminibufve viror: terræ male credita dudum,

Spem mentita, feges peiit, interiufque rigefcit.

Nec tantum intereunt rigidos arbufta per agros,

Sentibus et dumis et acutis horrida fpinis :

Vertumni decus omne ruit, variæque rofarum,

Myrtorum, florumque tribus e ftirpibus imis

Thurigeras ponunt animas: nec jam cypariffus

In conum affurgit viridantem, aut tortile buxus

In caput, iêta gelu.   Septis moriuntur in hortis

Et pyrus, et malus, feffis affueta per æftum

Umbriferam

Fishes benumb'd, and lazy sea-calves freeze
In crystal coalition with the deep.

THE hoary winter, beldam of the year
Unteeming, inly binds the frigid womb
Of all-productive earth. In frequent bands
The cattle perish, and the savage kind,
With each his food ; not moisture in the plants
Abides, nor verdure in the bladed grafs.
The feed, committed to the faithlefs glebe,
Belyes the peafant's hope, and, chill'd beneath,
Dies unprolific: nor through rigid fields
Neglected brambles, horrid, and perplex'd
With bryar-vines, and poifon-pointed thorns,
Alone decay: vertumnus, all thy pride
Falls in the ftem: the various families,
Of rofe trees, myrtles, and adopted flow'rs
Refign their odour-bearing fouls: nor now
The cyprefs rifes into verdant cone,
Nor into head the fafhionable box,
Smit by the froft. In gardens, though immur'd,
Or hedg'd, the pear, and apple-tree, late wont
From fummer-beams to yield a fhady dome

Umbriferam præftare domum, et fitientibus olim
Nectareos hauftus, auroque rubefcere vivo.

QUINETIAM patula nequicquam regia quercus
Objice ramorum, et fylvæ ftipata caterva,
Stat media, et cœli toties perpeffa ruinas,
Ventorumque minas, at atroces grandine nimbos,
Per fibras, ternæque plicas jam corticis acrem
Horrorem penitus bibit, et glaciale venenum.

INCASSUM volucres munimina mollia flabris
Eurorum objiciunt : plumofos perfurit artus
Frigus, et aerio pertentat vifcera telo :
Hæ pennis petiere polum, vitamque fub aftris
Algentem liquere ; avidis epulantur at illæ
Pabula luminibus : vitreis nitet efca pruinis,
Atque dolo fauces puro fubludit inanes :
Interea lenti languentes limine lethi
Expirant, fylvæque perit vox dædala vernæ.

NEQUICQUAM

To noon-tide fwain, and to the thirfty lip
Nectareous draughts, and blufh with orient gold,
Promifcuous dye.   The regal oak in vain
Objects its boughy fhield, encircled thick
With leffer fubjects of the wood, inur'd
To brave the ruins of inclement fkies,
The threats of winds, and tempefts, big with hail,
Deep through its fibres, and the triple bark
Imbibes the horror keen, and polar bane.

In vain the birds their plumy coats oppofe
To Boreal blafts: the penetrative cold
Pervades their downy limbs, and hearts, transfix'd
With lancet-air: thofe, upward foaring, leave
Their frozen lives beneath the ftars: but thefe
With eager eyes devour the luring bait,
That fhines, beneath an icy mirror barr'd,
And mocks with pure deceit their empty beaks·
They pining linger in the rigid gate
Of tardy death, and in their fall expires
The various mufic of the vernal grove.

In

Nequicquam cellas, et, multo ftramine texta,
'Tecta tenet gens acris apum: jam frigore tactæ
Ardentem amittunt animum, ftimulofque benigni
Ætheris, et fegnes moribundo murmure muffant.

At miferanda Fames, cœli crudelior ira,
Ingruit, inque dies ceriali munere vitæ
Deficiente, gravi mortales pallida luctu
Obruit, infolitaque quatit formidine cives,
Spe caffos, triviifque diu membra ægra trahentes.

Interea, vulgo fpirantes funera, venti
Ingeminant, rapidoque ruunt immane procellæ
Turbine; at ingenti ftridet nemus omne fragore;
Et freta velivolæ longe-refonantis aquai
Incandunt fpumis: imoque everfa profundo
Fervefcunt, liquidofque rotant ad fydera montes

Cum

In vain the race of animated bees
Maintain their waxen cells, and citadel
Of woven ftraw : benumb'd with cold, they lofe
Their inborn ardour, their etherial ftings,
And, flothful, murmur with a dying buzz.

But piteous Famine, the feverer fcourge
Of Heaven, advances, as the fruitful means
Of life decreafe: haggard, and pale, the fiend
With fullen grief and anguifh overwhelms
Afflicted mortals, and with wild amaze
Appalls defpairing citizens, aghaft,
Dragging with fickly pace a length of limbs.

Mean-while the winds, with rage redoubled, breathe
Death far and wide : with whirling eddy rufh
Loud-rending ftorms : each grove with hideous clafh
Re-echoes, and the long refounding waves
Of naval ocean, whitening into foam,
Boil from the nether bottom, and uprol
Succeffive, fluid mountains to the ftars.

Not

Cum fremitu: haud alias illifas littora puppes

Rupibus, aut fractas magis expofuere carinas.

Telluri fin quos advolvant æquora, motu

Vitali calidos, multoque humore fluentes,

Stant glacie, boreaque graves feriente medullas,

Aftricti faxis algentibus, obtorpefcunt.

At mox ætheræ gelida genetricis ab arce

Certatim increpitat lapidofa grandine nimbus

Plurimus, et niveis defcendit Jupiter alis.

Montibus affurgunt valles, et vellere campi

Albefcunt late fpiffo, neque cernere quicquam

Jam fas eft præter canam, immenfamque ruinam.

Nequicquam hinnitu cœlum ferit, et pede terram

Victoi equus, dominoque pio bos frontis honefti

Mugitu queritur vacua ad præfepia mœfto.

LANIGERIS

Not fandy fhores at other times expos'd
More fhatter'd prows, or billow-broken keels:
But, if the waves had haply roll'd to land
Some, warm with vital motion, and a-broach
With oozy brine, they ftiffen at the breath
Of Boreas, marrow-piercing, and adhere
In fenfelefs union, to the frozy rocks.

BUT from the tow'ring north, ingend'ring ice,
Impetuous rattle ftony fhow'rs of hail,
And wintry Jove on fnowy wings defcends.
The vallies, rifing into hills, and wide
The plains continuous whiten with a fleece
Condenfe, nor aught the pathlefs eye furveys,
But one vaft, hoar, interminable wafte.

IN vain the warrior-horfe with neighing fmites
High Heaven, and with his hoof the proftrate plain;
While to his pious lord the toilfome ox,
Of honeft front, with rueful afpect pours
At empty crib his bellowing complaint.

LANIGERIS vero balbatus edere triftes

Ne tantum gregibus 'fas eft ; hinc inde per arva

Mollibus urgentur niveis, penitufque fepulti

Vix tenuem accipiunt auram, et fpirabile frigus.

Hirfutis tandem contracti pellibus offa,

Exacuunt in fe rabidum fine more furorem,

Depaftique fuos jam villos, dentibus artus

Urgent, et laceri cognata pefte fruuntur.

PER glacies denfafque nives infractus et imbres,

Rufticus, incurvo jampridem membra labore,

Protinus ante lares geniales articulatim

Torpefcit, mulierque, domus tutela ruentis

Mollior, ut fpecies pario de marmore, prolem

Blanda manu, teneramque premens ad pectora curam,

Obftupet, infandum ! et medio fermone viciffim

Torpet: in æternum frigefcit lingua rigorem.

BUT

BUT fleecy flocks in vain would utter forth
Even doleful bleating: they, through devious paths
Opprefs'd with hoary heaps, receive a fcant
Of fubtil air, and cold, fcarce breatheable:
With fhrivel'd hides, contracted to the bone,
Againft themfelves unnatural they whet
Their hungry rage, and, paftur'd on the wool,
Invade their limbs with felf-confuming teeth
Rapacious, and enjoy the native peft.

THE fwain, unbroken with incumbent toils
Through fleaky froft, fharp ice, and cumbrous rain,
Sudden before the genial hearth expires,
Articulately numb'd, and, lo! the wife,
The fofter guardian of his falling houfe,
Sooths with her hand, clofe prefling to her breaft
The tender pledge of love, her infant babe;
When ftupid, motionlefs, as figur'd ftone,
She ftares: the faultring accents, on her tongue
Stiff, into filence everlafting freeze.

I N

REGIAS NUPTIAS

CARMEN GRATULATORIUM.

JAM cœli fileat rabies: meliora refurgant

Sydera.   Vos, toties animos experta Britannos

Belligerafque manus, Rectorem agnofcite veftrum,

Æquora; jam faltem tumidos cohibete furores,

Et canas lenite minas; dum regia puppis

Sulcat iter, ventifque volans per lubrica ponti

Labitur, et regni fpes altera fluctuat undis.

Non tam dives opum, nec tam felicibus audax

In patriam aufpiciis, delectos retulit Argo

Heroas:

Heroas: tantum cedit virtutibus aurum,
Et meritis fortuna fugax. Hinc, inde frequentes
Ductores, bello infignes, et vulnere crebro
Fortiter informes, nautæque, pericula paffi
Mille maris, primo fulgentem flore juventæ,
Sufpiciunt nympham : præftantis gratia formæ,
Puniceufque pudor vultus, frontifque ferenæ
Majeftas, facilifque decor, gravitate retenta,
Qualis gemma nitet, folidum quam circuit aurum
Regali in digito, pertentant mentis amore,
Ecce! pio, pariterque facra formidine cunctos.

AUDIN', ut infolitis gratantur plaufibus undæ
Virginis adventum! ut vafto, viden', ore dehifcunt
Mirantes, altæque tument, humilefque recumbunt,
Et gremio accipiunt, dominamque fatentur euntem!
In claffes, Ludovice, tuas affueta fuperbas
Cominus infremere, et repetito fulmine raptim
Fluctibus obruere avulfas, aut ducere captas,
Jam tormenta procul, regalis nuncia fponfæ,

Læta

Læta tonant, feſtoque fremunt maris alta tumultu,
Horrendumque placent: Hymæneis rauca refultant
Aſtra poli, fanctique canunt jam fœdera lecti.

VIRGINEUM interea, leviter fpirantibus auris,
Fertur onus, gentis cuſtos, Geniufque Britannæ
Dum regit ipfe ratem, nulli cernendus, opimam
Clauſtra per et fcopulos, et jam fe numine vertit
In formam vultufque viri, (a) quem dædala donis
Finxerat Euphrofyne, partes cui Cæfar amoris
Ipfe fui, fponfæque dedit de more petendæ
Grande miniſterium, et fefe patefecit in illo;
Finibus abductam patriis dulcique fuorum
Afpectu, nec dum fatis alma forte beatam,
Reginam tali folatur imagine regni.

ÆVI molle decus, magnifque parentibus orta,
(Qui quondam, pulchra pro libertate ruentes,
Romanas pepulere acies, qui vindice dextra

(a) Comitis de H———t.

A fferuere

Afferuere Deum, et violati numinis aras)
Te promiſſa manet tellus; ubi melle liquenti,
Ambroſio tum lacte fluunt juga, fœta metallis,
Divitiiſque onerant dominos, ubi turget ariſtis
Flava Ceres, pomiſque rubent redolentibus horti,
Vocibus et volucrum reſonant, et vere perenni
Prata virent, crebroque albeſcunt vellere campi;
Heroum nutrix, quondam celeberrima nymphis,
Dicta Deæ nemorum, et ſenibus luſtrata canoiis,
Emicat oceano, quam vallunt littora, et arces
Velivolæ ludunt circum, dominamque tuentui
Terrarum invictam, ſeu, vento mobile, bellum
Fulmineum, lugubre, ferunt impune profundi
Per freta, et extremum quatiunt terroribus orbem.

Hinc gens fida virum, claras exculta per artes,
Te poſcunt, avidiſque oculis et pectore toto
Jamdudum expectant. Ardentes agmine cives
Deſeruere Urbes, curvaque vagantur arena,
Et procul a terra, pictas, cœloque natantes,

Proſpiciunt

Profpiciunt nebulas, et avent pro puppibus umbras
Accelerare gradum, placidifque allabier oris.

Ipse fed imprimis Princeps pulcherrimus, altis
Dignus avis atavifque, diu defiderat abfens
Abfentem: quoties riguo dat membra fopori,
Et regni curas patrio fub pectore condit,
Te videt in fomnis, vacuifque amplectitur ulnis.
Mane vigil fervefcit amor: fibi conjugis optat
Ora dari, alloquioque frui: quo cardine cœli
Jam venti ftrident, et qua regione vocatæ
Afpirent auræ, velis votifque fecundæ,
Jam fpe, jamque metu notat, increpitatque finiftras
Sæpe moras, nec te referentes æquoris æftus.

Non olli citharæ, blandis non aula choreis,
Dulce ftrepunt, comitumve greges, procerumve nitentum
Grata minifteria, et lautæ convivia menfæ
Arrident; Virgo, nifi tecum purpura fqualet,
Pompa jacet, fordefcit Onyx, fordefcit Iafpis,

Eoufque

Eoufque Adamas liquida cum luce Smaragdi.

Tu lux atque comes, decus invariabile fceptri,

Unica Cæfareæ tu defis gemma coronæ.

HAUD Venus ante potens tales accendit amores ;

Haud Hymenæus ovans tales conjunxit amantes :

Tu fimul in populi plaufus et gaudia Regis,

Qualis ab oceano rofeis Aurora quadrigis

Purpureo invehitur curru, comitantibus Horis,

Lætitiamque diemque vagum fparfura per orbem,

Mitis, amœna venis.   Jam, jam, velut aureus ingens

Sol, vitæ lucifque fator, tibi debitus Heros

Ardet inire toros, caftifque caloribus ignes

Commifcere facros: hinc, O! Regina, falubres

Emanent radii, feries longiffima regum

Angligenum fceptro et folio fuccedat avito ;

Arma foris, pietafque domi, per fæcula fanctæ

Hinc vigeant leges, nec fævis rupta tyrannis

Jura focis, et cana fides, et libera virtus.

VOL. I.   M m m   Mo⌣

Mox autem advenies tectis ingentibus hofpes,

Haud ignota tamen ; princeps namque auribus haufit

Egregias animi dotes, et, confona formæ,

Dona pudicitiæ, cœleftia jugis amoris

Nutrimenta, faces vivas, et ahena jugalis

Vincla tori, poftquam verni decor aruit oris,

Horruit et Rifus, levibufque Cupidinis alis

Diffugere Joci, et flavi cecidere capilli.

Salve, mitis Hymen, verecundi fancte Lyæi

Legiferæque comes Cereris, gratiffima blandæ

Uraniæ, cœloque olim delapfa, propago,

In terras, requies hominum, et fpes fida nepotum !

Innumeri te, Dive, patres per munia vitæ,

Et matres, fratrumque manus comitantur ovantem ;

Virgineique chori tacita prece numen adorant.

Ardor at indomitus, ruptifque Licentia frænis

Horret atrox, refugitque diem, geftitque fub umbris

Luftra fequi nemorum, vitamque agitare ferinam.

Tecum

TECUM fæpe cafa fub paupere ruris iniqui
Durus arator opes animis orientis adæquat,
Nec late dominis, tenui conclufus agello,
Terrarum imperium, nec regibus invidet aulas.

TE fine regis onus geminata mole gravefcit;
Quod fi digna toris confors acceffit honeftis,
Qualis Nympha tuos florefcit, maxime Cæfar,
In thalamos, fpes alma fovet, curafque ferenat,
Et, fumpta folii jam majeftate, beatum
Prole virum exornat, meritifque recentibus auget:
Sic, ubi fublimi furrexit vertice quercus
Frugifero in campo, dubios quæ terminat agros,
Si valido, lætæ tenera propagine, trunco
Succrefcunt hederæ, tortifque amplexibus hærent,
Congugio fefe tollunt hinc, inde fequaci,
Implexæ ramis, avibufque per aera texunt
Umbrofum hofpitium, atque alieno robore regnant.
Frondet honore novo, revirefcit gloria quercus.

M m m 2

Glisce tua virtute, tua dulcedine vultus
Illius, qui cuncta fibi fubjecit, amandi
Molle loquax animi, raptæque ad fydera mentis,
O! Virgo, ante alias felix, cui contigit uni
Sors tam faufta tori, fociamque in regna vocavit
Imperialis amor, proprioque facravit honore!
Sed neque cafus erat, neque cæcæ teffera Divæ,
Aut vitreæ Veneris, refugive Cupidinis æftus,
At, foliis prælatus, Hymen, atque ætheris index.
Tuque adeo (jam tempus adeft) infignis amorum
Jam fpoliis victrix, palmifque ornata Britannis,
Aerias infifte vias, ac te quoque dignam
Finge viro, thalamifque novis, teque affere fceptro.

Et jam folicitant puræ præcordia flammæ,
Et firmata fides, et, paucis nota, voluptas,
Inque dies tibi crefcet amor, magnæque parenti
Grata nurus, parilique Heroum fanguine proles
Edita, veftalefque bibens ex conjuge flammas,
Exoriere recens aulai Cynthia cultæ
Cæfareos inter fratres, pulchrafque forores;

Qualis

Qualis, rore levi nutrita, tepentibus auris
Fota Jovis, patrioque virens e littore, Myrtus,
In regum traducta hortos, frondentia late
Thuriferas inter lauros jam brachia tendit,
Ambrosiosque nemus per amœnum spirat odores :
Talis honestatas meritis florentibus ædes
Augustas, Musisque sacrum virtutis asylum,
Perfundes, dulcique choro comitata tuorum,
Accipiens, reddensque decus, placido ore nitebis.

At jam primitias regni floremque juventæ
Ipse sacer Conjux, ultra fastigia rerum
Evectus terris, animisque ingentibus ardens,
Æmulus ille Numæ, melior non auspice ficto,
Legibus obstrinxit superis, cœloque dicavit.

Ille quidem, aligero curru pietatis in auras
Raptatus, qualem vates meminere ruenti
Turbine Triptolemum, rapidisque draconibus actum,
Nubila tranasse, et fruges fudisse per orbem.

Triticeas,

Triticeas, petit alta poli, et mortalibus infra,

Heu! macie miseris, divino munere vescas,

Spargit opes, et non periturae femina vitae.

    Nec minus Heroum ductor, victricia late

Arma movens, laurosque suas nexurus avitis,

Gallorum insidiis raptas, sibi vindicat oras,

Imperioque novas veteri fortissimus addit,

Terrarum, pelagique potens : qua thurea Ganges

Arva lavat, fluitatque auro, gemmaeque renident,

Purpureumque bibunt solem : qua sole cadente

Littora fervescunt, aliusque expanditur orbis,

Dives opum, frugumque ferax : qua tarda Bootes

Plaustra trahit, campique rigent, gelidisque sub undis

Montanos volvunt moles immania Cete :

Qua medio furit igne dies, et Phoebus anhelos

Urget equos, nimioque afflans nigrantibus Asiis

Numine torret agros, nitidaque tyrannide saevit.

Hujus

Hujus in adventum cognato fanguine gentes
Commaculare manus, prædafque referre nefandas
Bellorum folitæ, vivoque a vertice vulfas,
Heu! crudas capitum exuvias, manfuefcere difcunt,
Et fefe, fociofque horrent, victæque triumphant.

Hujus amicitiam, inter fe fera bella foventes,
Supplicibus reges votis et fœdera pofcunt :
Ille, fibi conftans, pacemque per arma fecutus,
Confulit Europæ, fociifque fidelibus hæret,
Invidiam virtute domans. Tu folus aperte
Arma amens, Ludovice, fremis, victufque laceffis
Victorem, et ventis jam verba ferocia jactas.

Sic ubi ferpentem, claro fub fole per umbras
Graminis infidiis latitantem, ac dira tumentem,
Intentus pecori, percuffit vimine paftor
Sæpius : ille oculos ignefcit faucius iris,
Horrefcitque jubis, et fibilat ore trilingui ;
Tum, tardo membra ægra movens tractu per humum, vim
Nequicquam effundit, mediaque in morte minatur.

Sic

Sɪc ruit in Præceps mens effera, fracta procumbit

Ambitio: ſic Marte tuus, Cᴀʀʟᴏᴛᴛᴀ, Maritus

Proterit, horrendis gaudentes cladibus, hoſtes,

Imperii ſine fine avidos, miſeraſque refulcit

Præſidio gentes, reficitque in prælia lapſas.

Iʟʟɪᴜs auxiliis opibuſque *(a)* Boruſſius Heros

Arma quatit, feſeque Deo probat auſpice dignum,

Impiger invictuſque animi, quem turpe tyranni

Hinc atque inde premunt, crebriſque aſſultibus urgent:

Ille, dolis cinctus, numeriſque oppreſſus iniquis,

Per cæcos rerum caſus triſteſque labores

Mentis inexhauſtæ vires, portentaque dextræ

Teſtatur, magnuſque cadit, majorque reſurgit.

Qᴜᴀʟɪs in Adriaci maris atro gurgite puppis

Ingens, armipotens, et belli fœta futuris

(a) Rex Pruſſiæ

Fulminibus,

Fulminibus, vario ventorum turbine et æftu
Multiplici rapitur, jamque imos acta videtur
Ad manes ferri, fubito quum fluctibus alte
Exfilit infanis, equitatque per æquora victrix.

SED quid in arma feror? quid atrocis prælia Martis
Attentare velim, cantufque ciere tubarum
Pro leni cithara, pro lætificis Hymenæis?

INTEREA, qualis laxo modo Cynthius arcu,
Depofitaque humeris pharetra, læta explicat ora,
Plectra gerens, fulget geniali Cæfar in aula,
Ignea quem ftimulat generofo in pectoie virtus,
Et proprium decus, et communis gloria gentis;
Cui conjuncta, Themis, tua proles, innuba pridem,
Ac terras exofa diu, nimis alma videii,
Nunc Aftræa redux, feu vult Carlotta vocari,
Humanam induitur fpeciem: præcordia cingunt
Dignus Honos, prifcufque Pudor: veftigia fignant
Et Charites choreas, et amantes otia Mufæ.

VOL. I.   N n n   AT

At, vobis late jam figna ferentibus orbi,
Felices animæ! ftabili quas fœdere numen
Duxit in imperium, et morum concordia vinxit,
Nos pigeat fcelerum, pudeat fregiffe viriles
Luxu animos, caftafque tori folviffe catenas.
Nec mora, clara ducum tantorum exempla fecuti,
Haud prætextati juvenes infignia gentis
Caffa gerent; quin mox, accenfi laudis amore,
Majorum ornabunt propriis virtutibus umbras:
Æmula tum plebes, tum duro pectore vulgus
Sentiet infufum patriæ telluris honorem:
Et quafi præfentis jam fentit numinis æftrum;
Spes fovet una omnes, agit omnes impetus idem.

Qualis, ab aerio decurrens vertice montis,
Quem, neque graminibus, nec amicum frugibus olim,
Agricolæ accendunt, Euro fimul acrior, ignis
Frondiferos ruit in faltus, et pabula flammis
Denfa rapit, totoque micant incendia luco.

Sorte

SORTE tua ingenti lætare, Britannia, feſtis

Infere, Diva, diem, quo cœli gratia terris

Indulſit, folioque ſuos advexit alumnos:

Et vos æternas amborum ad ſydera laudes

Tollite carminibus, famæque recondite faſtis,

Altiſoni vates, qui propter flumina Cami

Flectitis, aut lentum Thameſino in maigine curſum;

Quique Caledoniæ, vocales carmine, valles

Paſtorum incolitis, citharæque ſcientis Iernes

Fatidicos olim lucos, Divumque receſſus:

Vobis nempe datur patrios, regnantibus illis,

Inſtaurare modos, thyaſoſque inducere Phœbo;

Aut nunc Auſonii, nunc Graii viſere puros

Eloquii fontes, et circum carpere flores:

Ni potius libeat Naturæ exquirere leges,

Per terras, pelagique vias, et lucida cœli

Sydera, tum, flammis paſcentem ſydera, ſolem.

PANDITE

PANDITE jam, Nautæ, turgentia carbafa ventis ;

Ducite, Vectores, undofa per æquora tuti

Indigenas late merces, et utramque referte

Indiam in Albionem. Ducti melioribus aftris,

Findite tellurem ferro, fulcifque, Coloni,

Ne dubitate fuis jactatas credere fruges,

Plena redundanti rupturas horrea meffe.

NEC trahere, Angligenæ, pudeat vos candida, Matres,

Vellera, conjugibus puerifque audacibus olim

Purpureum decus, et manuum monumenta per orbem.

NEC vos, Hibernæ, carpentes penfa, puellæ,

Præcipites pigeat radios agitare rotarum,

Linigeramque colum niveis geftare fub ulnis,

Tenuiaque intorto deducere ftamina fufo,

Dignum opus Afcræo celebrari carmine! dignam

Inventrice Dea, fceptrifque tuentibus, artem !

ET

ET vos, dulce rudes, calamorum inflate cicutas,
Paftores, veftramque Palem, veftrumque canentes
Pana, novos jam nunc fertis intexite flores:
Ludere jam liceat vobis, viridique fub umbra
Rivorum ad lapfus fragrantes carpere fomnos;
Vos tantum e fomnis fragrantibus, ecce! ciebunt
Agnorum queftus, aut mugitus vitulorum:
Vos tantum in campo fpectabitis, acta furore,
Prælia taurorum cornutos propter amores,
Haud ullo litui perculfi murmure, et ira
Militis, armorumque fragoribus horrendorum:
Dum Bellona ferox alienas turbine gentes
Concutit attonitas, fufoque obfcœna cruore
Efferus arva lavat Mavors, quaffafque per urbes
Nuptarum exultat gemitu, lachrymifque parentum.

JAM vero videor folennes cernere pompas,
Antiquo de more datas, quibus ipfa, per urbem
Auguftam, ingentem, clara cum conjuge fertur
Regia Majeftas. Date thurea munera; flores

Spargite puɪpureos.   Procedunt ordine longo
Illuſtres cum prole patres, Matreſque pudicæ
Cum nuɪibus, textoque auro gemmiſque relucent:
Quam multi adverſo reſplendent ſole colores
Prata per, aut, vernis ridentcs floribus, **hortos**:
Quam multæ ſpectant pura ſub nocte bicornem
Reginam ſtellæ, cœlique per atria ſtipant.

Vɪɴᴛᴜᴍ eſt ad templum, jam jam ſurgentis ad aſtra,
Augurium impeɪii, regnique inſigne futuri,
Ore ſacro precibuſque piis ubi numen adorat
Flos Regum pubens, Divoque ſimillimus idem,
Ante aram ſupplex, pro libertate, Britanna
Pro re, pro patria, pro relligione tuenda
Cœlicolum Regi vovet inviolabile votum,
Immortale ferit fœdus: tuque, optima Conjux,
Conſpiras in ſancta Deo promiſſa Mariti
Ore ſacro precibuſque piis.   Felicis olivæ
Unctus uterque caput divino rore tenetis
Sceptɪ‌ɪ ſimul, gravidaſque auro gemmiſque coronas,
Ornamenta adytis, animiſque trophæa ferentum

Haud

Haud indigna quidem, tetra rubigine nunquam
Quos nec livor edax, nec fordibus oblinet ætas.

INTEREA cives, gemino pro munere, grates
Certatim effundunt animis, et carmine tollunt
Te, Pater omnipotens, immenfi rèctor Olympi,
Te læto clamore Deum, chorus omnis ovantum
Plenius undanti liquidarum vortice vocum
Te canit, æra Deum cava, tibia, barbiton edunt;
Ara Deum perculfa, Deum domus alta remugit.

END OF THE FIRST VOLUME.

Lightning Source UK Ltd.
Milton Keynes UK
UKOW07f0935051017

310457UK00008B/602/P

9 781170 150979